blue
rider
press

MENTAL

ALSO BY
JAIME LOWE

Digging for Dirt: The Life and Death of ODB

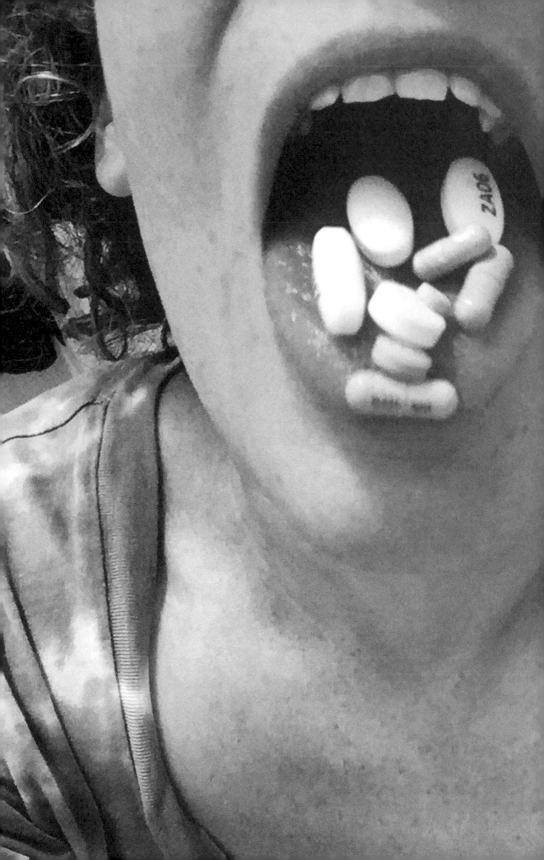

MENTAL

LITHIUM, LOVE,
AND LOSING
MY MIND

JAIME LOWE

BLUE RIDER PRESS

NEW YORK

**blue
rider
press**

An imprint of Penguin Random House LLC
375 Hudson Street
New York, New York 10014

Photograph on p. 172 courtesy Sam Polcer. All other photographs
courtesy Jaime Lowe.

Library of Congress Cataloging-in-Publication Data

Names: Lowe, Jaime, author.
Title: Mental : lithium, love, and losing my mind / Jaime Lowe.
Description: New York : Blue Rider Press, 2017.
Identifiers: LCCN 2017021267| ISBN 9780399574498
  (hardback) | ISBN 9780399574511 (eBook)
Subjects: LCSH: Lowe, Jaime—Mental health. | Manic-
  depressive Persons—United States—Biography. | Manic-
  depressive Illness—Chemotherapy—Biography. | Lithium—
  Therapeutic use. | BISAC: PSYCHOLOGY /
  Psychopathology / Bipolar Disorder. | BIOGRAPHY &
  AUTOBIOGRAPHY / Personal Memoirs. |
  PSYCHOLOGY / History.
Classification: LCC RC516 .L72 2017 |
  DDC 616.89/50092 [B]—dc23
LC record available at https://lccn.loc.gov/2017021267
p.   cm.

Printed in the United States of America
10 9 8 7 6 5 4 3 2 1

BOOK DESIGN BY MARYSARAH QUINN

*Penguin is committed to publishing works of quality and
integrity. In that spirit, we are proud to offer this book to
our readers; however, the story, the experiences, and
the words are the author's alone.*

FOR MY PARENTS
(ALL OF THEM)

CONTENTS

PART 1—EPISODE 1

PART 2—EPISODE 2

PART 3—THE TRANSITION

If you have any questions or complaints regarding your rights please contact:

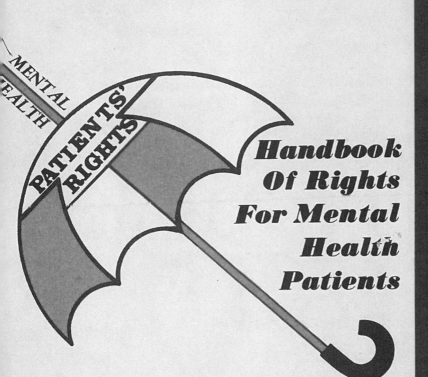

Handbook
Of Rights
For Mental
Health
Patients

CHAPTER 1

PAINT THE CEILING WITH ME AND I WILL SHOW YOU THE SECRET TUNNEL TO NEVERLAND

WHERE WAS THAT NUGGET of old, dried-up shit weed I bought on the Venice boardwalk two years ago from a vagrant dealer who may or may not have sold me a thimble full of dirt mixed with oregano?

I pounded on the volume button of my Costco-special Magnavox stereo. It was pulsating in syncopation with my anxiety. Cacophony doesn't describe it; it was so loud I could feel it traveling from my heels to my outer cranium, taking in the itching, the scratching, the clawing, the gridlock of atonal chords. It was loud and I needed it to be. I could feel the chorus like combat and I could deflect the harmony. Angels and peace and major chords weren't welcome, just the loud cheap stereo behind my slammed-shut door.

Where was it? Where was it? Where? I knew it was somewhere. The chords crashed on top of each other. I could see them. I could see the waves of sound cascading from speaker to skin. I could taste them.

It was not under my mattress or tucked into a corner of my pink floral Laura Ashley sheets (a present from my Bat Mitzvah). It was not in my jewelry box that my paternal grandparents, Oma and Opa, had given me when they traveled to Austria. The jewelry box (not the weed) had a tiny ballet dancer on a rusted metal gear that would spring to life and pirouette to canned music every time the lid was cracked. The lid was not cracked and the tiny dancer was crushed under a different sound, suffocating. Where was the nugget? Where was the nugget? Where was that nickel bag of shit weed? I bought it. I smoked it once on a Friday afternoon when no one was home. I felt nothing but fire in my throat, swallowing red hot embers. *I was good, I was great, I was perfect all the time.* But now I needed that chunk of bullshit weed so that I could get out of this terrifying place with no windows. Out of this castle of chords crashing down on me. A wall of terror, collapsing onto my skull, the way they had wanted it to. I had to get out, away from my tulip sheets, away from my delicate jewelry box, and very far away from my mask collection. The lips that moved in the night. It was subtle, I could see it. Those faces had something to say and would not shut the fuck up.

I hear you now, I am listening to you, I am leaving.

The popcorn tin! It was in the tin. The tin that once held caramel, cheddar, and butter and sat next to a life-sized penguin in our living room. My things that no one needed to know anything about. Behind my tiny rocking chair and boo boo bear. Stop looking at me, glass-eye.

I ripped off the tin lid. It smelled like popcorn; small stale kernels were wedged in around the edges. There was a folded-up piece of material. It was the key to my escape. I unfolded the material carefully like a curated item from a time capsule and, just like my vision, there was that shit-brown weed, barely more than seeds and stems. There it was, right where I had stashed it, my dirt fucking weed. It was in that forest-green tin wrapped in that original Venice beach baggie. I needed it now. It needed to be with me in my backpack. It needed to travel with me wherever I ended up. I could not leave without it. Essential item. Essential survival. Surviving. Surviving this. This war. This war with secret spies and reborn Nazis and people in masks, people who refused to take off their masks.

I grabbed it, buried it in my backpack, and laid my full body weight on top of my dog, Nature. My calm, calm, calming dog, immune to emotion. She accepted my love like the weather. It was there, nothing she could do about it but wait until it passed. I scratched behind her ears and above her tail. It wagged out of obligation and reflex. She had sad Labrador eyes and seemed empathetic to my plight, but she was indifferent. She didn't know war, she didn't know combat. She was even nice to the hissing opossum; she stood in front of the nocturnal beast licking her nose with her wet, pink tongue until *thwack*. That asshole opossum sideswiped her snout with a fistful of daggers. Claws. Nature was my soul mate, my partner in sad and lonely. She could not wear a mask and she could not throw a grenade or a gas bomb or knife. She had no opposable thumbs, so she was an ally. I could wiggle my nose in front of her wet muzzle and she sat patiently, collapsing on all fours to sleep like temporary death had struck her. She was so calm. Where I was going, she could not go. She would be eaten alive and maybe I would be too.

I *had* to go. I don't know why I was chosen to move out. I don't know why they wanted me to leave. But I knew it was absolutely essential to say good-bye to Nature, to escape the tightening parental grip of my controlling father, to run from the cascade of sound. My dad did not understand that Michael Jackson had communicated with me directly, and that I knew of a direct tunnel to Neverland, a not necessarily safe place but a place I could go, if needed. A last resort, Neverland. When I saw Michael Jackson, Michael Jackson wore masks upon masks and would remove each one, revealing different faces like a Russian doll shedding compartmental tiers of painted tiki.

I grabbed the shit weed and filled my backpack with several small cameras to document atrocities. It was a JanSport back-to-school backpack with a leather bottom (another Costco special). I packed a change of clothes and papers I had been working on, my manifestos about Nicaragua and the Holocaust and the Muppets, some drawings and diagrams.

I did not leave the house quietly; many doors slammed in my wake. I left my Magnavox on, waves of big guitars colliding, a tsunami of screeching sound. I was not communicating effectively with my dad. He did not understand anything. He yelled when I was suffocating in stereo but now I wanted him to know I was gone, going, forever, good-bye at age sixteen. My stepmom, Marilyn, was away, at her stepdad's Bar Mitzvah in Chicago. He was too old to be Bar Mitzvahed, but I respected his newfound love of the Torah, of God, of ritual, of holiness. I believed so deeply in God that I did not think a book could hold the majesty. Not scrolls. Not nothing. God had chosen me to be a savior and to be saved, which meant escape. And so I did.

I ran out the side door screaming, my dad chasing me. I think he yelled, I yelled back. I was that song, I was screaming those guitars. I was signaling something. He grabbed my backpack (MY BACKPACK!) and we struggled on the driveway near Marilyn's mustard-yellow Volvo station wagon. I was a prisoner, held back, held against my will, trapped in a house masked with shingles. Rights revoked. Violated. Eventually, I let go, the backpack didn't matter. Escape did.

He opened the small pouch and saw a handful of keychains

with cameras. No big deal. Except for the keychain that contained the key to my Honda Civic hatchback. He took that key. He opened the big compartment and rifled through until he saw the folded material. He unfolded it. And took my shit dirt weed. I screamed about unfairness and abuse; I needed my car but I needed that shit dirt weed more. It was like an oracle. Magic leaves so potent I didn't even want to smoke them. I screamed, "That is mine, I am a person with rights," and he grabbed my arm.

"You cannot go anywhere."

And I was gone. Hysterical and running down Beachwood Drive with a backpack full of shit but not my shit weed. My dad followed about three quarters of a block behind me, keeping up and keeping his distance. I was not so much crying as bellowing and heaving and crashing into the cement. I turned right on Rosewood and left onto Larchmont. I knew there was a pay phone on Larchmont and Beverly. I could call someone, I could get away. I could be free. I could go to Neverland. I could remove Michael Jackson's mask and find skin, humanity, a preserved and sweet boy aching for identity and autonomy. I could free him. I could see his real face, his real smooth skin.

The thing was, my dad wasn't the only person after me. The Nazis were after me. There was a violent war in Central America that had just ended, but I knew from Sandinista training with Salvadoran guerrillas that that war was far from over and I needed to be free to fight. I was on call to save the world. From the Nazis, the Contras, to free Michael Jackson (*oh wait, you thought Michael Jackson was free already? Hahahahaaaa. They got you to believe that*), and to free myself from my chasing-me dad who was clearly throwing a wrench in my self-determination.

I had an idea. It was a good one. If I stopped at a pay phone, my dad would try to get me home. But he could not make a scene. It was not in his nature. He was first-generation German. And Larchmont Boulevard would echo angry voices.

I saw activity at Prado, a restaurant we'd been to for dinner as a family. I had eaten soft-shell crabs to celebrate graduation or an anniversary or straight A's. Javier Prado, the owner, had opened the place two years before, in 1991, a fancy addition to our neighborhood. Javier was previously the head chef at The Ivy. I looked in the window and saw ladders and drop cloths and a handful of people painting the ceiling a deep dusky turquoise. They were expanding the dining room and technically closed. I opened the door and went in anyway, hot mess radiating in every direction. Javier sat me down, past the drop cloths and ladders by the kitchen, away from the ceiling painting. He gave me a glass of water. His wife listened to me. I told them my father had kidnapped me, abused me. That he was after me, that I had to run away. Then my dad showed up, a late-forties bespectacled lawyer with sparse, Jewish hair. He was out of breath and demanding to see me (frantic in his own calm-presentation-German-American way). They kept me sheltered away from him, my abuser. Though they did not know what to do with me, no explanation from my dad was sufficient. They did not know I was an unreliable narrator. I did not know that either.

So I sat with my water and eventually I called my mom from their phone at the hostess area. She was expecting this call. My stepdad, Jeff, and my mom had just gotten back from Maine—I flew home early to get ready for the school year. I was particularly taken with the loons, calling out to them as they shouted to each other, diving through the cold lake, inspired by their long runs under water. (*Did you know the loon plumage went gray in winter? Did you know loons have a salt gland near their eyes and can live in freshwater and salt water? Did you know they need a quarter-mile runway to take off and leave the lake when they migrate?*)

I sat in Prado's kitchen clutching my JanSport backpack, comforted by the dishes being washed and by a new friend. Javier's daughter was three years younger than I and had Down syndrome. The lilt of her voice made me think we were talking in code, that she understood me and that I understood her and that as long as things were being washed, we were both okay. I could read her thoughts. They were about math and school. I touched her hand and I felt, just by sitting in close proximity, that I understood her deeper than she had ever been understood before and that I could help her. And that she could help me. I felt bonded by trauma. I no longer had this urgency to battle and run from Nazis; I just wanted to talk to this girl who did not make it a practice to talk to many people. I was special; she was special; things were being washed.

I was calmer than I had been in three months. We were telepathically in a deep embrace, a mind-soul hug that went on for minutes, maybe decades, maybe never at all.

All summer I had been operating on a more efficient schedule, no sleep and little food. The past five days I had ramped up my regimen. I hadn't slept, not for a minute for the five nights previous to this one. I hadn't eaten much because most of what I was being fed was poison. I was running on vapors. Occasionally the late Jim Henson would come to me in a vision: warm, bearded, kind Jim Henson, an oracle for all things sensational, inspirational, celebrational, Muppetational.

But here, under a half-painted ceiling, I was still.

My mom pulled up to Prado with Jeff in the passenger seat. My dad was still hovering outside the restaurant, not allowed in, on my orders, shunned as an abuser. They regrouped, strategized. They had already formulated a plan. My mom had consulted with her therapist about what one does with a daughter full of demons. My dad went home and got his car. It was after dark and I got in my mom's silver sedan clutching my backpack full of end-of-world supplies. She pulled away from Prado, steering toward Westwood with my dad following. I thought that if I needed to, I could tutor Javier's daughter after school. I could make enough money to afford to pay for Yale. Maybe Javier would even spot me tuition for a year because obviously I was now estranged from my father. I had a plan to pay for Yale, a school I was determined and destined to go to. Javier could be one of my four corporate sponsors. He could be first up, sponsor a year of school and then I would work for him for a year. Wash dishes, tutor, whatever. Then I would have a second-year corporate sponsor like my uncle Steve. (He worked at Sweet'N Low.) And so on and so forth—an expensive education paid for. I had a plan, it would work, it was working. I was safe from my dad, a lane of traffic away. I had my backpack and my paperwork. Neverland could wait. For now. Yale would be next, next year this time exactly.

We arrived at the UCLA emergency room after dark, pulling into the curved brick driveway behind ambulances and EMTs. We didn't normally go to UCLA for emergencies. I was confused: Why were we going to the hospital at all? My mom said something to the effect of: We don't know what the fuck is going on. We don't know what to do. We are out of options. And we are fucking scared. There are doctors past those motion-sensored glass doors that know what to do. They are going to help you because we fucking can't anymore. My mom, though a tiny human, was fierce and forceful. She happily employed the vocabulary of her Teamster father.

I got out of the car cautiously. My mom said, in a tired, terse, exasperated, desperate, please-listen-to-me-demon-daughter way: "This hospital has a neuropsychiatric institute for adolescents." I did not register the implication of the statement. I just saw a waiting room full of masked faces in permanent grimace. This place was the place I was supposed to be, the place to engage in the war that haunted me. I had to crawl through the belly of a dark beast to see the shining graceful light of shelter. And so I agreed.

In the waiting room, I was pacing and agitated and I had a death grip on my backpack. There were people suffering from traumatic car accidents, broken limbs, bleeding out from fresh flesh wounds, and feverish babies wailing into the night. I was not bothered by their pain. I went up to each of them to ask the specifics of their condition, to understand why they were there and what their relationship to me could possibly be. (Everyone was related to me and my cause.) My mom saw this and intervened. She told me to stop talking to strangers, to stop talking closely to the other invalids. She purposely put limits on me and confined me. If she provoked me, I might have an outburst and get treated faster. If she told me no, I would wildly insist on yes. I wasn't just another shingles outbreak or sprained elbow. I was speaking in tongues and trying to heal these broken patients or enlist them in my army, I was channeling the Muppets and Michael Jackson to let them know that everything would be all right. I was murmuring to myself about poison, and electrified by the possibility of an elaborate escape plan . . . the waiting room responded with despondent heaves and sighs and groans of pain. People were suffering and I insisted on Uzis and rainbows. Reception noticed. I was escorted by antiseptic nurses and unfeeling night administrators past the doors and away from my parents to a gurney where I lay down willingly for strangers. I was nightgown-swaddled and buckled in.

I didn't fight. The night-shift psychiatrist was young and handsome and I remember feeling like a queen being rolled around the ER. Again, like at Prado, I felt instantly okay. War was on the outside. I was here to expand my psychological presence to return to the battlefield better equipped. I was smitten with this handsome ER doctor who was going to make me better, who was doing my bidding and not the other way around. The restraints were just proof of my importance, of my power. He asked me questions to determine my level of sanity. Questions of logic and determination. Questions that were like a test. There's no logic in this world, I thought, how can you test that? How can you know? But I knew how to game the system, I knew the right answers inherently. He did a physical exam, a neurological exam, lab work, a mental status examination, and a medical history. I refused the breast, rectal, and genital exam. I was rolled onto an elevator and kept in seclusion for a night.

The intake report said what was already obvious to everyone around me: I was exhibiting an "increased psychomotor rate, decreased need for sleep (about two to three hours a night), racing thoughts and paranoid ideation regarding her parents following her and watching her, as well as taping the phone calls that she was making."

I woke, groggy from sedation. The ER docs ruled out head trauma, other medical conditions, and use of drugs or intoxication. They determined that I was in need of psychiatric care and asked me about my mood, voices, my beliefs, if I was suicidal; they tested me with questions to determine how abstract my thoughts were and whether my mind was being controlled by other people. I thought, *I am going in deep, deep cover. I will find the evil in these neutral walls. I will exterminate before I'm exterminated. There is no guarantee of survival, but I must push on into this heart of darkness, penetrate the system, broadcast the corruption and be hailed a singular hero with omniscient knowledge of the universe past, present, future.*

I believed I had special powers, the report noted; I knew "when the end of the world was coming due to toxic substances" and felt that I was the only one who could stop it. I tried to tell everyone in the waiting room, but they were too busy crying over broken bones. This was the end of the world. This was not a drill. One persistent thought—a gut instinct—was that I was the *one, the only one*. A prophesized being, special, sent to earth with a mysterious mission—one that I was just now understanding with each passing day. I was Jesus, I was Bob Dylan, I was Hitler, I was John Wilkes Booth, Derrida, Marx, the Monkey Wrench Gang, a bear, a pile of glitter, and a galaxy. I was in an action movie, a war movie, a romcom—I was the protagonist in all of these, of course—I had to warn the population at large about the future, nuclear annihilation, war, genocide, apocalypse on the highest scale, bigger than biblical. I would fall in love along the way. I would recruit this love to fight the larger, epic war. The feeling was that of incredible pressure and responsibility. I could not believe I was tasked with this. I was only sixteen. I was an average teen. But this is how superheroes are born.

PULL BACK AND PICTURE this same person, this superhero twenty years later. She is stretched out, making angels in an endless desert, her wings imprinted on the Bolivian salt flats, the infinite, forever land of lithium. She is spellbound. She leaves an impression of her body in the cool, wet, iridescent, crystallized, cacti-marked terrain. She wonders if eating the salt crust will help or hurt. She is equipped with armor and weaponry and powers bestowed on her by chance. She has conquered demons, won the apocalypse, and now, stretched to the brink, she soaks and steeps in the element of her making. She knows it doesn't matter. This place, this pilgrimage is bigger than she is, bigger than anything she's known. She thinks back to the beginning when it was just a capsule and a cure, and she thinks to the future when it is corrupting her insides. This is what she is made of. This is who she is. This is how she came to be. She is there to be intimate with her keeper and her kryptonite, to marinate in it and rub it between her fingers, up to her forearms, into her pores. She walks barefoot. The lithium rises up through the soles of her feet, floods her body, and touches her brain.

C

I III I	**All** I have to say
I I I I I I I I	Is that you guys are lous~~y~~
I I I I I I I	at tricking me too stay
I	
I / I / I / I	I play and sing a song
I I I I I I I II	But NOOOOooo body sings along
I I I	

aaa II

su-ayetayeh

I' III	**All** I have to say
I' I' I	
I / I' I I	Is that ↑ you guys are lousy
~~III~~ I	at tricking me too stay

yoo-hoo

I pla-a-ay and sing ~~along~~ a s

But No-o-o-o-o-o body sings ~~a long~~

~~Ooooon~~

Ooooon ... Yeah ...

This is the reaeal world.

Intro II

CHAPTER 2

ADMITTANCE

I WAS ADMITTED to UCLA's Neuropsychiatric Institute on September 8, 1993. The discharge summary, a document that noted my progress from beginning to end, said that I had been suffering from increased paranoia and a lack of sleep, and that I had been hallucinating "people from the past." The report included my parents' interpretation of my erratic behavior the previous two months, which they described as increased "irritability, lability, and 'bossiness' with family members." Some time before the Night of the Hospital, I had filled out a questionnaire called the "Child Behavior Checklist for Ages 4–18." It was meant to be filled out by a parent, but I found it and filled it out myself. When the survey asked for an explanation in academic performance and why a "child is not being taught," I answered, "Because my father controls me." I listed "death" as an obsession, "cats" as a fear, and under the question of whether I ate or drank things that were not considered food, I wrote yes with the examples of "tequila and cigarettes." The fortieth question of the survey asked for a description of the "voices that aren't there." My response was "But they are there." Toward the end of the 113 questions, the survey asked for descriptions of any strange ideas, and for that I wrote "to kill everyone except for me and one other person." I was a mass murderer. I was Adam Lanza. Based on my answers, I seemed violent, vindictive, delusional, illogical, reckless, troubled, addicted; reading these answers years later, it's hard to believe I ever wrote them on a piece of paper. It's possible I was answering hyperbolically, playing into the absurdity of the questionnaire. I don't know; my intake report included a detailed account of auditory hallucinations and fears of the end of the world. It doesn't seem impossible that in my mind state I would have welcomed a worldwide do-over, an Adam and Eve scenario in which I got to start from scratch with everything. On the other hand, the fantasy fit perfectly with my line of thinking—the world was ending, I was tapped to start over with a fresh new society—a revolution and an apocalypse in one. On a personal scale, that's what hospitalization was to me, a quick shake of the Etch A Sketch to start over with a blank palette, me at the circular controls.

I entered NPI sedated but quickly began talking rapidly and incoherently. According to the report, I was not lucid. I was oriented to time but not place. And I was certain that my parents were not my parents, but agents impersonating my parents, on a mission to follow, watch, and record my phone calls—to monitor my behavior. I was assigned to Dr. Mark DeAntonio. He said later that when I was admitted, "Your state was altered; you couldn't function in that state on any level." He asked my parents about me. They said I was a top student at University High and that I had close friends, that I was confident, ambitious, creative, and generally engaged but that I hadn't been lately.

Dr. DeAntonio rocked in his office chair and twirled tufts of his hair, leaving horned curlicues jutting this way and that. He wore thick-soled motorcycle boots, faded black jeans, a collared shirt hastily tucked in, and earrings in his right ear. He had piercing blue eyes, like ice. He looked more punk than psychiatrist. His eyes squinted quizzically without hesitation. He had some of the mannerisms of a patient—tics and oddities—but he was, in fact, the head of adolescent psychiatry. We met and he asked me about my backpack, which I still had a death grip on. I carried it with me everywhere—to group, to doorways, to the lounge, to the dining area. He asked me what was in it. I would not reveal its contents; I would not crack under pressure. Dr. DeAntonio looked cool but he was still one of them, the head of them, maybe the most heinous and evil of them? Within days of my admittance, Dr. DeAntonio diagnosed me as manic depressive, the term used then for bipolar disorder. He said I was a classic case. I was one of the 44 million Americans who experience mental illness in any given year and one of the 5.7 million people diagnosed as bipolar.

He met with my parents—all four of them—for a family meeting. They described a period two years ago in 1991 that included "multiple psychosocial stressors." My older brother, Matt, had moved to Berkeley. I had started a new high school. They talked about the noticeable changes that happened gradually the summer before. My mom mentioned my behavior in Maine—I had been argumentative, intense, obsessed with the loons. I remember plunging into the cold water of Potash Cove on Lake Thompson and swimming through the still waters, communing with the fowl. Everything is a symptom in retrospect. I remember the rock that made a deep region shallow. I would swim out to where I could stand, where the tiny translucent fish would gently bump into my toes. I felt a rush of euphoria, a shock of cold. It wasn't especially weird but coupled with my lightning eyes and odd demeanor and unaccountable fixations, maybe it was. If you were to look at pictures of me that summer, you would have seen a laughing, relaxed rising senior with red curls that would not obey the dictates of a bob cut. I wore old flannel shirts, ripped jeans, and purple Doc Marten boots. I left Maine early that summer. My parents, worried, arranged for Joe, my stepmom's stepfather—a jovial and gracious school bus driver who loved to go dancing—to meet me during my layover at O'Hare in Chicago. I ate lunch with Joe and his girl-friend, Trudy, and we talked about Joe's job and the kids on his school bus. My mom made note of other oddities, like the time I came home with seventeen camera key chains from the Nature Company. I had figured that everyone I knew needed one to keep one in the glove compartment, in case of a car accident, obviously. They were meant to record the damages. I was an opinionated person but there was a new edge to my arguments, a passion that felt misplaced. I was journaling a lot. More than your average Indigo Girls–loving teen—my notebooks were covered in expansive and intricate doodles.

My parents explained that there was a clear shift in behavior. I'd always been an intense child, but the choices I was making—the conversations I was having and the way I was functioning—it was *off.* They described my sleep patterns as a child to Dr. DeAntonio. I was a precocious insomniac. After my parents' separation, when I was eighteen months old, I had night terrors regularly. In our first apartment on Almayo Avenue in West Los Angeles, our downstairs neighbor would pound a broom into her ceiling with each squall of hysteria. I grew up with sleeplessness, and night wandering stuck with me. My mom taught me to try to sleep. "Picture the waves," she would say. "Think about the ocean, the waves go in and they go out." As she soothed, I would breathe in and breathe out, matching the waves rolling in and out with visions in my head. My medical records noted two major traumas: my parents' divorce. And, when I was thirteen, I had been molested by a stranger at knifepoint. We were a verbal family, well versed in psychological discourse, but we didn't talk about the attack much. Immediately after it, I went to see a therapist named

Dr. G. My family referred to the sexual assault as "the incident," which simply meant we never used the phrase *the incident* again. In retrospect, the attack was connected with the breakdowns that followed, but at the time it was hard for me to see—and the psychiatric community favored genetic implications of mental illness over environmental issues. This thinking has evolved over the past couple of decades to incorporate both environmental and genetic factors, but it's a complicated and controversial determination to make. Is mental illness a result of nature or nurture? How many of these diseases are caused by experienced trauma, how many by a genetic lottery? How many by a combination of both?

Dr. DeAntonio asked for a family history. My parents told him that the only link to mental illness was with my maternal grandfather, Irving Tannenbaum, a barrel of a man who died with all his hair and all his teeth at age eighty-nine. He was a Teamster and spent most of his career dropping off kegs of Budweiser to local bars and liquor stores in West Los Angeles. He was surrounded by four chirping and loquacious ladies, his wife and three daughters, for most of his life, which left him inside himself. Irving would read mystery books in his striped brown velour chair; he had a gruff demeanor that belied an occasional inner twinkle. Two years before my hospitalization he had been hospitalized at NPI as well after a late-onset depressive episode. (We were the family that NPIed together!) After months of Howard Hughes–esque behavior—he refused to shower, cut his hair, clip his nails, or emerge from his bedroom—he was given Prozac, a transformative medication that took his personality from completely dysfunctional to congenial. He shed his gruff exterior and we all wondered at the time: What if Grandpa had been medicated earlier? He was the only clear link, substantiated by his family—a niece who committed suicide via a stab wound to the chest and siblings who were all on varying points of the spectrum. The niece's husband, an anesthesiologist at UCLA, thought his wife was an undiagnosed bipolar person. It never occurred to us that Grandpa's grumpiness was treatable; he was sane by comparison to his relatives, who were all estranged anyway.

For the first few days of my hospitalization, I was put on Mellaril and Ativan to control the acute mania and psychotic symptoms. They eventually switched me to Loxitane and Ativan, which I was meant to take two or three times a day and at night before bed. My dad, reluctant to accept a bipolar diagnosis, considered a second opinion. He didn't know what bipolar was, what it looked like. He couldn't imagine it was me. My symptoms got worse and I started to show signs of cycling again, at which point my dad consented to the diagnosis and to the treatment.

CHAPTER 3

IF NAZIS DON'T GET YOU, THE MOCCASINS WILL

I WAS SIXTEEN, young, at that time, to receive a bipolar diagnosis. The morning after I was driven to the hospital, I was volatile and irritated. The nurses said I was disturbing other patients. So I got a private room with four beds. There were about seven other teenagers in the ward, mostly girls with eating disorders and one boy. There were automatic double-locked doors next to the on-call nurses' terminal. Doctors could pass through; we could not. Immediately, I paged through my patient handbook, a small stapled brochure that outlined rights . . . very few, there were very few rights afforded to me. I explained that I was sixteen, old enough to drive, old enough to file to become an emancipated minor, old enough to know when certain nurses were trying to kill me. I demanded to be released; I would be seventeen in two months and I was too old not to make my own decisions, too old not to exercise free will. I already had too much responsibility to be stripped of choice. I had a part-time job wrapping gifts at a boutique owned by pothead lesbians, I was a Red Cross certified babysitter, I had a driver's license, I had been a camp counselor, a volunteer at a shelter for runaway teens, I'd campaigned for three Democratic presidential nominees and attended political rallies to protect a woman's right to choose. I was an autonomous latchkey kid. Here in the ward, I was a danger. I argued aggressively, pushing the point that my residency at this facility was a violation of my constitutional rights, my human rights. "I have been to Amnesty International concerts; this doesn't happen in this country," I said. A nurse politely pointed out, "A minor has no constitutional rights, no amnesty."

I eyed the double doors. I thought of escape.

NPI was a jail. The building was an imposing postwar brick behemoth shaped like a plus sign with wings extending in each geographical direction. The adolescent ward was in the west wing. Looking out the north-side windows I could see a power generator three stories tall and equally wide. If I looked past the metal grates, past the generator, I could see the bucolic hills of UCLA's campus and imagine the expansive green lawns with freshman students and stacks of books and backpacks full of purpose. Those rolling grass hills were not for us; we were locked in, double-locked in—no, triple. Those hills were not real to me anyway, just another movie set, a form of make-believe to mask an apocalyptic landscape—cratered earth swallowed by thick nefarious lava, a war-torn battlefield burning on the west side, an army of degenerate zombie serial killers thirsty for brain. Nothing good was happening on the outside. I was fixated on the generator—the pipes intertwined and shined, they were big and boisterous and volatile.

It was a maze of metal, menacing and alive. I watched those pipes like something was going to hatch—a plan, a spirit, a baby, a monster, a baby monster, a zombie serial killer, the Night Stalker, Richard Ramirez himself. The south side of the ward faced an equally awful image: a fenced-in asphalt volleyball court and recreation area that was wrapped in double-sided barbed wire. What kind of MacGyver move would it take to escape and save the world? Tuck and roll? A hysterical diversion? Sure. Maybe.

I tried to keep my head in the game by resisting meds, an obvious instrument of mind control. I would spit them out and run. I never made it far. Several nurses would tackle me in the hallway and pin me to the floor. They held my arms and my legs against the antiseptic linoleum. One nurse would peel back the waistband of my pants and stick a hypodermic needle into my left hip. In the needle was a cocktail of sedatives and antipsychotics. Nothing worked immediately. Those meds were appetizers to the medication that they would eventually give me in capsule form. Lithium.

But before the lithium, I was still a savior, a messiah, a renegade. I would stand outside the rec room door, whispering to another patient (TeeVee Dude) about the evils of TV, like a ghost speaking in tongues: *Back away, the rays, they are toxic, turn it off, it's not worth it, the TV, the fiber optics they will suck you in and spit you out, zombie, commercial, an evil corporate plan for brain hijacking. Stop letting them hijack your brain. They will take your soul. They will turn you into a sitcom character. They will turn you into a watch, a bomb, a drone. Step away, step away. I am here to help you. Don't be gassed, turn it off. Those rays, don't you see them? They are colorful and there is a laugh track but they are still noxious, the fumes will poison you. You see them. Don't breathe, don't move, I will save you.*

I was a doomsday preacher, I believed in my telepathic and all-knowing predictions. I believed I could save TeeVee Dude and that I could save me. I needed to save the world and I needed to save him. That was made even more clear in the visitors' lounge one afternoon when his stepmom sat in one folding chair and my aunt Carrie in another; they were old friends. The connection seemed uncanny to me, too coincidental. The boy was clearly sent to me as an ally, an inside support for revolution. Of course. I continued whispering in doorways about pipes and apocalypse. He continued not to hear. It was dark and crowded and chaotic. I was forced to go to group therapy, to appointments with people who grinned and said they could help.

I explained to Dr. DeAntonio that those pipes, those pipes outside were actually a vessel for death. He nodded, curious, but replied calmly: "Jaime, they are the generator for the building." Undeterred, a little exasperated, I repeated myself. There is a planned massacre in place, I explained, and it needs to be stopped. It would be the Holocaust all over again, teens and doctors gassed to death in the night. An asphalt volleyball court full of corpses. Gas seeping through Westwood village poisoning professors and tourists and crystal vendors alike. Could he not see it? Could he not feel it? It was imminent, it could be now! Those bodies would be on his hands. He had to let me go, I had to . . . *stop it*. Tuck and roll, escape, I explained. He could help me, I could sneak out through the volleyball courts. It was fate that my room faced north to the pipes; I could hear them breathing and sighing and steaming. *I could stop it*, I told Dr. DeAntonio confidently. It was up to me and I was up to the task. I left his office shouting loudly about the coming apocalypse, about the gas. If I was nuisance enough, maybe someone would let me go. That led to more tackling, more needles.

"Don't open the windows, don't turn on the TV," I told

TeeVee Dude and the other patients and nurses, enacting my own emergency evacuation. When I talked to Dr. DeAntonio years later, he remembered me being aggravated and annoyed, on edge and obsessed with Nicaragua, that I was hysterical about the apocalypse. He said I was particularly interested in disrupting other patients' routines, to tell them about the end of the world. But I was convinced I knew the truth; I was trying to save them. I refused medication. I would not take the Dixie cup full of pills that would sedate me—I needed to be sharp, aware, and ready. Once I raced away from some nurses. They followed. I thought it would be another hip check; I was ready to be tackled.

Instead, they took me to a room. Dr. DeAntonio called it seclusion, I remember it as solitary confinement. The difference was nomenclature—it was a four-by-four-foot room with no door handles on the inside and brown marbled padded walls. The pattern was streaked—khaki, poop brown, orange brown, brown brown— all muddled together in stripes that looked more like a swirl. A kind of ikat, using J. Crew catalog terminology. There was a double-paneled glass square window in the handleless door; I could not make out anything that was happening in the hall. I panicked. I hyperventilated. I clawed at the walls and threw myself against the door. I exhausted myself with hysteria. There was nothing left to do, no one to see. I sat down in a corner. I touched the soft walls. I imagined them absorbing my screams, and screams before mine. But then I was quiet. I could hear my older brother, Matt, whose sitcom catchphrase with me was "Jaime, *calm down*." His emphasis was slow and pointed. I hated when he said that. I collapsed on the floor. With no one to whisper to, no pipes to fear, no tunnels, no TV, no doctors, no teens, no hallucinations of Muppets, just me crumpled on the floor, tired in this variegated brown room, fetal and deflated.

It felt safe in there, like space. I was floating, tethered to a toxic world but letting go. I felt far away and secluded and deserted. I could sense a shift, I was alone, I needed to be alone. It was quiet in the soft, brown room with no doorknobs, and then it was quiet in my brain and quiet in my body. I just sat still for the first time in a long time. I could feel the padded walls. I knew what padded walls meant—I was dangerous, to myself and to others. In solitary, there was nothing I could do but fold. I was curled up in a ball, alone but attached to support, forming and developing all over again—like the early moments of life. Recalibrating, adjusting my brain, adjusting my place in the world. I was in so much trouble, the world was in trouble, everything was trouble. Not too long ago, I was a small, normal teenager who made earrings, bought overdyed jeans from Jet Rag, gossiped about first kisses that were never mine, hoped for a first kiss of my own, and stressed about chemistry tests.

My parents knew my behavior was not the norm. But adolescent psychosis raises the question: What is normal for a teenager? How do you distinguish between a kid encountering surging hormones and continuing physical and emotional development from one who is mentally ill? Adolescence has no logic, there is no norm. John Hughes's canon of teenage angst and dystopia barely scratches the surface of adolescent issues that have cropped up in the decades since. A child's brain was once thought to be structurally complete by age five or six, but more recent research shows that while 95 percent of the structure of the brain *has* been formed by then, the remaining 5 percent—including the prefrontal cortex, the area that controls mood, reason, and impulses—continues to develop. The teenage brain can "imprint" experiences. Certain triggers and experiences can change the way the brain works later in life. It's a period of time when "nurture" can modify "nature."

The irony of mental illness in adolescence—when many mental illnesses first emerge—is that the brain, according to Frances E. Jensen and Amy Ellis Nutt's *The Teenage Brain*, has to be mature enough to "do mental illness." Jensen and Nutt ask, "How, for instance, can you have adult-like schizophrenia that stems at least in part from abnormal frontal lobe activity if your frontal lobes aren't hooked up to the rest of your brain yet?"

My mind and body were incubating in solitary confinement. I had very recently been close to Jesus and carrying on idle conversation with Michael Jackson. But a new version of me was emerging—I was floating through a black hole, I was a supernova, eating and exploding and forming and circulating. I sat in solitary for hours; it felt like days. My brain, simmering and cooking and settling and emerging. Eventually I sat with limited awareness of my actual surroundings. I could see that there was no Michael Jackson, no secret tunnels, I couldn't hear voices anymore. I could just see the repeating pattern of the soft brown ikat walls.

I melted into the corner, my knees splayed, my body taking on a languid state. I waited. Waiting I learned is a big part of mental illness recovery. So is a kind of breaking—like breaking a wild horse or a baby elephant. I had to be restrained and I had to learn to operate within certain societal structures. I had to accept them. A day of seclusion broke me. One study that compared physical restraints to a seclusion room found that 82 percent of participants thought seclusion was less frightening than bed restraints, that they were able to reach a state of calm in a shorter period of time. I wasn't really into either, but solitary was good for one thing: I decided that the end of the world could wait. I stopped clawing at the door. And they let me out.

I was presented with a simple solution. Lithium, a mood stabilizer that can help stop and prevent manic cycles. It's usually the first medication tried with bipolar patients. It's effective for most of them. Including me. Dr. DeAntonio compared it to insulin, the hormone used to treat diabetes. Once it was explained that this was an element in everyone's body and that I just needed more, the three pink pills in the Dixie cup didn't seem so bad.

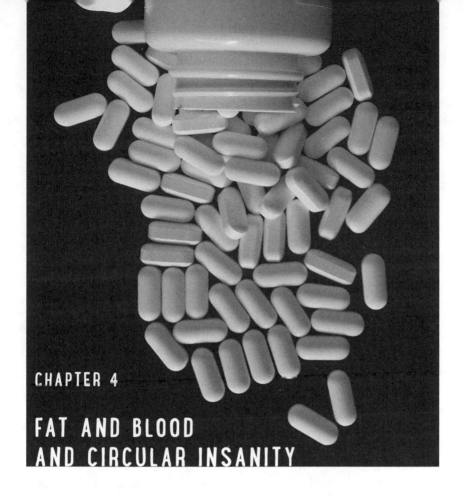

CHAPTER 4

FAT AND BLOOD
AND CIRCULAR INSANITY

MY DAD'S FRIEND LYNN, a Jungian analyst, told him when I was diagnosed, "She's just going to have big feelings." I knew about AIDS, everyone knew about AIDS in the early 1990s, but debilitating mental illness wasn't part of the larger conversation. I didn't know what I was or what was happening to my brain. I just knew that my judgment was horribly off, and that I believed things that were not real. It all hung on a delicate balance because it all *felt real*. Everything around me came into question: What was real, what was imaginary? What was genuine feeling and what was the disorder? Who was I in relationship to the disease? What was mental illness? How long had it been around?

Bipolar disorder is now defined by the National Institute of Mental Health as "a brain disorder that causes unusual shifts in mood, energy, activity levels, and the ability to carry out day-to-day tasks. There are four basic types of bipolar disorder; all of them involve clear changes in mood, energy, and activity levels. These moods range from periods of extremely 'up,' elated, and energized behavior (known as manic episodes) to very sad, 'down,' or hopeless periods (known as depressive episodes). Less severe manic periods are known as hypomanic episodes." The generic definition doesn't quite cover the extremes of the disease or its symptoms, which include inflated self-esteem, sleeplessness, loquaciousness, racing thoughts, and doing things that, according to the Mayo Clinic, have a high potential for painful consequences like unrestrained buying sprees, sexual indiscretions, or foolish business investments. The symptoms are weird and seemingly inexplicable, except that they all revolve around lowering inhibition. Hyperreligiosity is also a symptom—on the ward I insisted on some form of Shabbat celebration. I lit candles (which the nurses moved out of reach), I drank grape juice, and I said the Hamotzi over paper plates with bread. I was feeling Jesus and deeply Jewish simultaneously, and when my mania lifted, all that was gone, too.

There is a spiritual appeal to lithium for me, though it is historically medicinal. The use of lithium as a therapy for mental illness goes back to Greek and Roman times, at least, when people soaked in alkali-rich mineral springs to soothe both "melancholia" and "mania." Ancient writers are often credited with discovering the contemporary understanding that mental illness came from a biological perspective—the medical writers of the Hippocratic era considered the brain to be the root of the problem, denying explanations like demons or evil spirits. They viewed the brain as the seat of consciousness, emotion, intelligence, and wisdom and wrote that disorders involving these functions must be located in the brain and that they were not inflicted by the gods.

Roughly 2,500 years ago, Hippocrates, the "father of medicine," wrote what might be the first description of mania and melancholia: "The people ought to know that the brain is the sole origin of pleasures and joys, laughter and jests, sadness and worry as well as dysphoria and crying. Through the brain we can think, see, hear and differentiate between feeling ashamed, good, bad, happy. . . . Through the brain we become insane, enraged, we develop anxiety and fears, which can come in the night or during the day, we suffer from sleeplessness, we make mistakes and have unfounded worries, we lose the ability to recognize reality, we become apathetic and we cannot participate in social life. . . . We suffer all those mentioned above through the brain when it is ill."

That quote from Hippocrates is among the first pieces of medical writing describing any human disease—physical or mental. He was one of the first physicians to observe the human body in its entirety and to believe in rational explanations for illness. Through his research, Hippocrates formulated the first classifications of mental disorders—paranoia, melancholia, and mania. The physician Aretaeus of Cappadocia, a Roman doctor who was influenced by Hippocratic works, was the first physician to observe and describe the features of bipolar disorder in his two books *On the Aetiology and Symptomatology of Chronic Diseases* and *The Treatment of Chronic Diseases*. He wrote: "I think that melancholia is the beginning and a part of mania. . . . The development of a mania is really a worsening of the disease (melan-cholia) rather than a change into another disease," an early observation that not only takes psychology into account, it also considers the possibility of mania and depression as one disease. (For me, the mania came first, but how was Aretaeus to know?) Aretaeus described manic patients he observed in his chapter "On Madness" from *Chronic Diseases*:

> And they with whose madness joy is associated, laugh, play, dance night and day, and sometimes go openly to the market crowned, as if victors in some contest of skill; . . . At the height of the disease they have impure dreams, and irresistible desire of venery, without any shame and restraint as to sexual intercourse; and if roused to anger by admonition or restraint, they become wholly mad. Wherefore they are affected with madness in various shapes; some run along unrestrainedly, and, not knowing how, return again to the same spot; some, after a long time, come back to their relatives; others roar aloud, bewailing themselves as if they had experienced robbery or violence. Some flee the haunts of men, and going to the wilderness, live by themselves.
>
> If they should attain any relaxation of the evil, they become torpid, dull, sorrowful; for having come to a knowledge of the disease they are saddened with their own calamity.

His description could be a contemporary observation; parts of it were identical to my experience. Hippocratic physicians coined the term *hysteria*, which comes from the Greek word *hysterika*, meaning "uterus or womb." The Greeks believed that various female maladies—including hysteria—stemmed from a wandering womb. Aretaeus even characterized the womb as "an animal within an animal," an organ that "moved of itself hither and thither in the flanks." The Greeks and Romans defined the difference between the female and male temperaments. They attributed female pain and emotional angst to a migratory womb that would theoretically bump into internal organs, wreaking havoc—both mentally and physically.

It's not so far from the truth as to be implausible—there I was, out of my mind, admitted to a psych ward one year after I started puberty, my adolescent brain still in the process of formation, frothing at the mouth, suffering from the same symptoms that ancient Greeks, Romans, Chinese, Israelis, Egyptians, frontiersmen, industrialists, paupers, and kings had been suffering from since forever. I had that mental illness. It was not a classification I appreciated at first. No manic person—in the throes of omnipotence, ecstasy, and strategic warfare—wants to hear that they are . . . just sick. I would have sooner connected with a diagnosis of a wandering animal womb.

In the period between Greco-Roman innovation and the mid-nineteenth century, the understanding of mental illness and bipolar disorder progressed on a slow trajectory. Without listing everything that happened between then and 1854, here's a snapshot: A hospital dedicated to the treatment of the mentally ill opened in Jerusalem in AD 490; the first dedicated psychiatric hospitals built by Arab Muslims opened in Baghdad in 790. Under Islam, the mentally ill were considered incapable yet deserving of humane treatment and protection; in 1591, the Chinese writer Gao Lian described bipolar disorder in his work *Eight Treatises on the Nurturing of Life*; in the seventeenth century, Robert Burton wrote *The Anatomy of Melancholy*, which advocated for the use of music and dance as a form of treatment for melancholy (a condition he described as "nonspecific depression"); and later in the seventeenth century, Theophilus Bonet published *Sepulchretum*, a text about his experience performing three thousand autopsies. He linked mania and melancholy in a condition he called "manico-melancolicus."

The real progress was made starting in 1854 when French psychiatrist Jean-Pierre Falret recognized bipolar 1 disorder by calling it "folie circulaire" or "circular insanity," describing it as "characterized by a continuous cycle of depression, mania and free intervals of varying length." (People diagnosed with bipolar 2, introduced in 1994, suffer more intensely from depressive episodes.)

Around the same time, lithium was thought to cure gout and sometimes "brain gout," a lovely description for mania, extending the notion of swollen joints to a swollen brain. The element gets its name from *lithos*, the Greek word for "stone," and lithium is indeed found in granite—and in seawater, mineral springs, meteorites, the sun and every other star, and all humans. It is classified as a metal on the periodic table of elements. It was first identified as a solid in the form of petalite ore on the Swedish island Utö in 1817. A year later, scientists found that lithium, when ground into powder, turned flames crimson red—the key ingredient in red fireworks. Lithium is also stripped from the inside of batteries to make methamphetamines. Fiery and unstable, lithium somehow calms emotional states often characterized in the same way.

The term *bipolar*—which means "two poles," signifying the polar opposites of mania and depression—first appeared in the American Psychiatric Association's (APA) *Diagnostic and Statistical Manual of Mental Disorders* (DSM) in its third revision in 1980. I had very good timing. The era I was living in and the family I was born into meant I could get treatment. My mom worried I would not return to me. But once I was admitted to UCLA and diagnosed, the expectation was that I would get better.

I did, eventually.

I was not aware of bipolar disorder in particular, but I'd been made very aware of madness. I had a grasp on the language of psychology and the history of women and asylums. I had just never thought about insanity in terms of me. The best characters in literature, the most complex artists and musicians, the finest performances all seem to stem from extreme emotions (sometimes intertwined inevitably with addiction), and those were the characters I was drawn to. Isn't everyone? The *complicated*. I read *The Yellow Wallpaper* (written in response to eighteenth-century physician and psychiatrist Silas Weir Mitchell's bed-rest techniques) and *The Bell Jar*; I saw *Heathers* and *One Flew over the Cuckoo's Nest*. I could see wildness in Jack Nicholson's eyes, menace in the point of his sideburns. In Homer's *Iliad*—a doctor, Podalirius, says that he was the first "to recognize Ajax's flashing eyes and burdened spirit," before Ajax committed suicide. I never felt abnormal or out of control. I never felt different. But were those lightning-rod, wild eyes mine?

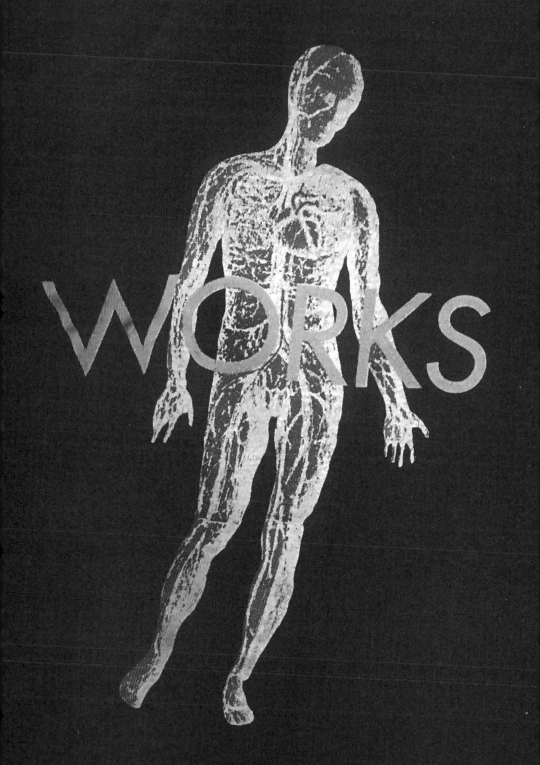

WORKS

CHAPTER 5

CLEAN NEEDLES NOW, ASPHALT VOLLEYBALL . . . NEVERMIND

ONCE I AGREED to take the meds, my urgency faded. My obsessions broke. My plans and paranoia still felt real but less frantic, like I made this bargain with myself and with NPI and with Dr. DeAntonio. I would pretend everything was fine. I would participate reluctantly—in group therapy, in individual therapy, in occupational therapy, and in recreational therapy. I would stop whispering in doorways and worshipping ghosts. I would take the Dixie cup full of pills and actually swallow them. I cooperated and engaged and as a result, I got better. It was just the easier thing to do. The ward's enforced daily structure was hard to resist—my hip hurt and was still bruised. I did not want to be tackled again. I did not want to be in a padded cell again. And so I relented. And relenting was easier than I thought. It might have been time passing, it might have been the meds, it might have been the ward, but I agreed to go along with the program, to pause on heroically stopping the gas massacre, to stop thinking about my telepathic connection to Michael Jackson. My two rabbis from Temple Isaiah—Rabbi Gan and Rabbi White—came to the hospital to see me during visiting hours. I still felt ever-so-slightly touched by God, but I now knew their visit did not mean I was a messiah, it just meant they were concerned. I was getting better. My friends Hana and Sarah J. came to visit me in the dining room, and we sat on folding chairs, pretending to be normal teens.

Occupational therapy was less of a struggle. I could paint. I took amber, ochre, umber, sunflower, and brown and made a painting of a deciduous, broad-leaved tree in the shape of Christmas. It was made with the colors of fauvism and stroked impressionistically. I made moccasins, sewing the suede pieces together and striating them with blue-lake-like paint strokes. I made a ceramic vase from a mold and refused to cut off the irregular lip. At night a nurse would hand me a Dixie cup with three pink lithium capsules. The Dixie cups were endless. I was told to swallow the 900 milligrams. I did. I would open my mouth wide and stick my tongue out and flip it over to prove it. I followed the routine and the rhythms of the ward. I woke up at seven a.m., had breakfast with TeeVee Dude and the eating-disorder girls. I had no restrictions on my food. They wanted me to eat more. (I had pared my diet down to essentials over the summer and lost about 15 pounds before I was admitted—I had wanted to be lean and ready for disaster.) But now, I reluctantly picked up my plastic utensils (no knives) and would eat the square meals. My mom, on my request, brought a homemade pasta dinner to the hospital. I missed the tomato sauce she made monthly in a witch's cauldron. I did all the things I was supposed to do. I even played volleyball.

And I continued to get better.

There were still moments of rigidity on the ward that made

me anxious and angry. One morning I put on my favorite concert T-shirt. It was black and long-sleeved and showed the outline of a man, with his veins and musculature and organs on the front. On the sleeve was a syringe with a needle and the words *free works*. The shirt was from a benefit concert for AIDS research and the word *works* signified the needle that heroin addicts use to shoot up. The concert itself was a social triumph for me, and I clung to the memory of that night, especially in the hospital as I was missing the first month of my senior year of high school.

Two years before I was hospitalized, in 1991, I switched from an out-of-zone magnet middle school (that I was bussed to) to my local high school, University High, a turn-of-the-century brick building that was originally built to feed students to UCLA. The campus was vast and sprawling, with a natural aquifer and a rambling stream that was once a sacred site for the Tongva people. Uni had been used as a set for everything from *My So-Called Life* to *Party of Five*, and the main brick building was even once blown up, thanks to passable post-production special effects, in an after-school special that I think our principal, in retrospect, regretted renting out the facility for. Students at the continuation school ate lunch by the stream; the friends I made ate on the grass by the administration building. I had pictured reinvention with my first day of tenth grade, but I just felt like an alien. The outcasts in *Some Kind of Wonderful* or *Pretty in Pink* were always full-lipped and glamorous and wore ugly hats that improbably looked perfect, their problems coated with cinematic sheen.

My tactic for making friends was to list music. "What do you like," I'd say; "what do you listen to?" We traded stories about the alterna-rock-funk scene curated by KROQ. The on-air DJs felt more like friends. We'd listen to Poorman and Dr. Drew. Morning hosts Kevin and Bean got us to school by arguing and shouting through our pop-off stereos. I was armed with a ready-made answer of who I'd listen to—The Smiths, Fishbone, Talking Heads, U2, Peter Gabriel, Indigo Girls, Cyndi Lauper, and sometimes Tom Waits for extra eclectic points, plus Madonna, always Madonna, forever Madonna. I worshipped her and would never let go of preteen choreographed pantomimed dance routines in my garage. With this arsenal of talking points, I made friends with a group of dark, smart alterna-girls who, like me and my friends from junior high, wore overdyed jeans, old dresses that fit like potato sacks, overalls and white V-neck T-shirts borrowed permanently from our fathers' drawers. We were a small group in size and stature—Alicia, Rebecca, Mara, Robin, and a token dude named David. We made mix tapes, we were good students, we drew winding doodles on Trapper Keepers.

The first semester went okay. But by winter break I started getting weird. I would call my older brother, Matt, late at night and speak in small, squeaky, little-girl voices. Like I was a character from *The Shining*. I couldn't sleep, I was haunted by Bob from *Twin Peaks*, the clown from Stephen King's *It*, and the Night Stalker, by men who lurked in mirrors, gutters, and alleyways. It was Matt's first year at Berkeley and I was stuck at home, on my own for the first time. I would also call Dr. G, the therapist I'd been seeing since my assault, during off-hours just to hear her calm, caramelly voice on the answering machine. She had a soothing, matronly, slow way of speaking. I called Dr. G a thousand times in a row, sometimes every hour on the hour all night long, just to hear her outgoing message. Our sessions became so fraught with stress that they almost always ended silently, eight or nine minutes early. I would fall asleep midsentence, to take a nap in her pink plaid chair surrounded by pastel wallpaper and the quiet, quiet, still, still, motionless, silence. Her office was like a pretty, feminine cocoon that I could curl up in. I wanted to stay longer than the fifty minutes, to hibernate. The frequency of my sessions with Dr. G increased to four times a week. When my symptoms first started, they were limited to anxiety and insomnia. She referred me to a meds-only psychiatrist and I would leave his office with refills or a scrip. There seemed to be a gap between my talk therapy and meds; my parents noticed it more than I did.

During winter break of my tenth-grade year, I was catatonic, confused, doped up on meds. For a brief period, I was basically on what my dad called horse tranquilizers. My tongue was so swollen from meds that when I spoke I could only feel a wall of flesh. I could articulate nothing. I spent a lot of time lurking on the bottom bunk of my brother's bunk beds watching our black-and-white TV and sleeping. I had eight weeks to recover—the school system was on a year-round schedule that year and I used my eight-week winter break stuck in an ad hoc asylum state. After eight weeks, I came out of it. I don't remember how. It seemed like lost time or a medicinal straitjacket. I made it back to Uni for my second semester of tenth grade with an amended schedule. I would take journalism after lunch.

My second semester was defined by—what I thought was—optional attendance. I did some normal teen things. I had crushes, wrote for the school newspaper (op-eds that were pro gun control, pro over-the-counter RU-486 birth control, and a very strongly worded piece on how the student body management reeked of fascism for enforcing "gang attire restrictions"). I wrote, I went to ceramics class, I competed on the tennis team, and I picked when I wanted to go to school. On April 29, 1992, I was at school when the verdict acquitting the four police officers in the Rodney King beating came in. I sat on the front lawn waiting for my mom to pick me up; the traffic going back to our apartment was so gridlocked I got out of the car and bought a frozen yogurt. My dad picked me up from my mom's around dusk and the traffic had entirely dissipated. As we drove east, the streets were empty, the city was on lockdown, the billboards and storefronts about to be on fire. I was outraged; the city was outraged. Dad's neighborhood near Paramount Studios was populated by older folks who felt the looting encroaching from Crenshaw or Western. When we turned left on Beachwood one grizzled old white dude stood at the corner of Beverly Boulevard and Beachwood Drive with a shotgun.

Tenth grade turned to eleventh. I took an SAT class with Urkel and Fred Savage and we learned how to game the results. The *Princeton Review* helpfully pointed out that the College Boards and standardized tests were developed as a way of measuring intelligence of World War II soldiers, in other words a test engineered for white men. ("The SAT will only measure how well you take the SAT," the tutors told us.) Our tutor rewarded us by playing a Beatles record backward at the end of the course—"Paul is dead, Paul is dead," the vinyl sang in a harsh alien monotone. Or not, it might have been something different. Some days I'd watch movies at the mall, two in a row. One afternoon, I bumped into a kid I knew at the discount department store Ross Dress for Less— he was looking for giant raver clown pants, something to buckle a pair of psychedelic rainbow suspenders on, and I was looking for cheap bras. We talked, we walked to his parents' apartment and smoked weed. We went to Subway, where he taught me about the munchies.

My friend Sarah J. would try to help mitigate my obsessive phone habits. I would call ten, fifteen, twenty times in a row to see if someone I had a crush on was home and hang up. Occasionally I would speak and crush-of-the-moment would speak back and we would have a cordial conversation. It was telemarketing style. Sarah would tell me when to stop, and most of the time I would. I spent dozens of afternoons at my dad's office in Santa Monica. One time, a full year after my sophmore-year breakdown, we both took a ditch day to watch Cal play in the Sweet Sixteen. We sat in a cavernous, dark, whiskey-drenched bar watching college ball on a beat-down TV at eleven in the morning when I should have been in Precalc or running SAT drills. I loved March Madness because it was orderly. Jason Kidd could see the court and move the ball. He was selfless and fast and precise and clutch. I could see the virtue in wanting something, in having a goal. My goal in tenth grade was to get through the year, and then the next year, and then to get myself to college. But, really, I was just looking for a place to be. I volunteered at a runaway shelter for teens called Stepping Stones and I remember some nights wanting to stay there because I liked the company. I felt close to the kids, my age for the most part; there was also a comfort in the concept of one house.

By April, Robin invited me to a concert on a Thursday night— everyone from the lunch group was going. I didn't have a ticket; they had had tickets for months. I scoured the classifieds, found a scalper, convinced my mom to go with me to meet him at a freeway off-ramp to exchange cash for one ticket—an amount that felt outrageous at the time, something like eighty bucks. I got the ticket and a ride to the Palladium and there I was, with a bunch of rock 'n' rollers. The lineup: Primus, Porno for Pyros, the Red Hot Chili Peppers, Fishbone, Rollins Band, and the Beastie Boys. Lakers Vlade Divac and Michael Cooper were in the audience (the Magic Johnson Foundation was one of the charities benefiting from the proceeds of the concert). I didn't see them, but I liked imagining their athletic bodies gesticulating in the mosh pit—the mosh pit that I had been in, running in circles to a throbbing and pulsating, loud, beat—their Laker heads ducked low like everyone else for once. We were all just a knot of limbs and frenzy, circling around nothing in particular, joined by forward motion and collision. We heard a live mix tape made up of every sweaty musician we could imagine, strumming atonal chords and bass lines plucked like roses.

Back in the hospital, a year and a half after that night, I gripped my needles T-shirt from the concert. I needed to be able to wear it; it felt as if I would lose the friends I had made—not because I was bat-shit crazy and institutionalized but because I was not allowed to wear the "free works" tee. It was more than "works," more than body; it was a well-worn, faded reminder of what was past and what was coming next—I had to deal with people again. My friends, when they visited me in the hospital, made a get-well card on poster board with puffy paint and exaggerated lettering. Those girls were hard-won prizes—friends! They were people I tasted alcohol with! Slept in their houses! Studied with! Listened to music with! Made mix tapes for! In fact, I had listened to Nirvana's *Nevermind* with them when it came out! That afternoon, when Robin showed us the CD and we listened on her Discman, all other music stopped. It was so guttural and base and fucked up. The guitars were reckless and chaotic and the drums just pounded persistently and primally. Kurt Cobain, unwilling tastemaker, brutal heartbreaker, old lady cardigan wearer, he was so deep and so dark and lazy and tired and he wore smudged eyeliner and was perpetually stuck in the darkest shadow of adolescent angst. He was manic onstage, depressed in his drawl, diagnosed manic depressive. He also wrote a song called "Lithium"—the flailing vocals, riotously emotional and insistent, paired with slow indifferent verses, pogo-ing between two emotional states, tethering and validating both frequencies. He was screaming what we were feeling as teenagers, validating my mind without naming it. He was prophetic—shouting about the medicine I would take. He would fight to wear the needles shirt too. Or maybe he wouldn't, maybe he wouldn't care enough to fight. Maybe it would fit in the category of *nevermind*.

But I did care, I would not take it off. I was well, I was getting weller with every day and every pink pill, every dose of lithium, but I would not give up my shirt. The hospital staff said this shirt was against dress code policy and insensitive and told me to change. I refused. I argued that it was against my First Amendment rights, and the nurses reminded me again that I had no rights. The ward had its own constitution and it did not include concert T-shirts glorifying heroin. I argued; I pointed to my dog-eared copy of "Handbook of Rights for Mental Health Patients." I pointed to specific passages like *You cannot be denied the right to wear your own clothes*. I was standing at a precipice, dangerously close to jumping off. Was the shirt worth more pain, was it worth doing more time? I still had an apple-sized bruise—purple, yellow, gray, and green—on my left hip from the multiple needle punctures that the nurses administered when I had been tackled. It seemed ironic that they were so anti-needles now. I argued for the needles T-shirt because it reminded me of before, that I had friends. It reminded me of the normal me, the one who would argue over a T-shirt and the First Amendment and who would hang on to ideals and rights. But I let go of the argument because I could tell I was close to leaving this place. The T-shirt was an argument that made sense on the outside, but not in here. Not in this place where confinement is cure. Soon I would jones for these restrictions.

CHAPTER 6

RABID MUTANT SQUIRRELS, FRONTAL LOBE, BEAST IN THE ATTIC

TOWARD THE END of my stay at NPI, my older brother, Matthew, flew down from Berkeley to visit. At that point I was a model patient—loved volleyball, embraced homework assignments in the afternoon, watched programs in the common room without shouting about death gases. I was allowed an off-site pass—a coveted status. Matt brought lunch so that we could eat on those grassy hills just past the mega-poison generator. (I still thought it was mega-poison . . . but I was open to the idea that it wasn't.) We sat and talked and I explained what had been explained to me. I had experienced a psychotic break, I was manic, I was manic depressive, I was on lithium, I would be better. He nodded and said he understood, he had met with Dr. DeAntonio and was briefed before we left the ward. All was fine. The food was good. It was nice to see him and to get out of a locked-in state.

It felt like an easy conversation, a return to normal. My brother cautiously danced around trigger questions. We talked about music:

Talking Heads, Skankin' Pickle, Tom Waits, Green Day, who were then just a band that performed at Berkeley co-op parties. Matt had put a lot of those bands on a mix tape for my sixteenth birthday, a tape I listened to obsessively until it ripped. I have always listened to music obsessively and on loop. Matt would pay me not to play certain songs out of fear that he would get sick of hearing them. We talked about his housing; he was living in a shack in the backyard of an apartment building in Berkeley. Sometimes an opossum lived with him on the inside corner of the roof, a good nocturnal roommate. (And I was the crazy one.) We talked about his friends who went abroad for their junior year. I had met them all and others—Stu, Lanchi, Steph, Tony, Chris—when I visited the Berkeley dorms during his freshman year. We talked about lithium, about how it was working—that I felt calmer and closer to me. He wasn't sure what that meant. I wasn't sure what that meant. I was hyperaware of getting better but still connected to the episode. We ate lunch and I was fine.

Sitting with Matt in the grass, outside the ward, I thought of the birthday mix tape. On it was Tom Waits's song "I Don't Wanna Grow Up," a coal miner's croaky anthem to regression, to the freedom of inhibition and youth. I think in a lot of ways, breakdowns are both a resistance to growing up and an acceleration of maturity. In his song Waits's chorus loops, an insistent, chanting anthem: "I don't wanna have to shout it out / I don't want my hair to fall out . . . I don't wanna grow up." That acid-throated voice was going through my head; I listened to it in the dayroom on my Walkman. I did not feel ready to grow up; I did not feel ready to be discharged from the ward, a place I had never wanted to be. It's possible I didn't even feel ready to have this day pass. To have this lunch with my brother. I could feel myself getting better; my manic and psychotic symptoms were diminished. Just having a sense of ever having been sick was thought of as real and important progress. But I wasn't sure how much of the episode lingered: How would it alter me fundamentally? Did it change my personality? Did my mood disorder—a disease of the brain—change me? How did I see myself? How did others—family and friends included—see me?

Lunatics have always been a curiosity. I could tell that Matt was curious, cautious. In eighteenth-century London, Bethlem Royal Hospital for the insane, aka Bedlam, was open to the public on visiting days, making all patients and residents more like zoo attractions than empathetic or equal humans. The idea was that civilians would bring "jollity and merriment" to otherwise depraved souls, but one visitor noted "a hundred people, at least, suffered, unattended to run rioting up and down the wards making sport of the miserable inhabitants." Decades later a Russian visitor described seeing patients who grunted like a bear and another who walked on all fours. Outside the doors of Bedlam were two carved figures—statues that represented melancholy and mania. Victorian literature had a habit of sequestering mad women from society, stashing them in towers or attics, where they might chew at the wallpaper, itching and wailing into the night. Just think about Charlotte Brontë's *Jane Eyre*, in which the heroine of the narrative is introduced to the "lunatic" wife of Mr. Rochester: "What it was, whether beast or human being, one could not, at first sight, tell . . . but it was covered with clothing, and a quantity of dark, grizzled hair, wild as a mane, hid its head and face . . . The maniac bellowed: she parted her shaggy locks from her visage, and gazed wildly at her visitors." The description is feral, animalistic, and wild—the pronoun Brontë uses is *it*, not *her*, as if the person is no longer present. When Matt came to visit, and when my friends tried to make idle conversation in the visitor's room, I felt gawked at. I'm sure they heard or knew or sensed that something very serious was wrong with me. I was in the *ward*.

In the late 1800s, as the medical field was looking toward more humane treatment, the mentally ill were still considered an enigma and sequestered into unfathomable conditions. In 1887 the journalist Nellie Bly, a pen name for Elizabeth Cochran Seaman, published an account of her undercover experience as a patient at Blackwell's Island Insane Asylum, which she documented in serial for the *New York World*. While the treatment she witnessed was appalling—she writes in detail of her experience with abuse, inhumane conditions, malnutrition, and rampant untreated sickness—she's most struck by the way the women are ignored. She writes, "I always had a desire to know asylum life more thoroughly—a desire to be convinced that the most helpless of God's creatures, the insane, were cared for kindly and properly." If I had been born in the late nineteenth century, when lithium was first being tested as a medicine, even to the most sympathetic ear—someone like Nellie Bly—I would have been considered among the most helpless of God's creatures, just a haunted body with a corrupt soul and an inconsolable mind. Or worse, from 1909 to 1979, California had a state law that authorized forced sterilization of people judged to have "mental disease, which may have been inherited." The researchers who uncovered the eugenics program (in my own state! still happening in my lifetime!) found that people were sterilized at very young ages, as young as seven. The average age of sterilization was the low teens—many of those sterilized were the same age I was when I was hospitalized. Maybe my paranoia was not so far off?

Temperament itself is so tempestuous. One year after *Jane Eyre* was published, a medical oddity revealed one of the first examples of the brain's effect on personality. On September 13, 1848, Phineas Gage was blasting rock while constructing a railroad in Vermont. While Gage was working, he brought his head near the blast hole and opened his mouth to speak. There was an explosion, and the large tamping iron rod was driven completely through his head, destroying much of his brain's left frontal lobe. But, miraculously, he survived and lived for another eleven years. The injury left a lasting and dramatic effect on his personality. His friends who knew him before the accident described him as "no longer Gage." After Gage's death, one of the doctors who treated him, John Harlow, described the difference: "The equilibrium or balance, so to speak, between his intellectual faculties and animal propensities, seems to have been destroyed. He is fitful, irreverent, indulging at times in the grossest profanity (which was not previously his custom), manifesting but little deference for his fellows, impatient of restraint or advice when it conflicts with his desires, at times pertinaciously obstinate, yet capricious and vacillating, devising many plans of future operations, which are no sooner arranged than they are abandoned in turn for others appearing more feasible. A child in his intellectual capacity and manifestations, he has the animal passions of a strong man. Previous to his injury, although untrained in the schools, he possessed a well-balanced mind, and was looked upon by those who knew him as a shrewd, smart businessman, very energetic and persistent in executing all his plans of operation."

The idea that the brain influenced personality and emotion wasn't new, but it wasn't proven either. The brain and its propensity to define and control personality and emotion was still a relative mystery. This seemed relevant to me because at the most basic level Gage represented two people, one brain. Even if I didn't have an actual rod through my brain, I felt like something had altered my personality. Something had shifted the direction of my thinking, my impulses. I was me, but I had been not me. Maybe I was permanently a different person because of the trauma of mania, and my brain was responding and forming around that?

But I was not born in an era when the mentally ill were pitied and hopeless; I was born in an era when the medical field was beginning to understand and to treat mental illness, an era when mental illness has almost been fetishized. Doctors could identify symptoms and prescribe remedies, which was a relatively new method. Just a few months before I was hospitalized, public figures like Patty Duke, who had published her book *A Brilliant Madness*, were emerging to talk about and advocate on behalf of this newly recognized group of people. Wild people, tamed with pills, who were reintroduced into civilian life.

Sitting on UCLA's lawn, one thing was clear: Matt could recognize a calmer me. I had a slight tremor from the cocktail of meds, which my brother noticed. Out of the corner of my eye, I saw a gang of muscular squirrels near our picnic spot and quickly explained that although I was fine and doing better, it looked like those squirrels had a plan and that we should probably flee the area. He laughed, I laughed, and then I said with urgency, "No really, we need to leave." I felt certain that the squirrels were collaborating and planning a rabid feast of flesh. Our flesh. They looked big, they were flexing, and I was betting on them. They stared with the intensity of a thousand suns. They started to look like kangaroos to me, growing more giant with each nose wiggle and acorn nibble. I was not hallucinating anymore, I was seeing actual satanic squirrels: aggressive, bloodthirsty rodents on steroids.

"Calm down," Matt said. "It's okay."

I was determined to be better and normal and okay. Our lunch expedition cut short, we scrambled out of the grassy hills with my view on squirrels permanently altered.

CHAPTER 7

IRRECONCILABLE DIFFERENCES
AND THE OMNIPOTENT DR. VISCOTT

BEFORE NEVERLAND, before mania, before bipolar, before
NPI and Dr. DeAntonio, before diagnosis, before my parents worried for my safety and for theirs, before I was predicting apocalypse
in public places, before I falsely accused my dad of abuse, I was just

Jaime. Sometimes Jaime Rose, occasionally Jaimer, or JR. I was born at Oakland Kaiser on November 20, 1976, the day before a big Michigan football game.

My mom always told me that Preston, their friend and OB-GYN, caught me in a catcher's mitt and that I didn't cry. I had thick curly hair. When they brought me home to our house in Berkeley, Matt, age three, faked nice but secretly had a stash of sticks ready to poke through my crib gate. My nursery was cloaked with curtains that my mom made: big orange ladybugs geometrically lodged against a kelly-green backdrop. We lived in the Berkeley hills next to an elderly neighbor named Mrs. Potter who had an elderly dog named Muffy; he was disabled and carted around his janky back legs on wheels through the neighborhood, where dewy mornings smelled like night-blooming jasmine and eucalyptus. My time in Berkeley was short. When I was eighteen months old my parents split up and we moved to Los Angeles. My mom moved into an apartment on Almayo Avenue in West Los Angeles and started her master's in screenwriting at the American Film Institute (AFI). *Irreconcilable differences* and *divorce* were words I used in sentences by age three.

My parents were divorced, but both partnered shortly after their separation—my mom met Jeff at the AFI, and my dad knew Marilyn from work. After a downstairs neighbor complained about my screaming from night terrors, my mom moved us into a duplex on Comstock Avenue near the Century City mall in West Los Angeles; my dad's house was on a tree-lined street abutted by Paramount Studios. They made nice, happy homes. We had two rooms, two closets full of toys, two closets full of clothes, a dog at my dad's house, a hamster at my mom's. We were kind of dumb kids when it came to food—we thought celery hearts were an extravagant treat and that carob was chocolate. My dad picked us up Thursdays and drove the thirty to forty-five minutes between the houses; we would shout out a song to the tallest building on Larchmont, the 3-2-1 song for the 3-2-1 building and that meant we were almost home.

I was a very verbal kid with unruly red hair that I refused to brush. Jack at Tipperary would scissor-cut my mane into a thick bowl, something that resembled a Michael Dukakis cut. I wore striped hand-me-downs from Matt, and I never wore matching socks. I was constantly mistaken for a boy. Freckles clustered on my face like constellations and I would say, objectively, that I was an impish troublemaker. My mom got me headshots and an agent like every other kid in LA. I posed in the orange tree in our backyard and grinned making sweet faces that were clearly forced. One picture looked real—an action shot of me in patchwork jeans, attacking a Wiffle ball with a yellow bat. Good swing, measured stance, fierce aggression and concentration. I auditioned for Jell-O commercials and hawked laundry detergent with other miniature hopefuls, but in my short three-month career—maybe eight auditions with two callbacks—I only landed one gig, as a leotard model for a catalog. It was obvious why: I had an outsized chubby belly, and when augmented by the dance clothes, I looked like a little piglet stuffed into spandex casing. I went to school. I had friends. I had Barbies. I made my Barbies have sex in the hot pink dream car with or without Ken. They were naked, they were headless, they lived tortured interior lives always striving for more and I continuously denied them fairy-tale happy endings. If Barbie was to live in the real world, my real world, she would have to work for success and contentment. Barbies had to learn about real life and disappointment and failure.

I grew up with swimming lessons; quartered oranges at soccer practice; sleepovers; doting grandparents and stepgrandparents

FROM LEFT TO RIGHT: MATTHEW, JEFF, MY MOM, LEEAN, AND ME IN MAINE.

and aunts and uncles and cousins; and loving, involved parents and stepparents. We'd visit Jeff's family on Lake Thompson in Maine.

We'd go to Yosemite with my dad and Marilyn. I would resist hiking and play "pizza" with Marilyn, a game that involved running and operating a pizza parlor that served ghost food to babies made out of blankets.

FROM LEFT TO RIGHT: MARILYN, MATT, ME, AND MY DAD, STEPHEN.

Matt and I would spend the six-hour drives up to the redwoods recording ourselves on portable cassette tapes. My mom got a deal on a rental car once, returning it to Berkeley. Driving up the 5, I would sing Madonna lyrics while Matt played a cassette tape of himself reading entries from the *Guinness Book of World Records*. While reciting improbable weights and feats of strength, he repeatedly mispronounced words, reading *lbs.* as "libbles." I only mention this because he was always smarter, more well read, and more academically diligent than I.

We were kids of the 1980s: we grew up with *The Muppet Show* and *Three's Company* and *Mork and Mindy*. My mom worked full time, so before I was old enough for kindergarten, I would be dropped off at an old lady's house across the street from West-wood Elementary. Mrs. Brown would flip on Richard Simmons' workout and I would lay on the carpet enchanted by his sequined short shorts and his high kicks. We listened to *Schoolhouse Rock* and we sang "Free to Be You and Me" like it was a Bible hymn. My mom had the original cast recording of *A Chorus Line*. I played that record till the grooves were dulled, dancing around the living room shouting, "Tits and ass won't get you jobs, unless they're youuuuuuuurs." And then in deep baritone, I'd sing, "Have 'em all done, honey take my word, go see the wizard at Park and Seventy-Third! For?" And I'd cup my ear in mock call and response to an audience of no one, standing as tall as I could on top of our maroon velour couch, then shout again, "Tits! and ass! Yes tits! And ass! Can't save your liiiiiiife, unless they're youuuuuuuurs." *Bah bah bada bada dum.* The fact that I was crooning about the glory of plastic surgery was lost on me. My dad had a more expansive record collection stacked with Sondheim and jazz and whatever hipster selections KCRW happened to be hawking that week. Our commutes were lessons in listening. One morning he popped in Tom Waits's *Bone Machine*, and I had never been so audibly repulsed in my life. Matt would play those cassettes on loop and Tom Waits's hangdog growl-shouting did not make sense to me. Not for a long time. Not until high school. Not until the ward, really. Not until I understood what it meant to not want to grow up. Not until I understood what it meant to love and to suffer and to disappear into a world of swordfish trombones. There was a loneliness to his voice but reassurance in knowing he always had an audience. He always had heart and heartbreak.

As children of divorce, we had to contend with a ferkakte schedule. Monday, Tuesday, and Wednesday we were at my mom's; Thursday and Friday we were at my dad's; and every other weekend we alternated houses. My favorite pastime was hitting a big red rubber ball against the driveway. My second favorite was hiding in a burro weed bush in the backyard in which I elected myself president of a "club" with no other members. On hot days at my mom's we would walk over to the Century Plaza Hotel and sneak in—as a family—to the pool. To make it more authentic Matt and I would fake New York accents and talk about our magical West Coast vacation with long-drawn-out vowel-dominant syllables. We always could entertain each other. There were moments of intensity that would devolve into hysteria and my brother would chant: "Calm down, Jaime. Calm down." Mary Karr once wrote, "In the entire history of anxiety worldwide, telling someone to calm down has worked zero times." "Calm down" should only be used in response to watching someone win the lottery. I was not calm. Would never be calm. I would never want to be calm. Calming down was for suckers.

At my dad's house I would scale the back fence to climb on top of the garage roof to eat tiny pickles from the local Italian deli. I exercised enough magical thinking that in my long afternoons I had fantastical visions of being crowned a handball champion or becoming president or someday landing that first teeth-clashing kiss or even, most improbably, scoring a goal in soccer. We were normal kids. We climbed trees; we scabbed knees; we outgrew clothing; we set small fires; we went to the beach; we Xeroxed our faces; we ate pancakes; we ate waffles; we listened to Michael Jackson. I was a normal kid. Aside from constantly commuting and being unhealthily obsessed with musical theater, my childhood was normal, normal, normal with lots of love from every direction.

When I asked my mom if there were ever any indications or hints at bipolar, she just laughed and said, "Well, you were a very dramatic kid." Then went on to describe a typical scenario. At dinner, I might be kicking Matthew under the table and my mom said she would send me to my room for punishment. Outraged, I would throw my napkin on the floor and march up the stairs to my room and slam the door. Thirty seconds later, she remembered me emerging red with rage spreading across my freckled face and screaming, "AND I'M NEVER COMING BACK." Then I would slam the door again, extra hard. About three minutes would pass and I would be back at the table eating homemade pizza. My mom said it was hard not to laugh at me, the tiny fury. "But that was just my personality, right?" I asked her. "Yeah, I mean that doesn't seem bipolar to me, that just seemed like you."

If someone had developed a genetic test (which Dr. John Kelsoe controversially did in 2008 in response to a rash of overdiagnosing children with bipolar disorder that peaked in the early 2000s) to determine if I was bipolar or likely to experience a bipolar episode, I wouldn't have even been given the test. I had none of the hallmark signs of mental illness. The disorder is thought to affect between 1 and 3 percent of Americans and tends to run in families, although no specific (or single) gene for it has been identified. Even the mental illness that ran through my grandfather's side of the family was thought to be a somewhat distant connection.

My normal childhood evolved into a normal junior high career. I was a gifted student and I argued passionately about politics. I hunted for vintage dresses, I valued overdyed purple jeans, and I made earrings with my friend Hana. I watched intentionally

FROM LEFT TO RIGHT: ME, DAVID, AND MATT IN YOSEMITE.

bad movies like *Cry-Baby* and ate pickles with Miriam. I was a little chubby and went to a teen weight-loss program called Kid-Shape. All of my parents came too and we learned about portion control and that juice is the sugary devil. When I was twelve, my dad and Marilyn had a baby, my little brother David. I changed his diapers and doted on him. I had nothing but unrequited love flowing toward him, but he was the little shit that bisected my already bisected life. I had grown from being a spunky, mismatched spitfire into a fat and anxious twelve-year-old. I was newly awkward—for the bulk of sixth and seventh grade I wore the same T-shirt every day; I also slept in it and I kept my hair pulled back except for three small braids framing the right side of my face. I was no longer cute and I didn't need to compete with a cute little baby, with a cute little smile, who made cute little noises. I went to a junior high magnet school in South Los Angeles called Los Angeles Center for Enriched Studies (LACES). We always thought the bloviated name was a misnomer, but we knew the words *bloviated* and *misnomer*, so who knows. It was founded in 1977 as the first magnet school in Los Angeles Unified School District (LAUSD) and was created as part of the district's voluntary integration program. We were all bussed to school on the site of the former Louis Pasteur junior high school on Eighteenth Street. The teachers offered self-selected elective classes, which meant I could take Gilbert and Sullivan or Japanese or roller skating as part of my curriculum. Leonardo DiCaprio rode my bus occasionally, Ms. Stringos taught aerobics in a G-string leotard and had Elvira hair, and the school cafeteria routinely produced the most delicious underbaked, steaming hot chocolate chip cookies.

I went to LACES from sixth grade until ninth grade. I played Pish-Tush in *The Mikado* against Rachel's Pooh-Bah and I never once felt dorky for wearing floral overalls, though I should have. I made close friends at LACES—Hana, Miriam, Sarah J., and Rachel.

One day, on my way to the school bus stop, I saw a man standing in the alley I passed just two blocks from my mom's apartment. I had seen him before—he was short, Latino, and young, probably not that much older than me. I smiled at him and waved, as I had done on previous days; only this time he gestured for me to come closer to where he was standing. I didn't know what to do or I thought he had something to tell me, and so I walked toward him. He showed me that he had a knife and held it against my side. He said that my father owed him some money and I explained that Jeff was not my father and that my father lived much farther away and that it seemed impossible for anyone to owe him money and if they did I would get the money for him. He stumbled on his words and continued to press the knife against my waist. I was wearing floral boxers from the Gap and a T-shirt. He pulled down the shorts and started fondling me. I had no feeling. I did not know what was happening. He asked me to spread my legs, and he said, "Let me just kiss it." He crouched down to kiss my vagina, at which point I screamed for him to stop. The scream was likely not much louder than a spoken word, but it was loud enough that he took his knife and ran up the alley.

I didn't cry. I pulled up my shorts and walked back to my mom's apartment. The building was painted yellow and our door was the color of rotten avocado. I put my key in the door and my mom came in the living room and asked why I wasn't on the bus. I started heaving-sobbing, and explained what had happened. She hugged me and we went to the police station to file a report. I described the guy in as much detail as I could remember for a composite drawing. My mom drove around with a butcher knife in her car for a day or two, in a blind fury. She didn't know what she was doing but was looking for revenge or justice or something. I missed school and one girl was certain it was because I had gotten my period. I was cold and calculated and measured when I told my friends what happened. Sometimes I was smiling: "I was molested." I didn't know how to talk about it. I didn't understand it. I had the vocabulary but nothing else. My friends didn't understand or believe me at first, even my closest friends. Why would they? I didn't know what it meant in the days that followed or even the years that followed. I wouldn't know for a long time. I still don't know because there is no alternate version. Nothing to compare it to. I was thirteen. I didn't get my period until three years after that. Sexuality was not in my worldview no matter how many health classes I took. My dad and Marilyn had been in Chicago and flew home. My dad didn't know how to talk about it. He bought me a pair of Air Jordans from Nordstrom and we sat in the Westside Pavilion silently, me clutching a shoebox and he desperately trying to make me feel better.

That was when my sessions with Dr. G started. I sat on her pastel plaid overstuffed chair. We mostly talked about the trauma of the divorce and the pressure of perfection, and most sessions I opted to express myself by forming creatures out of Fimo clay. Therapy was always a part of our lives. After the divorce, Matt and I went to a child psychologist, who suggested we work out our anger by pummeling each other with foam bats. My mom religiously listened to Dr. David Viscott on the radio. Analysis—about movies, art, music, self—was paramount. After dealing with the immediate effects of maladies, my mom would ask, *What are the psychosomatic symptoms that you're feeling? What do they represent?* A broken wrist was a reaction to my brother's birth; a cold could mean test anxiety. One of the many benefits to a psychologically mindful mother was that we could declare mental health days whenever we needed a break from school. For me those days involved my favorite video. My mom had recorded the first two thirds of the movie *Tootsie*, and that was enough. It was an early wormhole to New York—the New York of the 1980s. Cab strikes and desperate creatives living in lofts downtown, being mugged, working in a kitchen before there were foodies, Michael Dorsey's insistence on perfection in performance. I loved *Tootsie* and its original score even though it would be better matched to a toothpaste commercial.

By the end of ninth grade, most of my friends at LACES scattered, returning to their home high schools throughout LAUSD. Hana went to Hamilton High; Miriam went to Beverly Hills High; Rachel went to Palisades; Sarah J. went to Venice. And I went to University High in West Los Angeles. I don't remember having a choice, I was tethered to Matt's legacy. He did well there. I would too. He was already beloved by the journalism teacher, Monserrat Fontes, and by every other teacher at the school since he was a thorough and diligent student. He was a dork—competed in academic pentathlon in junior high and played the board game Diplomacy with all his dork friends in high school. (Apparently it was a good primer; he's now a professional diplomat.) I remember fantasizing about a fresh start at a new school with kids who didn't know me. I thought, if all the young adult books are correct, I will be the popular, unknown outsider who brings super cool to an otherwise deprived campus. The boys will swoon, my overdyed jeans will be heralded as a fashion breakthrough, and I will ace every test in between making out with the *most popular* boys.

The year I started high school was also the year Matt went to UC Berkeley. My grandmother knitted him a blanket, as she did for all the high school graduates in our family. But I don't think anyone could have predicted my reaction. Matt and I had one constant—each other. I didn't have a problem being independent from my parents, but being separated from Matthew felt like a psychic wound. I think Dr. Viscott would have labeled it a regression or a psychotic break or separation anxiety.

The timeline of collapse is simple. My parents split before I was two; in eighth grade I was assaulted; I started to see a therapist. In tenth grade I was undiagnosed but plagued with sleeplessness and agitation. In eleventh grade I held it together earning A's and B's and impressive SAT scores, making friends, going to parties, having a normal high school year. I was an All-City doubles tennis player and I won awards for on-the-spot journalism writing and editing. I had friends, crushes, lapses in judgment, and a keen sense for exceeding the bare minimum necessary to get into a University of California college. And I knew that with what I had managed in tenth and eleventh grade, I was probably already guaranteed a place.

So, in twelfth grade I broke. And I broke hard.

During my last few days in the ward, clutching the decorations that had lined the wall next to my bed, I wondered if I was ready. I was trying to make sense of this involuntary commitment. Was I cured by the diagnosis? What was lithium and would it work? Would there be side effects? Would the lithium be toxic later in life? Would I be able to have children? Would my kidneys and thyroid and brain survive? I survived a squirrel apocalypse, a personal holocaust, real abuse, imagined abuse, isolation, noxious gases, hallucinations of pop stars and serial killers, winding mazelike tunnels, spending sprees, war, killer teevees, gangs of evil nurses, and solitary confinement. Most importantly, I survived mandatory volleyball.

CHAPTER 8

"IT'S TIME TO START LIVIN'!"

I SAID GOOD-BYE to my eating-disorder friends and TeeVee Dude; I thanked the nurses and Dr. DeAntonio. I did not feel helpless, I did not feel different. I packed my symptoms in my duffel bag along with my moccasins, a colorful vase, my fauvist paintings, and concert T-shirts. I still believed what I experienced. It was, after all, real to me. People ask me if I remember, or if manic episodes exist in something like a blackout state. I do remember, and that feeling never fully dissipates. There's always a small question that persists: Maybe I was right about everything? Maybe I wasn't so far off? Maybe there is a germ of rational in what otherwise seems so far afield? It was like Nellie Bly's experience—I wasn't stuck for life on an island for the insane; I didn't have to plead my sanity, I didn't have to steal a set of keys to unlock the bars on the window or break down a door or trick nurses into a catastrophic mistake or enact my MacGyver fantasy tuck-and-rolls. I was crazy, I got a diagnosis, I got better. And now I was fine. Fine enough to go home. But I changed; the episode itself was traumatic. I no longer had a baseline for reality or even a way to fully trust myself. Two things shifted when I was discharged. One was that the psychiatric team at NPI felt that I should live in one house. So, my child-of-divorce schedule ended. I would stay primarily at my mom's house. The other shift was that my continued therapy would be handled by Dr. DeAntonio and I would attend an adolescent group therapy led by Dr. Arthur Sorosky across from a mini mall in Encino. My parents collectively felt that Dr. G had missed my diagnosis. My treatment with her ended when I left the hospital, and it felt like I had lost a parental figure.

I packed my bag and backpack and we drove back to our apartment. The same place where—just a month earlier—my mom had developed a nightly ritual in response to my psychosis. She would collect all of our kitchen knives, wrap them in a dish towel, and hide them in the back of a drawer beneath her bed. She didn't really fear for my safety or hers—but she didn't exactly know what to expect and she wasn't *sure*. Now, I was medicated. Now, it was safe to leave the knives unsheathed. My room was the same but neater. Paranoid poems I had written were neatly stacked in my closet. Diagrams I had written on my chalkboard wall were erased. My twin bed was made, army corners tucked in, and all my clothes were folded neatly and put away in drawers. The orange tree outside my window was just barely showing fruit. I put on my Clean Needles shirt and unpacked my vase, my moccasins, and my drawings.

We filled my prescription of lithium and I didn't recognize depression setting in. I was slow. I had gained weight and was thicker. It was hard to understand the difference between depression and not being manic, especially in the come-down of an episode. This is partly because my experience of bipolar disorder swings manic. My depressive periods are almost always in the wake of mania and almost never independent. I have plenty of anxiety, but I've never been deeply, clinically depressed unless it's in response to having been manic—in which case the depression runs deep. Most people who identify bipolar tend to experience much more extreme bouts of depression. Dr. DeAntonio described mania as similar to a cocaine high. Mania is overwhelming and intense; an enormous feeling of omnipotence coated in a glossy sheen of euphoria and sex. Everything is attractive, on fire, covered in rainbows and unicorns and deluded perfection. I have to take drugs to *not* feel this way.

I returned to civilian life armed with an explanation: I was bipolar. That didn't seem to mean much in high school. Or high school didn't seem to mean that much to me. I was told that other people who were bipolar changed the course of human history: people like Isaac Newton, Abraham Lincoln, Winston Churchill, Theodore Roosevelt, Pablo Picasso, Honoré de Balzac, George Frideric Handel, Ludwig van Beethoven, Robert Schumann, Leo Tolstoy, Charles Dickens, Virginia Woolf, Ernest Hemingway, Patty Duke, and Carrie Fisher. I was among the greats. It didn't feel like it. Even though Kurt Cobain was publicly teetering on the edge, courting the end, writing poetry about the very drug I was taking before bed every night. My pills felt limiting. I felt stunted and repressed. I was compliant, though. I carried a small pill box of pink pills. My mom, always a Girl Scout, wanted me prepared for any scenario including a stranding or—ironically—an apocalyptic event. I had enough lithium for four nights at all times.

I missed about a month of school and was behind in all my classes, including science and math. I dropped out of AP Physics and AP Calculus because I couldn't keep up with the homework in the hospital. (I wasn't bad at math; I only missed one math question on the SAT.) My schedule was light—nothing would be stressful, there would be no triggers. Before I was on the gifted AP and honors track, with homework assignments that took up many hours of every week night. Now I was hybrid, almost vocational. Out of all my classes—journalism, ceramics, photography, AP English, AP Government, and tennis—only two out of six actually required attendance. (Mr. Takagaki, the AP Government teacher believed that we—as nearly graduated students—could determine on our own whether we attended his class or not. He told us he was a staunch communist and imbued a sense of consequence and responsibility in his students. The consensus? No one went to AP Government or even took the final exam or the AP exam. We were too young for self-determination.)

For about a month, I rejoined my friends on the lawn and went to high school parties and gossiped about high school things. I had gained weight from the lithium and was feeling a little lethargic. I made an effort, I really tried. But every conversation was vacuous. I did not give a shit about high school—I could not fake interest in alcohol and make-out sessions and adolescent angst of mere mortals. I wanted to. I tried to. But with every conversation of crushes came the same realization—I was bipolar, I hallucinated Muppets, I imagined a fiery apocalyptic end and that I came back from the dead. I was taking lithium and acting normal but this high school shit was boring; I could not will myself to be interested.

I turned to invisibility.

I was calm, subdued, uncharacteristically compliant. When I wasn't feeling compliant, I ditched. My schedule allowed me to come and go as I pleased—and it did not take long for me to figure out how to go to school and leave by eleven a.m. without anyone noticing. Almost every day, at lunch, I walked out the front door of the administrative building, past the on-campus cop, the principal, teachers. No one questioned me—I was a good student, I was white, and I walked with a swagger that defied my actual purpose. On days when I was feeling less cocky, I'd sneak out the back fence. It wasn't hard—the continuation school for Uni, Indian Springs, was full of resourceful students who cut holes in the chain-link fence with dutiful regularity. I disappeared when it didn't matter, and it mostly didn't matter. It was high school.

My car became my home. I ate Subway sandwiches in my silver '81 Honda Accord; mustard and shredded lettuce dripped into the crevices of the automatic shift. Changes of clothes littered the backseat and empty fountain soda cups rolled around under the seats. The car was given to me by Matt, given to him by Opa. The brakes barely worked and the engine overheated so often, I kept a gallon of water in the backseat. The front hood would steam and hiss angrily, and I would pull over, water her down, and wait. Then get back on the road. When I wasn't at school, I would drive in one of two directions: east to the mall for movies or west to the beach for calming waves. I went to so many movies that the dude who worked at the frozen yogurt shop asked me which store I worked at, assuming I was on break. I'd see two movies a day and time it so that I'd get back to my mom's house on schedule as if I had gone to class. She worked at home as a script reader for Warner Brothers. Movies weren't a bad way to learn about the world. Romcoms in all their impossibility taught hope and love; fantasy taught wonder; thrillers taught caution; and all genres taught me critical thinking. It was a haven, yet I hated most movies and would go into excruciating detail about the plot flaws, the narrative arcs that never happened, the illogical character decisions, the stereotypes that rang untrue. I was a nightmare, a deeply unfun moviegoer. But, at the time, it was my way of interacting with the world, by feeling safe in the strobe—a finely curated ward of my own choosing.

On Monday nights, as determined by Dr. DeAntonio, I'd borrow my mom's car—to avoid overheating and breakdowns on Mulholland Drive—to go to what was essentially the Breakfast Club for the mentally ill, my adolescent group therapy. According to the neuroscientist Frances E. Jensen, between 20 and 60 percent of adults with bipolar disorder experience the initial symptoms of mental illness before they turn twenty, and severe mental health problems are more common in adolescents than either asthma or diabetes. At group, we discussed how hard it was to be the people we were, stuck in a place that could not accommodate our bottomless anxiety and feverish angst. There was the pretty girl who was bulimic in junior high, a charming dork who had ADD and was armed with a dime bag at all times, another girl who was a cutter, one with anger issues, and me. As I came to realize that my friends from high school were not my friends anymore, I had group. Week after week, it was the only thing I looked forward to. (In fact, I wish I had group now.) It was as much a social space as it was therapeutic. Peer counseling may even be more effective than some talk therapy, especially for teens. Adolescence is so isolating; we learned how to talk to each other and we learned how to listen. We'd talk about our weeks, one at a time, and on most Monday nights the ADD guy would roll a J and we'd all head up to the roof of our therapist's building to conclude our session by getting high.

When the tennis season ended, my mom asked what elective I would sign up for, and the only option was drama. I, in a diagnosed depressed state, was forced to try out for the spring musical *Pippin*, an orgiastic, anarchistic tale of a young prince who longs for passion and adventure in his life. I considered this to be an assault on every sense—*Pippin* was bad; its most defining feature was its sharp-limbed and exacting choreography by Bob Fosse, it was the show that launched jazz hands. I studied an old VHS recording of the musical from 1972 starring an unbelievably winsome Ben Vereen. I could not sing; I could not dance; I could not believe I had to try out for this monstrosity of a show. But I had vowed compliance, so I did. I was cast as a chorus girl. Our drama teacher was hell-bent on replicating the video, which included an actual orgy, so we all had to wear nude unitards and ripped net stockings and walk around onstage like hookers. I could not believe I was considered manic and this wasn't. It was weird, and my grandma came to the performances and said that we all looked very nice rolling around ecstatically singing about magic and sexual awakenings. I hated it but I liked having a place to go; I liked thinking that maybe the lead actress would get sick and I would play the princess, or Nora would fall off the swing, and I would have to step in as the carpe diem Granny, unafraid to live life swinging and singing: "Time to start livin', time to take a little from this world we're given, time to take time, 'cause spring will turn to fall."

There was one teacher I took seriously and that was because she took me seriously: Monserrat Fontes. A fierce, chain-smoking bull-riding-obsessed bowling ball of a woman with familial ties to Mexican royalty, she was my English and journalism teacher and I knew she would hurt me if I *didn't* do well. She was bat-shit crazy in the best way, a person so powerful that she was not afraid to wear sweatpants, crack a literal whip (made of bull's penis), and lecture high school kids on the efficacy of both William Faulkner's and Stephen King's prose. She was a woman so intense and dominant that she wouldn't take shit from anyone—students, teachers, or administrators. She just remained atop her perch, sitting cross-legged on a desk, reading and writing books doused in magical thinking and surrealism, speaking fast when she was excited and shouting angrily when she was pissed. (She was pissed often.) In journalism she pushed for truth, clarity, consistency, and cooperation, sometimes by standing on a desk and shouting it into the rafters.

She converted me to literature. I had her in tenth grade and for a long time thought the best way to win Monsy's affection was to turn in great essays. I found many great essays in a folder in our garage marked "Matt's English Papers." I would retype the first page with my name and change the date and hope the typeface and kerning aligned. Matt didn't have an essay for Flannery O'Connor's *Wise Blood*. So I *actually* read it. The best characters in literature are ones touched with fire—no one gets tattoos of Bartleby—and lucky for me and the world, Flannery O'Connor laced her literature with psychopathic eccentrics. In high school, I did not fit in, but I would have been just fine if I was born into an O'Connor short story. I wrote an essay about Enoch Emery, a profane, delusional, obsessive eighteen-year-old zookeeper, who seemed to have the same kind of crazy as me. (I didn't kill for a gorilla suit but I would have.) Emery, delusional and vigilant, was guided by "wise blood," a belief that his blood had instinct based on mystical intuition. (Bipolar here!) He preached redemption and guidance and stole, then worshipped a "new jesus," a mummified shrunken man from the zoo. (Bipolar here too!) He also managed to let a petty argument with "Gonga the Gorilla" become a transformative homicidal event. (Bipolar to the extreme!) I read about him; I could see me. I had no friends, but I felt communion with these characters—an innate belief in self was our shared symptom. That concept is particularly complicated for a teenager—to be told that confidence is a sign of sickness—at the very time when you are losing all confidence anyway. It's like a double hit of shattered self-esteem. I was already cowed by adolescence and now I was hyperaware of hyperactivity, of feeling too good, too complicated, too much.

CHAPTER 9

THE FACTS OF LIFE

A COUPLE OF MONTHS after my triumphant return to Uni High, I wrote an article about being bipolar, about my delusions of grandeur—thoughts that I possessed superior qualities like genius, fame, omnipotence, and wealth. Never one to undershare, I "interviewed" myself, a source I called a "student" who wished to remain anonymous and went by the pseudonym "Rose." Rose, my middle name, was a terrifically unsubtle way of saying it was me, I was Rose, I was interviewing me. This article was about my experience and functioned somewhere between a stilted confessional and a PSA. In it, I described my experience at the hospital, including the four nurses pinning me to the floor, and gave some examples of my grand delusions: "I refused to cooperate with any of the nurses because I thought they were mutant half-siblings who were trying to kill me for my imaginary fortune . . . after four days of not sleeping, I was convinced that I would inherit the world and that Jim Henson wasn't really dead, just locked up somewhere and that it was my duty to rescue him . . . for Kermit's sake." And then I elegantly ended the interview with myself saying, PSA-style: "I'm lucky I was diagnosed early . . . if your screaming thoughts reach an intolerable pitch, ask for help." Nathan, a friend of mine since elementary school, illustrated the article with a lunatic shouting about saving Muppets and a big sign pointing toward "The Mental Ward." I was shouting loudly about all the ways I wasn't normal. I was looking for an explanation myself; it was a battle cry, as if to say, *I survived war while you were busy crushing on someone who wasn't crushing on you.*

There's an irony in that message, because, for the article, I also reached out to a Uni High alumnus who had been in my older brother's graduating class—Mackenzie Astin. I knew him as the adorable kid from the sitcom *The Facts of Life*. He was part of a long TV tradition, the kid with a toothy smile who was tasked with breathing life and ratings into an ailing show. To write the article, I left my second-period journalism class to meet with him in his rented house on Benedict Canyon. He had just finished filming *Iron Will*, a movie about a fatherless teen who tries to raise money for his family by joining a cross-country dogsled race. The tagline for the movie was "It's not a question of age. Or strength. Or ability. It's a matter of will." Mack had winsome dimples, blue-gray eyes, and a warmth that betrayed his fame. He still had one of the dogs from the shoot and called him Kita. His mom, Patty Duke, also happened to be Hollywood's poster child for bipolar disorder. She was one of the first prominent figures to really describe the disease from a personal perspective. She bared all. She said when she was finally diagnosed at thirty-five and given lithium that it was a huge relief.

In 1989, a year after her autobiography came out, Patty Duke testified before Congress in support of the National Institute of Mental Health and National Alliance on Mental Illness in order to increase awareness, funding, and research for people with mental illness. She said, "In 1982, I was diagnosed as manic depressive. My mental illness is a genetic, chemical imbalance of the brain. It manifests itself in dramatic mood swings from states of euphoria or agitated out-of-control highs to disabling, often suicidal lows. From the onset of the symptoms of this illness in my late teens until proper diagnosis and treatment at the age of thirty-five, I rode the wild roller coaster." Part of the roller coaster included several attempts to commit suicide—Duke took pills, passing out with Mack and Sean in the house. She later said in an interview with *20/20* that she "knew at a very young age that something was not right . . . I thought it was just that I was not a good person, that

I didn't try hard enough . . . the very overt symptoms didn't start 'til my late teens and that was with a manic episode. . . . In mania I spent a great deal of money for things I didn't need . . . flights of fancy, meaning almost delusions of grandeur. You feel euphoric, you feel nothing you do has any kind of negative consequence. You can go anywhere, say anything, be anybody you want, marry anybody you want, I married somebody I had only known for thirteen days." She went on to say that as the cycles increased with frequency, they increased in intensity as well. She described the "depressive end lasting much longer, the deep black hole from which you cannot extricate yourself. This sort of depression goes even further than that and it's not based on any stimulus. . . . [I]n order to get on with your life you have to forgive yourself and you have to somehow do the best you can to make amends for the pain that you've caused. The toughest was feeling that I could ever be trusted again."

I interviewed Mack for the article and found the other side of what I went through. He was twelve when his mom was diagnosed. When I arrived at the house there was a semicircle of young beautiful degenerates, some smoking pot, some smoking cigarettes, some just sitting in a semicircle as if it had been ordained. It felt like a child actor's flophouse, and I breathed in the atmosphere like I belonged. I sat with the dog quietly in the corner kneading his coat. This living room, these people were much more interesting than class, much more real than high school, way more exciting than *Pippin* orgy rehearsals. A bong or a joint was passed to me, but I said no and explained that I had just been released from the mental ward. I had no filter and could only see it as a badge of honor, my entrée into this particular coven. The interview went well; Mack was friendly and nice because he knew my brother and he felt sorry for me. That semicircle was warm, and I started showing up at random times and crashing in his living room just to hang out.

There was an enthusiastic openness to Mack, with his bright eyes and tousled red hair. He was completely willing to engage without knowing the extent of what that meant. Sometimes after group, I would go out of my way to drive through his neighborhood, going down Mulholland, turning left, taking the long way through Benedict, driving under the stilted houses and past the cougars that lay in wait.

Some ditch days, I'd get a burger from Tommy's or one of my messy, dripping veggie sandwiches from Subway and drive down Benedict Canyon, hugging the switchbacks. I didn't always slow down at his house. Just passing. I was just passing by, back and forth, up the hill and down. I would drive by, religiously, daily, weekly, sometimes twice a day. I would just check to see if he was home and sometimes call to talk to him on the phone later. It was creepy; I was a little too interested. I had a crush and nothing else in my life—a dangerous combination. I'm sure Mack noticed, and he knew from firsthand experience how precarious a person like that could be.

I would think about him before I went to sleep. I imagined that if I kissed him, if we became intertwined, if he asked me to prom, if he just held my hand, I would be validated. I would have crossed over from the banality of high school, the insanity of being insane, and into something that felt more tangible. I would be a recognized person because another person recognized me. He was a new friend and that meant something. Even if the Benedict refuge was just a thespian flophouse full of slightly older pot-smoking dropouts and a panting Siberian husky, I wanted to be there. I didn't have to explain all the layers of who I had become, the person with bipolar embedded in my identity. I felt like Mack could somehow understand because he witnessed it before. He was special: my psychiatrists were clinical, my adolescent group therapy friends had different disorders and went to different high schools, my teachers had papers to grade, my parents were grateful I was alive, my junior high friends were absent entirely. No one really knew what being bipolar meant, but Mack did; he was born into it. And so, in a gesture that signaled totally normal teenage behavior, I wrote terrible embarrassing awful poetry about him:

> *I see your name on the rusted grill of a truck*
> *You are the first syllable of my favorite food*
> *The small dated picture I possess says you*
> *So are you talking to me because I get secret esoteric messages*
>   *from my local UPS*
> *They warn me . . . you throw stones*
> *and suck leaves. You'll never call*
> *I look at the fallen brick*
> *the debris of relationships*
> *with foundation we can build a fireplace*
> *We've got the Bunsen burner—all we need*
> *is the chemistry set.*

I WAS LANGUISHING in the adolescence of it all, rolling around in angst. Decades later I can say this: macaroni and cheese was never my favorite food. Obviously, Mack wasn't real to me, so I sat in the circle and passed the bong and petted the dog and listened to Marley and smelled the misty chaparral and lupine of Benedict Canyon. I drove by like a phantom and called like a ghost, hanging up when it was too much me. Sometimes I knew. Sometimes I didn't.

On January 17, 1994, at four thirty in the morning, deep under Northridge, California, the tectonic plates shifted violently, and the people of LA were jolted from their slumber by a magnitude 6.7 earthquake. One aftershock was immediate. The most formal definition of an earthquake, according to the U.S. Geological Survey, is when "the tectonic plates get stuck at their edges due to friction. When the stress on the edge overcomes the friction, there is an earthquake that releases energy in waves that travel through the earth's crust and cause the shaking that we feel." Not dissimilar to a manic episode—a release of energy. The ground was unstable, the earth moving. Pulling back, earthquakes form continents, our world. Manic episodes did that to me. I was staying at my dad's house in Hollywood, closer to the epicenter in Reseda. My brother Matt was in town from Berkeley for his winter break. Nothing in our house was broken. Things shifted, our dog Nature cowered in a corner, the hair on her hackles standing straight up. My immediate thought was of Mack in the canyon and his house built on the side of a mountain. I tried to go back to sleep but I had to make sure my Benedict Canyon posse (not my posse at all) was okay. They were fine, but when I showed up may have been the moment Mack realized that our friendship was probably bad for both of us—for me to have expectations of him, and for him to have a fresh-off-the-boat bipolar girl (underage to boot) hanging around his house for unclear reasons.

Eventually my mom figured out what was happening and she told me that I couldn't drive to Benedict Canyon anymore. I still hoped that Mack would resurrect my number and call me in May to go to prom in June, a John Hughes fantasy that never came to be. I knew I wasn't going to prom, but I bought two dresses on the off chance that I might. (Both long, black, and velvet.) I did not want to participate in high school, *but of course I did*. I was pleasantly shocked when I won a senior superlative for Celebrity Look-Alike. The student body had voted me as an Annie clone, and I was more than happy to take the picture with a Leapin' Lizards pin attached to my hoodie. I thought about prom—how great would it be if I showed up with Mackenzie Astin, driving a dogsled full of Akitas and malamutes and Siberian huskies through the Hilton Airport ballroom. Fuck prom queen, I would be adorned in a full wolfskin onesie, howling at the lunar eclipse. I was depressed, alone, bored, but I still had fantasies. *I only had fantasy.* Recent studies have shown that one of the main characteristics that separate humans from animals is the ability to think and plan and fantasize about a future. And Mack was that for me—a fantastical, abstract future. He was the person I thought of when I sat in the dark, listening to my Magnavox stereo (at normal volume now), to the same song over and over—Peter Gabriel's "Washing of the Water." I lay shuttered in darkness, taken away by the spare drum and his solemn voice, a wish to go back "to the place where" he came from; Peter Gabriel sings: "Will you take me on your back for a ride / If I should fall, would you swallow me deep inside? . . . I feel like I'm sinking down."

When I talked with Mack decades later, he didn't remember my stalking or much about our friendship except that I had been around and that we had talked about his mom. We had pancakes at Du-par's and he was exactly as I'd remembered, open and willing and expansive and generous in sharing with me what he had been through, his view from the outside that I could never experience. It gave me a better understanding of my mom, my dad, Marilyn, Jeff, Matt, David, Monsy, Sarah J., Hana, Rachel, Miriam, everyone I came in contact with who had to deal with me while I was internally lit. They had to endure the uneasiness of the unknown; they had to navigate being the complement to crazy.

Mack and I spoke again about what it was like to grow up with a mother who was bipolar. And he had a loving but pained reaction, one that was familiar. There were things he couldn't forgive even though he'd tried. He intellectually understood the dips and turns of the disorder. He even emotionally and experientially empathized, but he couldn't fully absolve his mom of her actions and forgive the consequent weight that defined their relationship. Understandable. A month after Mack and I spoke, Patty Duke passed away. I asked Mack if he still held on to some of the frustrations and difficulties that came with their relationship. He wrote in an email, "Do I have a better understanding of the difficulties she had raising us? I don't know if it's possible for me to truly do that until (and if) I have kids. We're a real handful, we kids. And until I walk somewhat of her journey in shoes somewhat like hers, I don't think I'll ever really understand what she was up against. I can imagine it. But until I've lived it, it's just imagination. Same with the chemical imbalance. If I suffered in the same manner she had, perhaps it'd be easier to understand, and in doing so, forgive. But both those experiences—parenthood and a chemical imbalance—are still at more-than-arm's-length for me. I don't know. I'm still figuring it out." He went on to write that, "She gave so much of herself, I think, that she had very little of herself left for her. And, for all the shit I've given her about the shit she gave me and my brother, the impact she had on others is incalculably good. She *deserves* to be heralded. And, heartless though it may sound, it's easier for me to do so now that she's not around." When I got out of the hospital, I was relatively uninformed, I didn't have kids, responsibility; I wasn't yet worried about being trusted again, I wasn't worried about my relationships. Parents forgive and high school friends don't always last forever.

Diagnosis and medication gave me clarity and a cure, respectively, but they also posed some harsh existential questions: Who was I if my actions and thoughts didn't represent me? What if they did represent me? What if they were extensions of me, rooted in a subconscious realm? What if the me from before I was on lithium was the real me? What if I would need lithium—for forever—just to function? I didn't let these questions sink in; I was not in any position to think on the complexities of identity. Like every other seventeen-year-old, I was just beginning to form an identity—to figure out who I was and who I wanted to be. I couldn't absorb whether I was in fact shaped by my mania or medication. It had happened; like the assault, there was no longer an alternate narrative. I now knew that I could hallucinate without drugs; justify a spending spree on key chains; talk to God; and be persecuted by televisions, pipes, and squirrels. I just wanted to get through high school. And I found an unknowable well of superhero-like qualities raging in the recesses of my neurological development. I took solace in self-imposed seclusion when the canyon became off-limits. I had to relearn myself. Dark movie houses, crashing of saltwater waves, and the collapse of Subway sandwiches—that was my reality. Solitary confinement without walls. I don't think it was ever clear I would come back. I don't think anyone could say for certain that I would be the same, and I wasn't.

Once, I heard Iggy Pop describe being at the beach like this: "It was so quiet, and nobody knew who I was, and there was the beach. There was the ocean, there was the end of all the tension and complications." And that is what made sense to me when I left the ward: being at the edge of nothing. At the edge of everything.

CHAPTER 10

REACH FOR THE SKY

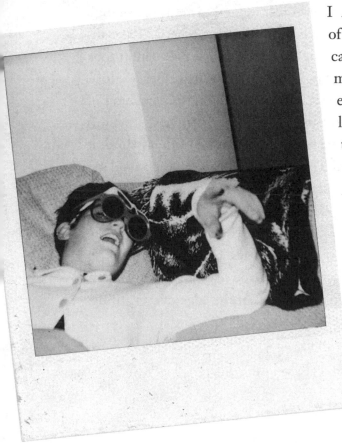

I APPLIED TO a handful of University of California campuses and got into most with a devastating essay on what it was like to lose my mind. I parlayed trauma into acceptance. I visited campuses—Santa Cruz, Berkeley, and Davis—each one more of a dream than the next. In Santa Cruz, I hoped to see a fleshy banana slug but spent most of the visit riding old wooden roller coasters dipping and diving over breaking waves. Berkeley was too familiar with my older brother and his friends populating the good burrito shops and Cody's, the legendary bookstore on Telegraph Avenue. The air smelled too familiar with dewey eucalyptus haunting the hills. Davis won me over with one impression—an incredibly hairy hippie emerging from a geodesic dome (one of the off-campus housing options), lifting his arms high overhead (past a dreaded beard, a tie-dyed V-neck, and long guru hair). He lifted his hands toward the ethereal sunrise—soaking in energy and rays and power—his limbs nearly touching branches. A latticework of shade covered his closed-eyed face. He just reached high into the sky. And then he was gone, back in the dome after a greeting of the day. *Yes, this is my place*, I thought, *geodesic dome hippies.* I didn't even know about the fistulated cows (cows with portholes in their sides that allow for monitoring of various functions). There was a distinct and persistent smell of fertilizer. This was the only school at which you could major in viticulture and enology. Yes, yes, yes.

I walked at my high school graduation—reluctant but proud—fuck if I wasn't shocked that I actually graduated and that I got into my first-choice college, UC Davis. I spent the summer before college interning at the tabloid news show *Hard Copy*. The program was supposed to be on hiatus, and then O.J. happened. My job—which had been confined to sitting in a dark corner "logging the competition" and occasionally organizing the archives—shifted dramatically. I was only seventeen, but a tragedy that included race, football, blondes, Brentwood, and every Hollywood lawyer required all hands on deck and a return from hiatus for all the tabloid shows like *Inside Edition*, *A Current Affair*, and our program. The talking heads who anchored the show wore blazers and airbrushed faces and big hair that defied gravity or logic; they were camera-ready from the waist up; below the lens view, they wore jeans or sweatpants. Psycho up top, comfy from below. I was deployed to Kato Kaelin's press conference and sent with crews to search for trails of blood staining otherwise pristine Brentwood sidewalks. I tried to find exclusives or breaking information, but I mostly just tagged along in between shifts of my other more appropriate job scooping ice cream at Ben & Jerry's. They say one way to ease pain is to feel pain, more pronounced and sudden, in another area of the body. Distraction, really. I was on to someone else's tragedy; their bloodbath felt worse than my strange brain. I could deal with hallucinating Muppets. Slowly, I got used to the lithium, to being the person who takes lithium.

I arrived at the UC Davis dorms with a meal plan (unlimited soft serve and cereal), a bunk bed (in a dorm room shared with a girl named Nina), and a pair of patchwork overalls that I bought on the corner of La Brea and Beverly (perfect for a geodesic dome party). I also had a three-month supply of lithium, three 300-milligram pink pills to be taken every night. What I didn't realize was that this was the dawning of the age of the psychopharmaceuticals! I was like Queen Fancy Lithium and had an entrée to every party. "Hey, man, I'm on drugs, what combo do you take?" According to the *New York Times*, "From 1994 to 2006, the percentage of students treated at college counseling centers who were using antidepressants nearly tripled, from 9 percent to over 23 percent. In part this reflects the introduction of S.S.R.I. antidepressants, a new class of drugs thought to be safer and have fewer side effects than their predecessors." Every goddamn person I met was on some kind of prescription cocktail to help with sleep, anxiety, ADHD, OCD, depression. Lithium was hella exotic. According to the Centers for Disease Control and Prevention (CDC), "From 1988–1994 through 2005–2008, the rate of antidepressant use in the United States among all ages increased nearly 400 percent." There was a new method of addressing madness and it was through a flurry of pharmaceuticals.

Once I got into a rhythm with lithium, it was just a pink pill. On a day-to-day basis, I never thought of myself as defined by my disease or my drug, but that's dumb. Of course I was and am. Looking back at my college career, I made video art interviewing friends on meds, calling it "Pill-ars." When I interviewed myself (*again*), the shot was composed in stark black-and-white, almost like a security cam, and I spoke so sadly about my time in the hospital, my voice gravelly and dramatic. In my sculpture class I made a wooden box with bars that rested on top of a pedestal raised to brain height; inside the box were long branches stripped and then stained red, busting out in every direction but still jailed and contained like bursting blood rivers. I made a painting of a cartoonish me running away, hospital gown flailing. What I did in college was a thinly veiled attempt to work through what had happened. I wrote a short story about a mental hospital in the style of Thomas Pynchon and interviewed Elizabeth Wurtzel for my nonfiction writing class. (She stood me up for our first meeting in San Francisco but then took me out for a very chatty dinner at Chez Panisse in which she bewitched the waiter with so many detailed questions about the menu that we almost didn't order. Her book *Prozac Nation* had been published the year I graduated high school and was one of the few comparable accounts of what I went through. Kay Redfield Jamison's books *Touched with Fire* and *An Unquiet Mind* were among the others.)

I did other things, more college-y things. I finally achieved a first kiss with my brother's best friend, Stu. It was who I imagined it with (I had loved the idea of Stu for years) but not quite *how* I imagined it. Just after we kissed, he barfed all over the bathroom and passed out; to be fair, it was his twenty-first birthday party, and it was at the end of a long night of drinking and weed. Matt was mad. "Don't fuck with Stu," he kept saying. But Stu called me once I was back in Davis to say he didn't regret it and was just sorry about the barfing. I had friends in college, good friends; I vomited up gallons of cherry-pink jungle juice on my way home from frat parties; I obsessively skateboarded from downtown to the outer reaches of East Davis and back again; I shaved my head; I ate eggs at Delta of Venus; I learned that musicals were not cool, and Op Ivy was, this according to my roommate/BFF Autumn, whose dad was a roadie for Willie Nelson. I sold coffee at a mystery bookstore; shroomed in the arboretum; had drug-induced auditory hallucinations that made me think a helicopter was following me; vomited more exotic combinations of alcohol; smoked many trees of Humboldt green; skipped class; wrote papers at four a.m. about books I had never read; wrote a column named "SPAMCO" for the *Daily Aggie*; wrote about music; saw a lot of free concerts using my press pass, which was why I chose to write about music in the first place; went to a secret Beastie Boys show at a skate park after MCA borrowed my friend's skateboard and put us on the list; I lived in Edinburgh for a year and learned to love the twenty-four-hour light on the summer solstice when I camped by myself on Orkney; ate wine gums till my teeth were sticky. I was introduced to Jean Rhys and the melancholy prose of *Good Morning, Midnight*; I went to half a dozen Beck shows and hundreds of shitty ska shows; I obsessed over KDVS DJs who went on to become Solesides musicians, then Quannum musicians, like MCs in Blackalicious and DJ Shadow and Latyrx; I named a pet bunny Coco and hoped for bunny babies; I listened to live music next to the too-tall speakers blasting directly to my gut; I got good grades; I got bad grades; I cared more about my painting critiques than I did about my English Lit classes; I interned at the *LA Weekly* and got my first bylines; I dreamed of working at the *LA Weekly* someday and being as pierced as Ron

Athey and as badass as my editors; I saw the movie *Kids* with the manager of my Ben & Jerry's who used to deal weed out of the walk-in freezer and would occasionally pass out from inhaling too many whip-its; I lost my virginity in Istanbul to a Chilean traveler named Arturo whose only English was "You are zee feesh. I am zee piranyah"; I was freaked out by dating and so I didn't; I kissed a *South Park* writer in the parking lot of Smalls; he dipped me low to the asphalt after last call and asked me to go with him to his Hollywood apartment; I was scared, so I didn't; I protested the regents' decision to end affirmative action with Autumn and fellow activists Joel and Fraser; I saw salmon spawn for the first time; I listened to demo CDs; I flailed through more mosh pits; I listened and loved early 1990s hip-hop—Tribe, Wu, Outkast, Biggie, Nas, Missy, the Fugees—it all seeped into my spongy brain and I painted. I loved Davis. I loved those four years.

I did one thing that fell into no particular category. I created an alter ego superhero named Silver Girl—I made plaster breastplates studded with rhinestones, a hat with curlicue antennae, armbands, and fanciful silver tights, and I just strolled through campus occasionally in full regalia as if I were on metallic patrol. Lithium metal, its state in nature when not a compound, is soft enough to be cut with a knife. When cut, it possesses a silvery-white color that quickly changes to gray as it oxidizes to lithium oxide. While it has one of the lowest melting points among all metals at 180°C, it has the highest melting and boiling points of the alkali metals. I subconsciously took the element inside of me and wore it on the outside. This was normal enough for me, normal enough for the quad on campus. It was around the same time that Berkeley had their own Naked Guy.

I was not manic. I was still on lithium. Inventing Silver Girl was just what I wanted to do.

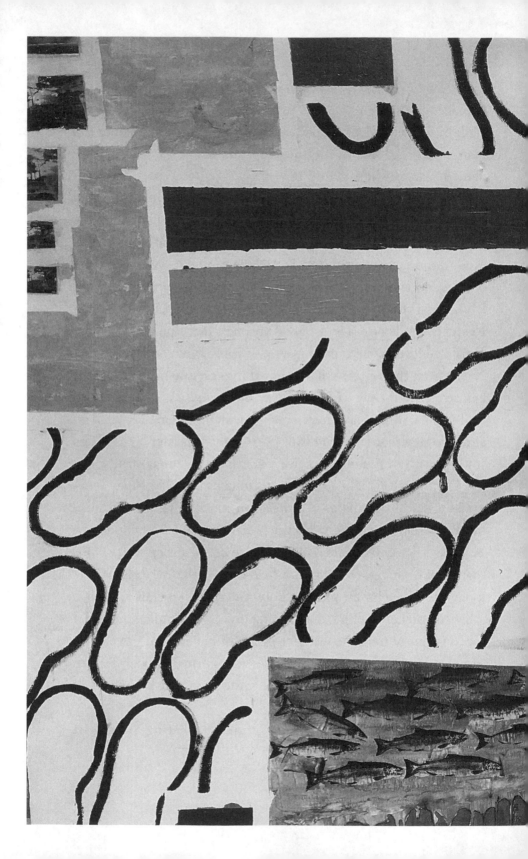

PART 2 — EPISODE 2

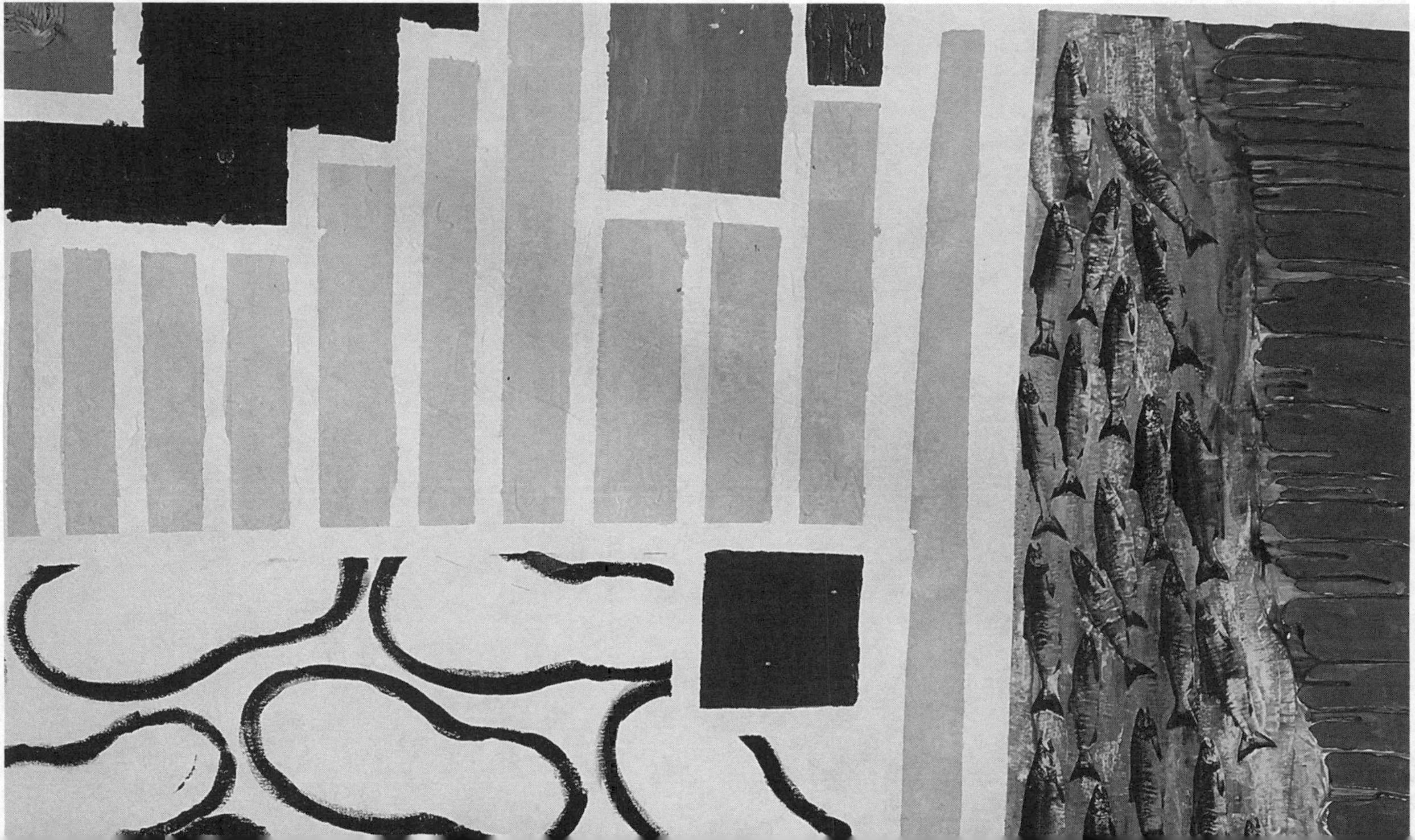

CHAPTER 11

MIDNIGHT COWGIRL: 1; *HOUSE & GARDEN*: 0

"MAKE SURE to go to the deli two doors down and not the one on the corner," Hana said over the phone the night before I left Portland, Maine, in September 1998. She didn't have a cell; I didn't have a cell; the whole city didn't have a cell. She had four different jobs: hostess, waitress, babysitter, and assistant to the feminist writer Marilyn French. Hana had offered to let me sleep in the sixth-floor walk-up apartment in the East Village she shared with her cousin Sarah P. and a third roommate. I was in Maine, visiting relatives and dragging two duffel bags full of my move-to-New-York essentials around. A skirt suit for entry-level interviews, flannels, ripped jeans, ill-fitting vintage finds, and one pair of slacks. My duffel bags were dramatic and enormous. Set against the scenery of the Portland Greyhound station, I looked more like a teen serial killer, schlepping bodies instead of schmatas.

I had an image of arriving, face pressed up against a Greyhound window, everybody looking at me. My three reference points of New York were *Midnight Cowboy*, the first two thirds of *Tootsie*, and *The David Letterman Show*. I wished I had worn cowboy boots. It's not the best New York arrival fantasy—to wish to be Jon Voight strutting through Manhattan with a fringe jacket and high-water pants and a comically small cowhide suitcase in the hopes of becoming a high-paid street gigolo. But Voight had bluster; he left Texas. His tragedy was not yet evident. He did what he wanted and he still had the humanity of a country boy (just like me!). While he was on that bus, he still aimed to strive and arrive. I got into Port Authority, stupid as hell. This was my logic: After summers of writing for the *LA Weekly* and *Film Threat* magazine and working on the daily campus newspaper, I thought, I will make my living as a writer. I will work in publishing. Publishing is in New York. I must go to New York to write. My parents did not object. My brother Matt sternly said I should not go, warning me of all kinds of failure or destruction or you're-gonna-lose-your-mind-again. I did not hesitate. In fact, I flatly ignored him and may have even called *him* hysterical.

When I asked him what his memory of this phone call was, he wrote: "I did worry about you; NY was far away, we had little support network there, and we had only been there once before in our lives. It seemed like you were taking a huge leap, and making the first year of post-college life more difficult than it needed to be, especially with the threat of episodes lingering. But you were adamant; you wanted to get the hell out, and you were convinced you would be okay. You had a lot of confidence, and even though I didn't think you had thought it out at all, and had only half-assed your plans, you expressed little doubt. In fact, I got the sense that my skepticism only hardened your determination."

My brother and I are different. He is cautious and rational; he had to be sane when I wasn't. I wondered if his objection was that I didn't think too hard on failure, or that I was more willing to "get the hell out" of LA, something that was stressful for me to navigate and related to our parent's divorce. Los Angeles was my home, but after four years of stable living in Davis, going back to Los Angeles felt impossible. I did not want to commute between parents or feel guilty for choosing a place to live on one side of town over another. I also had been to New York on my own. I stayed with Hana, Miriam, and Karen in a walk-through apartment in the East Village for a few days just after my first year of college, the highlights of which I journaled about—"a cold shower in the middle of the kitchen, going the wrong way on the subway, ice coffee, and the Cloisters! I wound up mistakenly at the World Trade Center. The view from the 107th floor is beyond magnificent. It encompasses Liberty, Jersey, and the New York skyline, which seems like it should be in my future." New York was somehow easier—I didn't think twice. I was going to New York. I was not nervous on the bus ride. I was not nervous about hailing a yellow cab. I was not nervous about tipping appropriately. I was not nervous about the dirt and the noise and the pushback of the city. I was prepared; the city's mania suited me. I had my bags and about seven hundred dollars. I was ready to build a life. A rich life, full of poverty and drama and art and music and fights and drinking too much and smoking too much and generally being a fucked-up early-twenties human on the hustle.

I got to Hana's, collected her keys. I saw my reflection in the door at 516 E. Eleventh Street. My hair was terrible—still the length of a stunted Chia pet from having shaved it two years before. (I had some idea that if I shaved my head, skateboarding would be more aerodynamic. It took two years to get to this length, one in which my only options for styling were bobby pins, spit, glue, and fanciful hats.) I dragged both bags up the short stoop. I opened the first door but there was only room for one duffel bag inside. That did not seem architecturally possible. The East Village is the capital of architecturally impossible but I did not anticipate this squeeze; I could not get both bags in the door. At that point I panicked. I was unclear on what to do next. I whimpered. *How am I going to get my two duffel bags—TWO enormous duffel bags—up six flights of stairs?* I was certain someone would steal one bag if I left it on the stoop while I dragged the other bag up to the sixth floor, but it was my only choice. I chose the bag with the preprofessional suit in it to drag up first. I dropped it and ran down the six flights of stairs to find what I've found every time I've doubted the humanity of the city . . . my second bag was still on the stoop. I sat relieved and thrilled and in love with New York.

I didn't have a job, I didn't have a room: two things I needed to call this jigsaw city my home. When I first arrived my friends made me feel like a sponsored celebrity; Hana showed me the shortcuts and gave me a breakdown of where to get work clothes on the cheap (Joyce Leslie, Strawberry, Century 21); her cousin Sarah P. clued me into the free-drink bartenders, and her neighbors would meet us where the roofs were tarred together for ad hoc wine and cheese parties. Hana and I shared a bed, and each

morning, as the week began, I would go to David's Bagels on Second Avenue. I bought one bagel with cream cheese and one plain
bagel; I redistributed the excessive cream cheese application to
the two bagels and ate half of one while I stuffed résumés into
envelopes and made calls from pay phones to HR departments. I
saved the other half of the bagel for an afternoon snack to meet
my food budget of $1.50 before five p.m. The second bagel was for
the next day, a little stale but practically free. I could not believe
people said New York was expensive! The bagels were huge,
THERE WAS SO MUCH CREAM CHEESE!

It was easy to get a job as a twenty-one-year-old—entry-level

SCRAPBOOK OF MY EARLY YEARS IN NEW YORK. PICTURED:
HANA, SARAH P., AND EFFIE (BEHIND THE LEAVES).

work was largely meritocratic, as long as you didn't care where you worked. My first preprofessional interview was with Condé Nast's human resources department—they told me I might be a good fit for *Women's Sports and Fitness* (which I later realized was code for "not fit for fashion" and "not Ivy League enough for the *New Yorker* or *Vanity Fair*" and "not a man, so not *GQ*"). I got a second interview, and, as foretold, the HR rep told me to prepare for a meeting with the managing editor of *Women's Sports and Fitness* in two days. The pace of this was excellent since I was running out of money and David's Bagels and hospitality karma. I had monologues about sports rolling through my brain. I would talk about the radio project I did about discrimination and female athletes in high school; I would discuss my love of the Lakers and the Dodgers. I wore a skirt and blazer and applied lip gloss. I arrived at the HR department and met managing editor Alice Siempelkamp—the managing editor of *House & Garden*. There was some HR mix-up, but I didn't care and she didn't seem to either. A job was a job was a job. I explained to Alice that I would be happy to talk about softball. She asked me a few basic questions, about my art degree and year of studying art history in Edinburgh. Can you order lunch and convince the taco guy to include margaritas? Can you file? Can you deliver things? Can you stomach a certain amount of absurdity? She sat me down to a familiar monologue: *Are you sure you want to do this?* I flashed back to the moment when Pam Klein, the editor who hired me to be an intern at the *LA Weekly*, ran down all the reasons I should want to run away from publishing, alternative publishing in particular.

Pam told me, "This newspaper is supported by sex phone lines and porn ads and you have to believe that that is okay."

I told her, "That is fine with me, that is something I get."

Pam explained that alternative media was the kind of publishing fighting against mainstream media; it was creative and energetic and it gave a voice to those who couldn't be heard.

She stressed it again. "But the ads are how we make our money. That is part of alternative journalism."

Siempelkamp wasn't warning me of soft porn, but something else, something more corrupted in my mind—luxury goods and consumption, the gilded class. This magazine was a fantasy for the masses to look at on glossy pages but to never touch or live in. I think she sensed that *House & Garden* might not be the best fit for me. She saw through my preprofessional skirt suit and my awkward walk in low heels. She could probably see the bedazzled Silver Girl psycho underneath the layer of corpo gray flammable material. But she didn't care. We talked antiques and rugs. She hired me for a position that was split between reception and as the second assistant to the editor in chief, Dominique Browning. I was a bargain at $21,000 a year plus overtime. The other assistants at *House & Garden* included the daughter of a Condé Nast executive and the daughter of someone else whose status was lofty but unknown—they both were towering creatures of elongated beauty and poise, carrying leather satchels that clearly did not come from sample sales or Joyce Leslie. I mostly avoided them. I did not seek what I did not understand.

Around the same time that the job came through, an apartment lead landed in my lap. The space was perfect, a sublet in a commercial loft over Mustang Sally's on Seventh Avenue. It was a bed and room for $630 a month. The stairway leading up was lopsided and covered in stained gray commercial carpeting. The apartment itself was dark; there was one bathroom for many people and a black toilet in that bathroom. My future roommates told me that Timothy "Speed" Levitch, the tour guide, poet, speaker, philosopher, and New York character had crashed for weeks on the futon. Apparently, no one who actually lived there knew him and he was eventually asked to leave. A pharmaceutical consultant lived in the front half of the space; a startup company was using one room as a meeting space in the back. There were twice-weekly aerobics classes directly above my soon-to-be-bed. And one window with a limited view of outside life—the frosted glass led to a fire escape/roof landing that faced a Chinese manufacturing space, a hybrid oasis of *Mad Max* and *West Side Story*. I had been shown rooms with no windows; rooms in Williamsburg with tilted linoleum floors and small lions guarding their stoops; rooms in dance studios; rooms inside other rooms. This one was it—the fire escape was my balcony, the aerobics class was my alarm; the room was a twenty-four-minute walk away from the old Condé Nast building and so I never had to pay for subway fare (tokens at the time). I just walked everywhere. I walked the city until I saw something I had never seen before (which was in every direction).

Once I defied the impossible—finding a cheap room and a job before I ran out of my seven hundred dollars—New York became real. The first three months included a serious adjustment to uncomfortable work clothing, a near-pathological need to drink at the Eleventh Street Pub and the Village Idiot, and a scrambled brain constantly packing and unpacking this idea of working poverty and working on a magazine that celebrated an opulent lifestyle. I tried to understand why anyone went to college to do this: Every morning, I was instructed to clip the horoscopes from the *Daily News* and the *New York Post* for Browning (something that at the time felt like a badass request made simply as a show of power, it turned out she was considering hiring the legendary Sally Brompton and needed a crash course in astrology), and then I would sit behind a desk and wait to interact with whoever and whatever showed up—Condé

CONDÉ NAST ART PROJECT, OR WHAT I REALLY DID AS A RECEPTIONIST FOR *HOUSE & GARDEN*.

Nast executives, messengers, food deliveries, photo books, free samples, flowers. I killed time by making art projects on the color Xerox machine and by abusing the Sharpies.

Sometimes I would walk Condé Nast's editorial director, James Truman, into Dominique's office, and sometimes it was Si Newhouse himself; the latter never made eye contact, but both of them were nice enough to me. By Christmas, I was realizing that my absolute drive to get a job—any job—in publishing was potentially misguided. I was outraged by the amount of drudge work I had to do. I sent out issues and clips to every person who contributed to the magazine. I opened and sorted mail. In college, I had been writing and getting published and all of a sudden all I was doing was managing daily astrological forecasts. Then Christmas came. My family—so shocked and impressed that I had gotten a job and an apartment—came to visit. We were intending to spend Christmas Eve together. Instead, I was asked to hand deliver a Christmas present to every contributing writer and contributing editor who lived in New York.

Snow was coming; the air was crisp and the winter sky was gray. Just as I was loading the dozens of ceramic candles wrapped in iridescent paper into the backseat, flurries twinkled down. The start of a blizzard. I mapped out a course with the help of my driver and by ten p.m. we delivered as many as we could—there was no Google Maps or GPS. I missed Christmas Eve dinner with my dad and Marilyn and David but they understood; editorial assistant duties called and this was the reality of Condé Nast assistanting. One photographer opened the door to his apartment, looked at me dusted in snowflakes, and shook his head. He apologized, thanked me, took the candle, and sent me back to the car.

CHAPTER 12

SEX 'N' EGG 'N' CHEESE

BY MARCH 1999, I had stolen a lot of office supplies; dragged home all the free paint, lampshades, and wallpaper samples I could; and doodled as many creative Post-it collages as humanly possible. Alice asked if I would be interested in working with the photo department; their assistant had given notice. Yes, without hesitation.

Matt was not wrong about the downside of moving quickly and without a plan. I mourned Davis like a death in the family; college

felt like a phantom limb. My friends had dispersed, the town wasn't mine, and I didn't have a weekly column or music to go to or an art studio to spend all night in, wrapped up with blank canvases. No one cared if I was Silver Girl in New York; that was just a regular Tuesday near the Liberty Inn. This new city was more about day-to-day survival: achieving a delicate balance of not hitting the overdraft charge, ordering enough lunch for the editors so that there were weekend leftovers for me to take home, and saving enough cigarettes to smoke on the roof when it all felt like hell. My home on Seventh Avenue was a dirty cesspool surrounded by rag shops, furriers, Irish bars, and Madison Square Garden. The occasional homeless person slept in our vestibule and I made rent, I ran at the McBurney YMCA (which is now a seven-thousand-square-foot duplex valued at $14 million), I went to art

MOOD BOARD, CIRCA 1999.

openings, and I pined for a painter who was in the Yale graduate program.

He had been a graduate student when I was an undergraduate at Davis and transferred when I moved. He was not interested in me, but we would talk on the phone about artists, emerging and otherwise. I wanted to impress him with small drawings made with taped-off lines. He was distant, like his paintings.

My twin desires were to be a working writer and a functional dater, neither of which seemed likely or even remotely possible at the time. I worked very late nights; overtime was the only possible way to afford my deluxe lifestyle, which I considered to be raucous and rich despite no cents to my name. In late January 1999, after the candle-delivering blizzard of '98, I went, at the suggestion of Dr. DeAntonio, to meet with Dr. Schwartz, a psychiatrist on the Upper West Side. This cemented my move to New York. (I believe his recommendation was so emphatic that Dr. DeAntonio said, "He's treated my family members, he's *very* good.") I arrived late and we went over basics. Schwartz's office was a study in what I assume is stereotypical analyst decoration replete with oddly shaped vases, a tissue box near the soft mid-century sofa, Asian rugs, and modern art photography. One photo—a black-and-white shot of the interior of a movie theater—was of a blank, bright white screen, illuminated seats, and an empty audience. The brain, I thought, with an audience of no one. He had a window in the center of the east-facing wall; it overlooked the Central Park Reservoir. It was a beautiful space. Not a womb like Dr. G's, more like the next level, like Freud could have analyzed Dora here.

We talked about my family, my episode in high school, my sexual history, my current anxiety over dating (more precisely, not dating), my terrible job, how much I could pay per session, how much insurance covered—all this according to his session notes, which he shared with me for this book—I'll call them The Notes. The first mention of lithium in our sessions came a month later on February 19, 1999, when we discussed whether I wanted to decrease my dosage or stop taking lithium altogether. My first reaction was anxiety, according to him. I wasn't ready but it was something that I wanted to consider, since I had been fine through college. Here I was in New York delivering packages for fancy editors and worrying about my inability to date. These were not bipolar concerns. This was life.

By June 1999, I decided I wanted to get off the lithium. Dr. Schwartz said in his notes that he called Dr. DeAntonio, who "described her as floridly psychotic during her episode in 9/93 but no repeat episodes or even instability. He feels she has done well enough for long enough to be tried off lithium." In my early days of seeing Dr. Schwartz, his notes most often describe me as "damn assertive," "late," "aggressive," "controlling," "angry," or "frustrated." It's unclear to me if this was a hallmark of the disease or just my personality but I was unwilling and unable to conform, in general. We would talk about my work frustrations in sessions and my unrequited loves—I preferred wild crushes to reality. We never addressed how the attack effected my dating, how my parents' divorce may have influenced me and my dating habits, how my hospitalization may have affected me—I wouldn't have passed a Bechdel test; all I talked about were boys. I wasn't very deep. In reviewing The Notes, I am embarrassed. I deserved better than session upon session devoted to boy drama. But I never learned boy drama; I went from babysitting and obsessive phone calls to collegiate avoidance to New York drunk.

When I moved to New York, adolescence was thought to be over in the teens; scientists found that the brain was done (or close to done) developing. I was expected to be an adult, to process information as an adult and to be responsible, as an adult. In 2016, however, a study by Dartmouth found that "adolescent-specific behavior may be driven by an imbalance in activity between the prefrontal cortex (PFC), an area of the brain involved in cognitive control and inhibition, which does not fully develop until the late teens/early 20s," which could explain why most early-twenties individuals lack the self-control of adults. I'm not sure why science had to prove that being in your twenties is an extension of adolescence—it seems anecdotally self-evident.

My early years in New York included some wild behavior. I slept with some random-ass people, mostly colleagues or late-night drinkers at the Village Idiot, a bar that used to stink up the meatpacking district back when there were actual bovine carcasses hanging from racks. I slept with an art school model who had to shave his entire body but when we had sex it was growing back and was prickly (I almost kicked him out of bed for fear of full-body rash); someone who urinated on my rug; someone who was so drunk after a magazine party, he thought I was his co-worker (I was not); someone who was married with kids; someone who was a photographer who could spot-check that I was wearing H&M panties (which seemed weird, too much time spent styling photo shoots); men with bad pickup lines ("I like your dress, but I'd like it crumpled on my floor"); many people I do not remember. The ghosts of my vagina past.

My main problem was that while I kept this going, I pined for suitors far away and unavailable, and I was completely repulsed by anyone who liked me. I was twenty-two and my physical life in college was limited to skateboarding and living inside a Silver Girl suit. Perhaps this early New York life *was* a delayed adolescence?

If this was adolescence and the experience that I missed while

I was in my sad Subway sandwich high school phase, that was fine. It was a time in publishing when there were still parties. The Lad mags had especially lavish budgets and expansive guest lists— Madonna was at a *Stuff* party! *Maxim*, *Stuff*, *Details* all outselling each other in ads and spending it down on lowly paid assistants and their friends (me). Their parties were almost all the same— free booze and a room full of dudes. I was fixated on a fantasy and stunted by reality—in therapy we talked repeatedly about why I slept with people who offered no second-date future. A lot of the notes from those years circle around coupling as a goal, but in retrospect I wonder why having a relationship had to be the goal at all. I was exercising. It was practice.

I think the most frustrating thing for Dr. Schwartz was the very clear pattern of who I didn't sleep with—those who might return, those who might care, those who might leave after caring. It sounds so reductive and hooey, but that was that. The first example of this trope was Jeremy, one of my best friends in college who I kissed once and told him, "I think you are kissing me wrong," and we never kissed again. He was now living in the loft and still one of my best friends. He took out the dead mouse carcasses and collected vinyl and worked at Sony Records and was a calm counter to my frenzy. Jeremy made elaborate creatures out of Fimo modeling clay and had the ability to quietly and comically riot. (I was always on the floor laughing when I was around him.) Another example of the too-nice guy was an editorial assistant, who worked at *Details*, a men's magazine located on the same floor as *House & Garden*. I described him in a personal essay in the *Village Voice* in September 2004:

> Dave was one of my first New York friends—one that I
> met post-college. He was the only person at Condé Nast

who wasn't intimidating, largely because he didn't wear stilettos. . . . I'd call him on Sundays while he was watching cartoons; we'd meet at delis and eat fatty pastrami and drink Cel-Ray sodas, go to Blockbusters, stand next to each other at concerts, drink through our respective office parties. We were surrogate dates.

Dave was always my therapist's favorite. Dr. Schwartz would mention him first when I complained about boys and their badness and their badness toward me. He still talks about Dave because Dave was the only boy in my stable of self-obsessed flakes who actually stood me on a corner and said unequivocally, "I have a crush on you."

I remember that Upper West Side corner. It was September 1999; it was technically my first intentional date. It was one of the only seemingly formal dates I've been on, kind of a dork prom; we were both so green and ecstatic to see Tom Waits. I wore a skirt. Dave got the tickets for the show at the Beacon Theater. I imagine he thought very clearly about the best way to win me over, and he was right. We sat, tiny, young, and ready to marvel at the Waitsian duality—the somber lullaby swooner that morphed into the circus barker, punk rock shouter of the absurd.

The theater was dark, darker than dark. It was a moonless sky in which the stars fell off. Silence reigned. Anticipation perspired through the walls. The electricity between Dave and me could have been mistaken as a "between" but I only felt it for Waits. A thick, persistent drumbeat began. Boom, *boom*. Boom, *boom*. Then a single spotlight shone at one of the two doors in the back of the auditorium. Boom, *boom*. Boom, *boom*. A mic'd gravelly voice—one that was very familiar—joined the drums. Boom, *boom*. "Arrrgh, arggh." And a door in the back of the auditorium flung open as if possessed by spirits. Waits entered the spotlight, walking methodically, each step measured to the drums. With each beat, he threw out a handful of glitter that caught the spotlight's glare and cascaded fancifully from hand to floor like a comet's tail. Boom, *boom*. Argh, argh. Glitter bomb, glitter bomb. Until he made his way from the back of the theater to the stage, where he *performed*. I am a piece of shit when it comes to being an audience member—I criticize, I analyze, I am not satisfied. But this was stunning to me, a performance so perfect. It was even okay that I was sitting next to Dave, who I felt much less rapturous about. Tom Waits played the last song of his second encore—"Take It with Me." He sang slow and sweetly, touching the piano. Lyrics of love, a long love, a deep love, a Russian doll of love, a lifetime of love: Waits finished the song with instructive lyrics, telling no one in particular, "It's got to be more than flesh and bone / All that you've loved is all that you own." And with that I freaked out. I did not have access to love. I did not have access to *that* kind of love. That kind of love had always been on a stage, in a box, far away from me. *But it was what I wanted.*

And so when Dave and I stood on that corner, right on the curb and he kissed me and said he had a crush on me, I made some excuse and told him no. There were moments I thought Dave and I could date, I was convincing myself. Tom Waits described his wife, Kathleen Brennan, who co-writes many of his lyrics, as "a remarkable collaborator, and she's a shiksa goddess and a trapeze artist, all of that. She can fix the truck. Expert on the African violet and all that. She's outta this world. I don't know what to say. I'm a lucky man. She has a remarkable imagination. And that's the nation where I live. She's bold, inventive and fearless. That's who you wanna go in the woods with, right? Somebody who finishes your sentences for you." Dave was not that to me. I told him something along the lines of, *I don't date people who are normal and that I actually like*. And I think ultimately I was not convinced he really liked me. And so I fell back on aggression. As I told Dr. Schwartz later that week, I found Dave "weak and dorky." I dug into the idea that I could only date the unobtainables. I wasn't ready to date. And no one, certainly not Dave, was going to wrestle me away from bad decisions and greasy breakfasts with strangers. This phase seemed doomed to last for forever. It felt that way to me. And I think it did to Dr. Schwartz. In the same session, Dr. Schwartz asked in a parenthetical in his notes, "Is she a lesbian?"

A week after the Tom Waits date with Dave, I talked with Dr. Schwartz about being molested. Up until then, it was more of a plot point in my therapy sessions, just something that happened to happen. In real life—beyond the Oriental rugs, dramatic photography, and turquoise sculptures of Dr. Schwartz's office—it never came up. From Dr. Schwartz's notes: "We tried to delve into the relationship between molestation and later difficulties with men. She went over what happened and seemed upset recalling how frightened she was . . . she wondered why she hadn't realized why the knife wasn't sharp . . . she agreed that her 'aggressiveness' now could be a consequence of wishing she had been more aggressive then . . . she also agreed that she repeats the experience in some ways with the strangers she has slept with and that she lacks the ability to feel relaxed."

CHAPTER 13

HYSTERICAL METAMORPHOSIS

LACKS THE ABILITY TO FEEL RELAXED. It was true. I defy anyone who has lost hold of themselves to feel relaxed, in a relationship and otherwise. And I defy any man to say that to a woman who has had any kind of sexual trauma. Part of my inability to date was because I couldn't trust myself. How could I trust someone else? *Lacks the ability to feel relaxed.* It was true! In 2011, the CDC released an exhaustive survey that found that one in five women had been a victim of "rape or attempted rape" in the previous twelve months. *Feel relaxed* was code for *calm down*, a phrase I'd heard my entire life and I didn't know *how to calm down*. Part of that might have been due to my sexual assault. Lisa James, director of health for Futures Without Violence, told the *New York Times* that she'd seen chronic health conditions associated with assault before. I was aggressive and angry and frustrated and I did have big feelings. I didn't know why.

It turns out there is a long history of women who had a hard time relaxing, and given historical sexism, and the variety of "treatments," who could blame them? Just look at "The Yellow Wallpaper." Charlotte Perkins Gilman explained in the introduction why she wrote the short story in the first place: "For many years I suffered from a severe and continuous breakdown tending to melancholia—and beyond. During about the third year of this trouble I went, in devout faith and some faint stir of hope, to a noted specialist in nervous diseases, the best known in the country. This wise man put me to bed and applied the rest cure. . . . [He] concluded there was nothing much the matter with me, and sent me home with solemn advice to 'live as domestic a life as possible,' to 'have but two hours' intellectual life a day,' and 'never to touch pen, brush, or pencil again' as long as I lived. . . . I went home and obeyed those directions . . . and came so near the borderline of utter mental ruin." The story she wrote in response is one of the most famous fictionalized recollections of how misguided "treatment" can be. It doesn't surprise me that Weil, her famed doctor; her husband (also a physician); and her brother were all complicit in the treatment. Resting all the time doesn't address a wild mind. A wild mind is much more complicated than that.

There was a label for women like Gilman. There are words assigned to their condition: melancholia and hysteria. One of the first examples of hysteria was observed by Thomas Sydenham in 1681. According to the historian David Healy, Sydenham's originally observed patient was a woman who "shrieks irregularly and inarticulately, and strikes her breast and has to be held down by the united efforts of the bystanders . . . fear, anger, jealousy, suspicion, and the worst passions of the mind arise without cause."

Healy goes on to say that what Sydenham was describing was an early version of mood disorders—specifically borderline personality disorder or bipolar disorder. Sydenham called it hysteria. Several leading psychiatrists at the same time were diagnosing psychiatric disorders by examining the unconscious or at least considering it. And attitudes toward the mentally ill were changing: French physician Philippe Pinel began reforming asylums by unchaining patients, pioneering humane treatment of psychiatric patients, and was one of the first physicians to demand evidence-based medicine. Pinel, according to a paper written by Healy, distinguished general insanity from mania in his paper titled "Medico-Philosophical Treatise on Mental Alienation" in 1809. It established the possibility for a distinct mood disorder, and by the 1830s Jean-Étienne Dominique Esquirol, a student of Pinel's, wrote about deep sadness.

In the nineteenth century, the French neurologists Jean-Martin Charcot and Pierre Janet introduced the idea of the unconscious mind. They went on to identify types of hysteria—modern concepts of mental and emotional disorders involving anxiety, phobias, and other abnormal behavior. Charcot's student Sigmund Freud then radically and controversially changed the landscape of hysteria altogether with "talk therapy" or psychoanalysis. Erika Kinetz wrote, "Freud's innovation was to explain *why* hysterics swooned and seized. He coined the term 'conversion' to describe the mechanism by which unresolved, unconscious conflict might be transformed into symbolic physical symptoms. His fundamental insight—that the body might be playing out the dramas of the mind."

In 2012, four researchers wrote, "Hysteria is undoubtedly the first mental disorder attributable to women, accurately described in the second millennium BC, and until Freud, considered an exclusively female disease. Over 4000 years of history, this disease was considered from two perspectives: scientific and demonological. It was cured with herbs, sex or sexual abstinence, punished and purified with fire for its association with sorcery and finally, clinically studied as a disease and treated with innovative therapies." Hysteria (as is the case with many female illnesses) has always been tethered to sex and sexual appetites or lack thereof. The paper describes two female doctors in the Middle Ages who both had a sense of hysteria and later melancholia, if not a grip on exactly what it means.

> But we cannot talk about women's health in the Middle Ages without citing Trotula de Ruggiero from Salerno (11th century). While as a woman she could never become a magister, Trotula is considered the first female doctor in Christian Europe. . . . Trotula was an expert in women's diseases and disorders. Recognizing women as being more vulnerable than men, she explained how the suffering related to gynecological diseases was "intimate": women often, out of shame, do not reveal their troubles to the doctor. Her best known work, *De passionibus mulierum ante, in et post partum*, deals with female problems, including hysteria. . . . Trotula works at a time when women are still considered inferior to men because of their physiological and anatomical differences. Hildegard of Bingen (1098–1179), German abbess and mystic, was another female doctor. Her work is very important for the attempt to reconcile science with faith, that happens at the expense of science. Hildegard resumes the "humoral theory" of Hippocrates and attributes the origin of black bile to the original sin. In her view, melancholy is a defect of

the soul originated from Evil and the doctor must accept
the incurability of this disease.

IN THE EARLY 1400s, medieval Europeans allowed the mentally
ill freedom, assuming those people weren't witches, in which case
a common treatment was "casting out devils." By the fifteenth
century asylums started popping up outside London and in Va-
lencia and Padua. By the seventeenth century, the male medical
community "treated" hysteria by massaging a patient's clitoris
until orgasm. A medical publication on hysteria from 1653 cites
the following medical notes that described a standard practice
from the time:

> When these symptoms indicate, we think it is necessary
> to ask a midwife to assist, so that she can massage the
> genitalia with one finger inside, using oil of lilies, musk
> root, crocus, or [something] similar. And in this way the
> afflicted woman can be aroused to the paroxysm.

This practice—of doctors and midwives massaging female
clitorises—carried on for centuries. Physicians didn't consider
women capable of orgasm, which is why the treatment described
was so clinical, without even a reference to sexuality. By the
early twentieth century, doctors began complaining about their
fingers hurting from the therapeutic practice which, combined
with the invention of electricity, led to a new invention: the
vibrator.

Historically, mental illness has been categorized in three basic
ways: supernatural, somatogenic, and psychogenic. Aspects of all
three are relevant, and I find myself asking: Why am I bipolar?

Psychiatry has included environmental histories and stressors in diagnosis for most of the twentieth century, though less so since the advent of psychopharmacology in the last twenty years. This feels especially true in cases like mine, where the genetic link is weak (my grandfather and his family are clearly a genetic link, but most psychiatrists look for a link within one generation, like my mom or my dad). I took the lithium, I relied on it, I took the diagnosis and rarely questioned either. But the words "lacks the ability to feel relaxed" echo in my head. A few years ago, the Mayo Clinic conducted a comprehensive study on the relationship between sexual abuse and whether a history of abuse can lead to psychiatric disorders. The researchers found that a history of sexual abuse is associated with an increased risk of a lifetime diagnosis of multiple psychiatric disorders and that medical literature has long reported an association between sexual abuse and psychiatric symptoms.

A study published in 2016 by the *British Journal of Psychiatry* found that childhood traumas were linked with later diagnoses of bipolar disorder and that people who are bipolar are 2.63 times as likely to have experienced some type of abuse. What this means, in theory, is that the disease is not purely genetic; it is environmental as well. The ability to assign a beginning to the madness, to redistribute the weight of responsibility, felt like a relief. I thought of when I was attacked, the childhood molestation that occurred during the formative years of my brain. Post-traumatic stress disorder from sexual trauma and PTSD from war trauma are different, but they share common ground in that both are relatively unstudied. Dr. Farris Tuma, a National Institute of Mental Health psychiatrist, described PTSD to me as "someone's stress response system or view of the world essentially hijacked, and it has to do with how memory works. PTSD is a disorder where people can't forget, and it becomes a physiological response. There are intense feelings of horror and panic. When you bring back a memory, you are essentially experiencing it again." There are times when my brain feels hijacked by panic and agitation, and I imagine for the women centuries and millennia before me who didn't even have the benefit of diagnosis, it felt even worse.

CHAPTER 14

TAPER MEDS,
THANKSGIVING IN MAINE,
KYRGYZSTANI MAN

WHEN I MOVED to New York, I was not manic, I was not depressed, but I was in a frenzy. Maybe it was the kind of frenzy that
people go through, that transformation from coddled college life
to real-not-real adult life. My form of psychological frenzy did not

match well with my day job, but when my job switched to the photo department, I had allies: a boss, Dana, who acted as a mentor and champion; a colleague, Amy, who was a hippie goddess with dramatic bangles and colorful swing skirts, closer to me than any of the Condé ladies. I knew Amy's husband, Donnell, from the *LA Weekly*, and I had been to a barbecue at Amy's house in LA when I was a summer intern, which felt like the best kind of small-town coincidence ever.

Magazines were still in their glorious excessive heyday. Jay McInerney was our wine columnist, and we had a contributing editor whose main job was to smuggle unpasteurized cheeses in from France. When we moved to 4 Times Square, Dominique hired a Feng Shui expert clad in marigolds and caftans to bless the halls. I worked in the electronic sign shaped like a can, filing chromes (large-format negatives) from photo shoots that cost thousands of dollars to produce. Occasionally I'd step out on location to assist in the luxury pet shoots, or I'd scout an interior. I scoffed at the money spent and hauled home whatever I could carry from the free pile. To Dominique's credit, I pitched relentlessly within *House & Garden* and wrote a few small things that kick-started my national magazine career—a piece on animal print rugs, one on artist installations, and I produced a shoot of Matthew Ritchie installing a wall drawing. I was building clips (realizing one half of my aforementioned goal: becoming a working writer).

I even wrote for Dave after he went from being an assistant at *Details* to an assistant at *Maxim*. By August 1999, Dr. Schwartz and I began talking again about tapering off lithium with the idea of eventually not taking it at all. "Today she arrived late talking about bipolar disorder as being a form of spirituality or inspiration or something that didn't make sense." It didn't make sense to him, but when I think of being bipolar, I always think of it as something that elevates me, that has taken me to spheres of the universe otherwise unknown (for better and worse). I got so religious in high school, my experience felt more godly than anything I'd known. I didn't do drugs, I didn't need ayahuasca, I didn't trip on LSD because I had done all that without ingesting anything. When I did cocaine for the first time, I thought, *This is it?* Coke was closer to Bud Light Lime than mania. (Dr. DeAntonio was slightly off in his initial analogy: mania is more like unbridled dizzying love or the first sparkling spring day when daffodils are bursting and everything is coated in warm rays and looking like a rainbow paradise, prisms of iridescence beaming.) Being bipolar meant I had access to the other side. But there were still functional kinks to work out—living with daily tasks was sometimes a challenge. I was anxious, short, and impatient, and unable to draw straight lines. "She seemed to want to be talking about getting off the lithium . . . she strongly disagreed with me, saying that wasn't the issue—she's still irked by my having called her 'damn assertive,'" Dr. Schwartz wrote.

My solution to everything was wild and disorganized and forceful. I continued my practice of crushing out on unavailable dudes and supplemented that absence with one-night stands. But if I needed to sleep with some strangers to get to the other side of a painful experience, I'm not sure that was the worst thing in the world. Dr. Schwartz and I talked about relationships and dating, but that was far from possible. I just wasn't ready, it wasn't in my vocabulary. (And according to Dr. Schwartz, I was too aggressive anyway.) Maybe a relationship would have validated me, made me feel normal and unscarred? But I doubt it. I wasn't alone entirely. We—my friends, my roommates, my colleagues—were incubating. We had parties at the loft almost every month, my roommates were now a bunch of attractive dudes who had attractive dude friends, and my friends were single and we lived in bars until closing time and sometimes walked home as the summer sun cracked the horizon line, glowing against the city's geometry.

Things were changing with me. What was purely physical, a punch card of experience, was becoming emotional. Through all of this, lithium was something I took without thinking, something that worked without question, something I kept in a pill box with me at all times just in case I ended up in someone else's bed. I was growing and lithium was helping me to grow by being quiet and in the background. I did what I wanted and a new creature was emerging.

I imagine a butterfly's life from minuscule to breaking free—the egg laid on a milkweed leaf. An insect at first, a caterpillar, long, thick, stubby, systemically eating the green she was born to. She grows, and she hangs from a milkweed stem until a pupa forms around her body. Inside the pupa, tissue, limbs, and organs form, pushing against the casing—a metamorphosis from crawler to flight. The change is protected by a silky cocoon until that protective cocoon is shed. But there's a struggle behind that change, there's violence and transformation. I could feel that coming and I could feel wings growing too.

I was bad at my job. Being drunk half the time didn't help. My basic tasks were organization and mailing things and addressing envelopes en masse. I could never pay my bills on time or manage to organize a sock drawer or even wear matching socks, let alone manage thousands of photography shoots that I would have to pull and present at will. My most terrifying moments were when Dominique remembered an interior and asked to see it; I would go to the chromes storage and the interior was gone; chaos would ensue while I looked for the project until Dominique was distracted by something else. But she took note, and everyone knew I was not meant to be a photo assistant. I loved photography and taking

photos. I took advantage of the fact that I was responsible for sign-
ing off on printing invoices and shot every weekend. Sometimes I
would blow three rolls on one building corner. I started using my
color Xerox machine art collages as invitations to parties that I
mailed to my friends and colleagues and complete strangers.

By November 1999, I told Dr. Schwartz what was clear to me,
that painting didn't feel like a career path but publishing did. In
the same session we decided "to get off lithium. We planned to go
to 600 mg every other week from 900 mg, starting right away." A
month later I was down to 600 milligrams and I felt a little twinge
of giddiness. Having hit the year anniversary of my employment
(a crucial benchmark for first jobs), I started looking for another
job. I got my first music review published. The *Village Voice*'s music
editor Chuck Eddy let me write a bordering-on-offensive analysis
of Korean pop, and I felt like I had a chance to become a freelance
writer if I could cobble together a few different sources of income.
I wrote about Blackalicious and I carved a niche of obscurish indie
Bay Area rap reviews along with whatever was being overlooked
or unknown by East Coast music writers and editors. I tried to fill
in gaps with my pitches, things that weren't going to be covered by
actual music writers. I still harbored fantasies of being an artist.
In therapy, I talked about a project I imagined. I wanted to deco-
rate and paint and take over an entire subway car, living in one
portion and interacting with strap-hangers as they commuted, for
a week or a month or a year. I just didn't know how to go about it.
I was more interested in art than work and would routinely visit
Charles, aka Stanley, aka the receptionist at the *New Yorker* on the
twenty-second floor. He held himself with gravitas and had a
booming voice that rivaled James Earl Jones. He and I would talk
and I convinced him to hang one of my resin triptyches in a group
show that he curated in the lobby. It was about my stay at NPI and

included one section of pipes, one of the grassy squirrel knoll, and one of the actual building. The placards were painted red and had words etched in gold that described various phrases of fear. (It was my first and only piece of art in an art show.)

I was getting in trouble more frequently at work, for losing chromes or not knowing where they were in the first place or being completely disengaged with our mission to present a narrative of luxury interiors. I thought about quitting in April after some disaster or another, no doubt caused by my inability to organize. We continued the decrease of lithium and as the dosage went down my plans to escape Condé Nast were forged. I became friends with the research editor and begged her to teach me how to fact-check. I pitched relentlessly, and hoped that when I was fired/quit I could rely on some writing work and some freelance fact-checking. In May, I preemptively quit. (I was clearly going to be asked to leave and I just decided it was better if I did it for them. I mean I probably would have been asked to fire myself anyway.) The art and photo department had a sad nacho party for my good-bye event, and there was little to do except slink out the side door with as many office supplies and custom tote bags as I could carry. I started fact-checking at *Stuff* magazine and writing short front-of-book articles for *Maxim* and *Stuff* and I had regular music reviews in the *Village Voice*. By mid-November I was on the lowest dose of lithium possible before entirely eliminating it. Dr. Schwartz wrote: "She informed me today that she decreased the lithium and wondered if the new improvements in her life since then were related. She felt better about herself and her work, she's lost weight and goes to the gym, and she's changed the clothes and hairdo—generally making herself more attractive. She decreased her drinking and decreased the one-night stands."

I had a new life and a fabulous gay hairdresser who cut my

ME, TAKING MORE SELF-PORTRAITS THAN USUAL, STANDING IN FRONT OF THE POPPY MURAL I
PAINTED ON THE LOFT'S DINING-ROOM WALL.

unkempt, frizzy hair into a lioness mane. He plucked my eyebrows. I was no longer tethered to an everyday office job. And I was off my meds. I would visit Stanley at the *New Yorker*, I would shop for fresh vegetables and fall gourds, and I had a new morning routine. Light a few candles and take myself through self-guided yoga. I would breathe calmly and with the feeling of enlightenment, as if all the heartache and stress had come from the lithium. I felt happy again, motivated and unworried by life or logic. I had energy. I had ideas. I did thirty push-ups and thirty sit-ups and ended every morning with a headstand against the wall; I could feel the day rush by before it even happened. A close friend of my dad's cousin Pam (my cousin too, but more like an aunt) ran the National Coalition Against Censorship (NCAC) and they were looking for a communications director. I interviewed for the job but did not get it. However, and this is the biggest HOW-EVER possible, it left a big impression. Censorship became my cause, my central focus. I devised a plan to write a book, do fundraisers, and raise awareness about First Amendment rights and censorship issues in general. I invited my friend Josh, a fellow editor, to join the team, which I named RedSpark Productions. I gave him an impassioned pitch.

"First Amendment rights are the only thing you should care about."

"I care about the First Amendment," he said.

"They are crucial, the backbone of our industry. A free press. A real N.E.A. How much money do you need?"

"I'm really more interested in just being a writer or editing," he said calmly.

"Fifty K?"

"I need to make more money than what you are offering."

I had not one dollar to actually pay him. And upped the offer. He still said no.

It did not deter me.

By November 22, Dr. Schwartz's notes indicated that I got the job offer from NCAC. From The Notes: "Jaime seemed thrilled because the NCAC would pay her to do the book project she planned on doing anyway," he writes. "She began discussing a benefit for them that will involve lots of art stars and musicians which they could do at the Playboy Mansion. She envisions herself hobnobbing with Beck and Matthew Ritchie. We discussed whether her excitement could lead to mania, but she feels well within her self-control for now." The most notable thing about this is that I never got a job offer from the NCAC and they never offered to publish a book on censorship. I must have been con-

fused or conflating an imaginary future with one that I was trying to will into existence.

For Thanksgiving, Hana, Sarah P., and I drove up to Maine.
We cooked Brussels sprouts that were so organic they had worms
crawling out of their crowns; I insisted on not washing them, it
was simply more protein. We roasted gourds, so many gourds.
We drank cheap red wine and ran naked from the sauna to the
cold freshwater lake in snow boots, our skin streaked red from
heat, our bodies and spirits pliable.

I continued my morning routine, only adding what Sarah re-
calls as "300 sit-ups and pushups a day. You encouraged Hana and
I to follow suit but we were a little bit too lazy." Hana remembered

ME, GREETING LAKE THOMPSON IN NOVEMBER.

my waking up at five thirty a.m. with the sun and that I was obsessed with the loons and the loon calls—their echo against the lake. We had an animated discussion about little people and performance. I can't remember my exact argument but it probably went something like this: *I am not in favor of anyone being taken advantage of, but if little people want to perform, they should perform; if they feel there are significantly less opportunities because they are little people, that is fucked up.* I think this was a two- to three-hour argument, mostly because I was fired up and increasingly argumentative. I was also taking rolls and rolls of photos, some nudes, some double exposures, some shots of trees overlapping trees like a plaid made of branches, a psychedelic canopy of bark. I told Hana and Sarah they would all be published in the *New Yorker.* My meetings for coffee with Stanley had morphed into this idea that my photos would be *in* the *New Yorker* and that eventually my writing would be, too. Hana and I drove home after dropping Sarah off in Boston and we got so lost that we ended up in Albany.

In another entry a week later, I told Dr. Schwartz that I did not feel carried away with big ideas; nevertheless the big ideas continued to develop. Now there was a movie attached to the book, fund-raising, and an awareness campaign. Additionally, I told Dr. Schwartz, this would all end with my marrying Beck. He writes, "Ultimately she wants power, money, fame, and Beck."

Just before Christmas, Dave published an article in *Marie Claire* that included some references to our frustrated and nonexistent relationship. It was also a chapter in a book he wrote years later. He didn't tell me about the article (or the book). The article didn't bother me; I was a little flattered. At the same time that he published the account, I was distracted by a rare one-night crush that cut deeper than most. I met a Peace Corps volunteer who had just returned from Kyrgyzstan at the Village Idiot. The Pabst hole that was dirty, dizzy, and perfect for certain needs; you could always find someone if you waited long enough. I was drunk and smitten, and he was just drunk. "Every 10 minutes or so a garbage truck would hurl through the driveway," I wrote a month later for a personal essay for the *Voice*. "Lighting our chins and the trail of spit between our mouths, spider webbing its way from shoulder to ear to throat to teeth to temple . . . In my bed we talked of tiger force, had squirrelly cuddles and loud lap dancing. He asked, 'Did you feel the shocks? Did you feel them?' I smiled. I didn't have to say yes." I felt with him—a glimpse of love. Lust, yes, but also body, spirit, mind sharing, the kind of feeling that elevates and creates a rainbow sheen on life. Dr. Schwartz said in his notes that I felt "spectacular, that it was spectacular." Weeks later, I thought I might be pregnant even though we didn't actually have sex. It was part of some immaculate theory. (No one flagged this as a grand delusion . . .)

I was still—even more so—obsessed with my First Amendment project. I had dinner with Aaron, my old roommate, who had since moved to Los Angeles, and basically told him I was producing a benefit concert with Sting and others. I shouted my manifesto to anyone who would listen, including Dr. Schwartz, who noted that I "yelled" the mission statement at him during a session.

The introductory letter of a twelve-page packet that I had put together explained the project Censor This and ended with a rallying cry:

> It is time for a pre-emptive strike, a change in thought, action, and responsibility. It is time for the arts communities to band together to nurture creativity and freedom of expression. . . .
>
> The answer lies in a grassroots movement of, for, and by the artist. It is time to take on Tipper and Joe [Gore and Lieberman, respectively], it is time to demand an

explanation of the MPAA ratings system, it is time to fill the void where the NEA once existed, it is time for a revolution.

This is a call to arms. But rather than resorting to guns and ammo, let us use the resources at hand. The following proposal requires three things: funding, participation, and a belief that the first amendment is the crux and livelihood of creativity and education in America.

To paraphrase Springsteen, it takes a spark to light a fire, and baby, I'll be your gun for hire.

I HAD A LIST of about 250 people I was planning to send the packet to. I was determined to involve everyone I knew in the project, including a rabbi, half of the media, and anyone whose address I had access to, including authors, artists, politicians, and every press relations person I had any contact with in my brief time as a music reporter. Anyone. I was jacked about my Lollapalooza-of-speech-freedom event and irritated by many everyday concerns.

For Christmas 2000, I bought dozens of tiny Buddhas from Pearl River and gave them to everyone I could think of, including Dr. Schwartz. My moods were pushing and pulling like a current—tense, then calm, elated, then angry. I got in fights with friends—my friend Effie and I stopped talking altogether—but I continued my yoga-stand-on-my-head ritual. I told Dr. Schwartz I quit my health insurance, which I had actually done months prior. I was angered by my bank and started to develop a barter system—I decided I would operate without money. The truth was I had very little money anyway. I could trade for necessities, I thought. I made granola religiously and started filling my pockets with the cereal so that I could share grains with the world. I was wandering into doorways and talking with the neighborhood's longtime residents—furriers, garment sellers, and one outsider artist who packed decades of work into a ground-floor storefront around the corner from my apartment.

I was feeling otherworldly but was not functioning in this world at all.

CHAPTER 15

AND NOW FOR A PSYCHOTIC BREAK . . .
OR THAT TIME I ALMOST GOT MARRIED
ON TOP OF THE WORLD TRADE CENTER

WHEN I ROUNDED the corner of Twenty-Eighth and Sixth, I knew. I saw the lights at the end of the block, I saw the flash rounding around the corner and bending toward me. I walked slow and then fast and then slow again, thinking, no, those lights weren't for me. Sirens in New York are as common as bagels, as native as egg 'n' cheeses and drop-and-fold laundry. I was fine, it was okay. I was wearing Marilyn's sealskin boots lined with wool from the 1970s, a wraparound fluorescent floral skirt over long johns, and my coiffed red 'fro. I had just been interviewed for a job to be an editor at *Blender* magazine. I told Andy, the editor in chief, that I was not interested in a cumbersome job, a daily job, but that if he would like to collaborate on my Censor This project, I would consider letting him in on the action. I gave him some pocket granola and left. I took photos in the hallway of *Blender*'s offices—of their fire escape, fire signs, the poles that crisscrossed on the ceiling of the emergency stairwell. I did double exposures—it was a crisp winter day with harsh light. The blues and reds came through in high relief, carving out details of prewar buildings that seemed tall and mighty when they were erected.

Then on my walk home, I got to the end of my street and turned left, where three fire engines blocked traffic on Seventh Avenue. *They couldn't be for me.* I walked faster again.

I counted the floors calmly, each time coming to the conclusion that the burnt-out cave with broken windows and splintered beams was not my apartment. I did not live there. That was the floor above or the floor below but absolutely not where I slept every night. And I counted again, and everyone looked at me as if it was my apartment. I counted again.

"Jaime, that's your apartment," a voice said. And I shook my head no. No, that is not where I live.

And then, with my legs buckling under me, and my knees hitting the hard, dirty ice, I passed out. Cold. I remember the freezing sensation of falling and the

MY APARTMENT ON FIRE.

inability to use my muscles to hold my body upright. I collapsed on the hard, dirt-caked ice. Mike squatted next to me. "Are you okay? Do you need to call anyone? Are you okay?"

I was not. I called my roommates from the camera store across the street; Jeremy was calm, my other roommate (the investment banker) understandably less so. For some reason I called Andy at *Blender*, who said I should call my parents; I called my parents. My mom was not surprised because of various elevated e-mails I'd been sending. I went to see the apartment and was struck by the suffocating smell of char. I couldn't get the burn off my hands. I couldn't see the apartment I lived in under the wet wreckage. A mural of poppies I'd painted directly on the dining room wall was streaked with brown and black. My clothes were half burned from the bottom up and soaked. My papers, computer, bed, everything. All my art was burned. One piece that lived in a Plexiglas box, recycled from a *House & Garden* shoot, looked like a moonscape— melted resin dripping and sagging like a thick-lipped smile. This fire was clearly a sign from God that I should be living possession-free, that I was being communicated to by a higher power, a pagan power, a fiery force of nature.

Mike and I had met once before. Mike worked downstairs in a tech start-up. He had a goatee and a sweet smile that extended to his eyes. I didn't have a cell phone; I had a strong argument against them. I didn't want brain cancer, to be tracked, or to be reached at all times. But now I needed one—the catastrophe I had been preparing for had happened. Mike scrawled his landline on a piece of paper and gave me his cell phone. Hana came over to make sure I was okay and we took pictures, making hand shadow puppets against the burnt walls. She held out a dress tiered with melted sequins. All of my hand-me-downs from my aunt Carrie were charred. I didn't care.

I spent the first night after the fire sleeping on a futon that belonged to my extremely generous downstairs neighbors (ani-mators) on the second floor. They let me sleep on the couch and we drank whiskey and felt burnt inside and out. One of them let me borrow clothes and I slept under his painting of Ray Charles. It said *Grace*. That night I went back upstairs in the dark, where people were rummaging through the mess—pickers, they're called—salvaging anything worth stealing. I had a fancy watch from my aunt and tiny diamond earrings from my grand-mother, and I saw one soot-covered man holding them. I could only see the whites of his eyes. I told him to take them. I didn't care. I told everyone to take whatever they wanted. I did not need things.

Mike called his own phone to check on me but I didn't know how to answer, so it stayed blinking in my bag through the night. I woke up the next day and ordered seven hundred dollars' worth of butternut squash and lavender hand cream and healing balms to be delivered to my second-floor neighbors. After that, they—and everyone in the building—decided it would be best for me to stay elsewhere, farther from the fire. Hana called my dad and my mom, telling them I was not acting normal. My dad got on a plane; Matt booked a ticket on Amtrak from Washington, D.C., where he was in graduate school. The landlord and firefighters were saying that they found a lot of candles in my apartment, a potential cause for the fire. My neighbors and roommates were blaming me, and that made sense. Jeremy never blamed me be-cause he is the most chill human ever and the most forgiving per-son, even though I burned half his record collection. By the time my dad arrived, he and my brother tried to mitigate the chaos. I stayed with them at the Chelsea Savoy Hotel on Twenty-Third and Seventh Avenue next to the Chelsea Hotel, where I imagined, once I explained my circumstances, I would be immediately given an artist residency. (This did not happen.)

Two days after the fire, I went to see Dr. Schwartz and told him that yes I had candles but that they weren't the cause of the fire. My landlord thought otherwise; so did the fire department, though they did not officially pinpoint an exact cause. I was convinced it was shitty electrical wiring, since nothing had been updated in decades. Evidence in my favor: loose wires. Evidence against me: the week before I found dozens of large table candles in a box on the street and I took them up to the loft for a potential future party. There were other candles (including a couple from the blizzard of '98) that I lit for my makeshift yoga and exercise routine. Unlit candles and lit candles look the same after a fire— melted as if they had been in use. Dr. Schwartz wrote that I was "sedate and unruffled and spoke in an overly calm manner." I had taken rolls and rolls of film of the fire aftermath, and I shared them with him. I told Dr. Schwartz that I had solved a complex math problem involving prime numbers. He suggested I resume taking the lithium. I refused.

Mania began again. (Or maybe something closer to hypomania, when a patient is ramping up toward the inevitable flourish.) I sat in the brown leather wingback chair and I was calm because I had determined the answer to a difficult algebra equation. I had connected with the mysteries of infinity and the ever-enduring unknowability of the number zero. They were one and the same— a philosophy, a future, an unknown that only I knew, *another grand delusion*. I was up all night thinking about numbers and equations and solving problems and I walked, lit from within, knowing that I—and only I—could solve those problems. And so I calmly explained this new piece of information to Dr. Schwartz.

I had also been at the apartment the night before with Mike. We went back to shoot footage of what was left. And I knew I wasn't fully manic because I felt sad. In this moment, I did care. I felt sad that this weird nest of art and music and debauchery and people had been torched. After some documentation of the carnage, Mike and I sat in the stairwell, on top of charcoal footsteps over torn cardboard. We huddled in the corner under our jackets. We kissed for the first time and lay in the hollowed-out burn.

My dad and Matt moved my charred belongings into a storage locker. (My vision of the fire had changed after the initial shock wore off. I would not let things go— everything that was

ME, PHOTOGRAPHING EVERYTHING BEFORE AND AFTER THE FIRE.

left was an artifact.) I took half-burned sweaters and wore them, walking furiously through the streets of Manhattan wrapped in a cloak of smoke. I always had some charcoal streak on my cheek or hands like a warrior or a coal miner. Black ashy residue collected under my nails. I was getting thinner and thinner, dipping below 100 pounds and only buying clothes at flea markets or used-clothing shops. My outfits were gilded, bedazzled, fluorescent, multipatterned, multitiered, lovingly very 1980s. My look: if Cher swallowed Mick Jagger who had eaten Cyndi Lauper and Madonna with a touch of righteous Michael Jackson and Liza Minnelli sprinkled on top. And cowboy. And Indian. And shaman. And God. I clasped about a thousand necklaces all at once across my upper breast, again like a warrior. A breastplate. My dad came to my next Dr. Schwartz appointment, and they both tried to convince me that I should take the lithium again before it was too late. I refused, saying that lithium changed me. It took me away from my true self. I could not allow that to happen again. We (my dad and Matt) finished putting everything in storage, and my dad was trying to convince me to go to LA. I wanted to throw a party. My dad, exasperated, bought stacks of pizza and had them delivered to the Village Idiot. Hana came, colleagues came, we gave pizza to pool-playing strangers. We gave pizza to everyone. Dave was there, and so was Mike.

By then, Mike and I were yoked to each other. We disappeared around the corner to "shoot more important camcorder footage for the censorship project," which at this point had come to include a second documentary about my burnt apartment. On the sidewalk, we kissed again, which seemed to be the real point. He returned me back to the Chelsea Savoy at five a.m. and we kissed, again, good-bye. "See ya," he said in a tone so casual it belied what was clear to me. I had met my soul mate. I was going to LA the next day to visit, but not to stay, and he was my fire neighbor. He was intrigued, addicted to the mania, and devoted, following me around with his video camera, recording impromptu dance recitals and monologues. Mania or even the beginnings of mania will do this. There's a magnetism to that kind of high, and I knew I could draw people to me. I had drawn in Mike.

I had plans. I had a concept of myself as an anarchistic cult leader in a gold tutu. If Mike wanted to be part of that, fine. If not, I would find another Mike. On camera, I talked about a utopia I planned to build and rule. A place where inhibition was not welcome, a place where creativity reigned. To get there, we had to break through the norms of society, to end censorship to make free speech, freer than water. To be naked in body and soul. I yelled about the people I admired, like Chris Ofili, like NWA, like Eminem. I thought about Eminem's lyrics constantly, on loop, I am whatever you say I am . . . or even more direct arguments against censorship like his lyrics from "Who Knew?": "There must be a mix-up/You want me to fix up lyrics while the president gets his dick sucked?"

Eminem, the number zero, living in a utopia in the trees and morphing into fairy creatures: I could see the next steps past the pizza party, and so, while clomping through the meatpacking district, passing transgender prostitutes and Florent, I could feel my luminous future and Mike was tangled in it. As Sylvia Plath wrote, "When you are insane, you are busy being insane—all the time." Mike had a camera; he could document it all. I asked him to film everything and he obliged. Mike was new to the city; he went to school in Vermont and grew up in Chicago and had this perfect all-American face. He looked like the Gerber baby grown up, perfect, spherical, and Aryan. Big blue eyes and tousled blond hair; he fucked with his face by growing that awful goatee but I didn't care. I felt like he was an extension of my Peace Corps man, maybe even the same person—someone I was drawn to and who was drawn to me. It was a new feeling, heightened by being an all-powerful magic fairy creature, one hundred percent clad in gold lamé and gilded medallions. My dad was desperate to get me on a plane home. I realized the Grammys were being held in Los Angeles later that week and that I could start recruiting rock stars and rappers for ENDING CENSORSHIP FOREVER, and so I said yes. I was amped to start with Eminem since I thought I could get an audience with his PR dude. I told Dave that I could do an interview with Marilyn Manson or Eminem or the *South Park* guys for *Maxim*, and tried to sell him on assigning it to me. He agreed, tentatively, to a short interview with Trey Parker and Matt Stone. They had a live-action show—*"That's My Bush!"*—scheduled for debut, and Dave thought I might be able to get an interview that he couldn't get through regular PR channels. He thought this because I told him my mom's house was across the street from their production offices and that I used to see them shooting hoops in the parking lot. I could just show up and ask, I said. Unusual ambush technique, but Dave agreed. So I decided to go back to LA. Dr. Schwartz and I struck a deal—he prescribed me Klonopin and Risperdal and said I should fill the prescriptions and that I could decide if I needed to take them, if I felt "edgy."

Yeah, right.

I was in Los Angeles between January 26 and February 13, 2001. I saw Dr. DeAntonio for several appointments and he recommended I go back on lithium; I didn't. I bought clothes and bartered for clothes. My aunt gave me a metallic gold swing skirt that paired perfectly with one hundred thousand necklaces. I did not stop "freelance writing." I called Dave several times to inform him of my progress on the *"That's My Bush!"* profile, which in fact did not exist. We got into a screaming fight on the phone. He was uncertain of what the fuck I was doing on behalf of the magazine, and I felt certain that he was spineless and did not belong in my revolution. I went to the *LA Weekly* to visit my mentors, editors Tom Christie and Pam Klein. Tom remembered "the necklaces and glitter—the day you showed up at the *Weekly* wearing more of that than I've ever seen on anyone, your mom in tow." I called up the skateboard company Sector 9 and told them I was a pro skater. I also said I was looking for sponsorship and new boards since my decks had burned in the fire. My mom got on the other landline during this particular call and said loudly and firmly to ignore me. She spoke over my voice even though the nice gentleman was actually hearing me out and concerned, and had offered to send me a new board. "Do not send her a skateboard. She does not skateboard. She is having a manic episode," my mom said.

The thing about mania is that all the hippie, glitter, and glow comes with an aggressive intensity that could make a planet reverse rotation. Maniacs breathe fire. I literally had started smoking a pack of American Spirits a day, having barely smoked before. My mom hated smoking but put out an ashtray and made me sit on the curb in my gold lamé, looking like a Dumpster pixie. For special occasions, I'd get Fantasia smokes in rainbow colors and leave bright butts in various stubbed arrangements.

The argument with Dave over *"That's My Bush!,"* which should have been a warning, did not stop me from showing up in Gabe Tesoriero's Universal Music office asking for an interview with Em.

"Could I guarantee the cover?"

"Sure! When can he sit for a photographer?"

I'm pretty sure Dave had already called Gabe and apologized or asked him to ignore or block my access on behalf of *Maxim*, but that didn't matter, outcome wasn't the point. *Maxim* wasn't the point, if I could just talk to Eminem. I worked the editor from my interview at *Blender*, Andy, with sixteen pitches—all one- or two-sentence hot-flash ideas, including an oral history of the song "Come and Knock on My Door . . ." from *Three's Company*. My tone was always confident and insistent and thoroughly underresearched, like, "5) Pinknoises.com, online collective of female DJs and MCs. Superfly talent and hot ladies. Launched a week or so ago, would be good to get it in ASAP." I ended my note to Andy with *alright, I think this is enough. Tell me what to start working on. I'm on it. I have more ideas but I don't want to overwhelm you with too much shit.* He did not respond immediately or otherwise, and then I ended up getting extremely sick. I was in a feverish state, topping out at 103 degrees for about five days, a fire within. On February 5, still feverish, I wrote Andy, *a couple more thoughts for you. I know you are starting with a bare bones staff and I intend to do the freelance dance and write whatever you assign me, happily . . . however when* Blender *is a flourishing, unstoppable success, can I please be considered for the West Coast Editor position? That, eventually would be an ideal position for me. . . . I am returning to New York Feb. 13 and will contact you when I land somewhere. It's kind of fun to be a nomad.* The pitches weren't wildly off-base, they just weren't thorough. There were too many and they all basically had a subject with no story. When I asked Andy later what his impression was, it was kinder than my assumption, which was that I'd caused myself pure professional embarrassment: "I would not say that you were 'full-on' crazy, as you put it. You were definitely eccentric and quite driven and energetic, but by the wonderfully forgiving standards of a) the music business b) New York and c) writers, hardly 'off the charts.' All the best writers were a bit bonkers. At least I always thought so (and still do)."

At the turn of the century when Carl Jung entered his apprenticeship at Burghölzli, the psychiatric hospital at the University of Zürich, he wrote that his interest and research was dominated by the "burning question: 'What actually takes place inside the mentally ill?'" I can tell you what was happening in me. I turned into a comet or a supernova, bursting, going in no particular direction, aimed at nothing but intensely moving forward on a trajectory to nowhere and everywhere at the same time. Everything was eclipsed by me. I was the sun, the moon, the solar system, the beginning of time and the end.

What actually was taking place on a more realistic level was the beginning of a two-month manic cycle. I   NOTES TO ANDY AND *STUFF FROM CALIFORNIA.*

Dear Stuff,
   Hello again from Cali.
I am finally heald from
the crash and burn I'll
be back in March and
we can party like i'nit's
   1999.

♡ Jaime

Dear Andy,
   Things are well
in Cali. No house burned
down yet.
   I'll call when I'm back
in March.

♡) Jaime
(JAIME LOVE)

believed everything I spouted (*I am God! I am a rock star! I love you! And you!*) to be true. I remembered most of it; I had no inhibitions or boundaries or fear. My family, meanwhile, was scrambling to make shit work and to make sure I didn't accidentally set everything on fire—physically or metaphorically. Marilyn went through stacks of files and was on the phone for hours to get my COBRA health insurance from Condé Nast reinstated.

"How can you say she willfully stopped paying the bills when stopping paying the bills is part of the disease—a symptom?" she would ask. Again and again and again until the insurance company relented. Can you imagine the tenacity it takes to break down the bureaucracy of insurance, to file the paperwork and jump through the impossible maze? Marilyn did it. She still has a thick file. There were logistical hoops and hard moments, but bright spots too. In particular Cody.

My dad and Marilyn had gotten a puppy, a Wheaten terrier named Cody. When I met him, he was a shaggy Muppet creature that looked like a boy in a dog suit. I believed he could talk to me, and I believed he understood me in a way many people couldn't (like Nature before him, but deeper. We had a real connection.). I talked with Mike every night and we made plans for the future. I made it clear that I would return to New York to be with him. I fell in love with Mike and Cody simultaneously, and I told Mike that Cody looked just like him. (I also told Cody he looked just like Mike.) *They had the same hair*, the same scruffy goatee. I held Cody until I could hold Mike.

Things were teetering on bad, but I was well enough that Marilyn and Dad let me go on a short drive through the Hollywood Hills with David, who was just on the other side of Bar Mitzvahed. We drove up to the end of Beachwood Canyon to pay homage to the Hollywood sign. We lifted our arms and took a series of conquer-

LOVE AT FIRST SIGHT. ME, WITH CODY.

the-world photos, our hands reaching toward an ethereal Los Angeles sky, lording over mountains and cityscape and hills. I look deathly thin and overly enthusiastic in bell bottoms that were intended for a child. I could feel the flip from elevated, magnetic energy to agitation, scattered thoughts, distraction, obsession, anxiety.

I had to be back in New York for Valentine's Day to collect my bride (Mike, obviously). No one thought this was a good idea. No one could stop me. I had a plan for Eden. I went to Oma and Opa's house off Mulholland and picked bags and bags of kumquats to bring back to the city. I went to my maternal grandma's house on Wade Street, near the Santa Monica airport where I used to take naps under the flight pattern, and picked avocados from her trees. Carrying the genetic seeds of the fruit trees seemed especially important to me. Both fruits: good barter potential and useful for winter survival. I bought cigarettes. I packed the few clothes I owned and told Mike I was coming.

On Valentine's Day Eve, I arrived at Garfield and Sixth Avenue in Park Slope. We went to a bar.

"If I draw a really good portrait of you, can we get free drinks?" I asked the bartender. He would not engage. Mike ordered beers in the normal way. I drew a really unflattering picture of the bartender on a napkin. He was stone-faced. But we did not pay for the beer. We went back to Mike's apartment to get his video camera. I looked like Janis Joplin had risen from the grave and dipped herself in gold.

The video starts with us sitting on Mike's stoop, talking with a group of moonfaced teenagers. I already had the "marry Mike" campaign going because I got each of those kids to say, "You should marry Jaime." In my hip-hop drawl—I was starting to absorb Eminem's talking pattern and the cigarettes were making me sound like Harvey Fierstein—I recited lines from *Romeo and Juliet*. Then the kids chanted with me: "Roses smelling sweet!" You can see they're mesmerized and confused by this pseudo-adult, crazed, clad in a tutu. At the end of the exchange I said, "You babies are all right!" Then I jumped into some Eminem lyrics.

The next scene on the tape is of me showing the camera different album covers and singing songs from each album. I'm wearing a cowboy hat, gold pants, the same fluorescent flower skirt from the day of the fire, and all the necklaces in the world. I pause at *Sweeney Todd* and say, "Oh, this one's about eating people, soooooo, that's cool." Mike, off-camera, peppered me with questions, asking me to hold the record albums higher or lower or to the side.

The next morning, I went to the bodega on the corner to get

Mike flowers. I set up the camera so the lens's point of view shows what I've made—kumquat-and-avocado salad, cubed PowerBars, and a glass of wine. The first ceremonial meal of the cult of Jaime. I videotaped Mike waking up. On film, he looks pissed, groggy, and confused—like a normal person. He negotiated for more sleeping time. I clearly hadn't slept at all and was now wearing a silver-flecked red bra and the gold skirt. I tried to get him to eat and he finally acknowledged me by eating a chunk of a Power-Bar. I said *Baruch atah Adonai* over the cup of wine, borrowing from the Hebrew prayer. I hushed it as if my voice were a direct line to God. It felt that way. Mike asked me what I was going to do that day.

"Today, I'm going to contact MTV to debate Gore, Bush, or Tipper Gore. I hope it's Tipper. I have a lot of work to do today." Pause. "I have to change the world." Ironically, Tipper Gore had been a strong mental illness advocate, if not a champion of free speech.

Mike asked me why I was holding an avocado pit in my hand. "I saved the pit so we could plant it wherever we decide to land," I said. Then I started talking about a singing toilet bowl, a scene I was still working on from the musical I had written. I had performed it the night before in the Prospect Park Amphitheater to an audience of raccoons. It was, naturally, a musical about poop.

That morning, we rode the F train to Mike's office, one floor below my old burnt-out apartment. Mike told me that I talked to everyone on the subway, that I kept asking people what they did and there was this woman in her thirties who said, "I'm a lawyer." I said, "This is Mike, you guys should definitely talk." I gave her a pile of Mike's business cards and introduced them. "The thing was she really liked you. She was into it." When we got to Mike's office, which was launching its site the next day, I put him on the couch and took his desk so that I could arrange my debate with Tipper Gore. I intended to use the *Village Voice* as a potential sponsor and began calling my editors to see if they could set it up stat.

Mike, relegated to the couch, had to work and I had many, many things to accomplish as well. I had changed back into the same skirt I'd been wearing most days since the fire—the wrap-around number with fluorescent flowers and one pocket. I had been keeping handfuls of granola in that pocket for weeks and today was no exception. I went upstairs. My apartment was cold and cleaned out and apocalyptic. It smelled like devastation. Like rotted flesh. Everything was gone. It wasn't my apartment anymore, just bones.

I took a walk toward Fourteenth Street with my pocket full of granola and a couple of stray kumquats left over from breakfast. I was ecstatic in love and every day was kaleidoscopic. I stopped at a bakery a couple of blocks north of Fourteenth because an elderly man with rainbow-colored eyeglass frames was hovering outside. He had a gray beard and I thought he was homeless, so I offered him a kumquat. He accepted, introduced himself as Bobby, and offered me a chocolate-covered rice cake probably thinking *I* was homeless (which was accurate). We kibitzed together over this strange makeshift snack. He was not homeless; he was a poet. And he had written a poem for his girlfriend, Peggy, and submitted it to a contest and won. The contest was sponsored by Windows on the World, the restaurant on top of the World Trade Center that, every Valentine's Day, would marry a couple every half hour, all day long. Bobby and Peggy would be married, but Bobby was having second thoughts. He loved his girlfriend but had no idea why, this late in life, they needed to be married. I was in favor of his marriage. I was full of unbridled love for everything, and we talked on the corner with our sour kumquat faces about the ceremony that would happen later in the day.

"Well, why did you write the poem in the first place? Why did you submit it?"

"I'm a poet and she wants to get married. I thought, why not?"

"Then get married," I said.

I found his nerves and hesitation comforting. Like love's first flutters never die. By the end of our conversation, Bobby invited me to the wedding at five o'clock; they hadn't invited anyone and needed a witness.

"Yes," I said. "I'll see you at the World Trade Center, five o'clock."

With that small suggestion, I decided that Mike and I should and would get married, as well, on top of the World Trade Center with Bobby and Peggy at five o'clock. This decision, without consulting Mike or the wedding coordinators at the World Trade Center, was extremely exciting. There was a lot to do. I called my older brother in DC and left a message, "Matt, I'm getting married, if you want to come, it's gonna be on the top floor of the World Trade Center at five today. DON'T TELL MOM."

I called my best friend, Hana, and left her a message. *I was getting married!* If they could, they should come to the World Trade Center at five o'clock and be at my wedding! My wedding! *I was getting married.* I needed flowers and white shoes and an outfit that could pass. I went to Rags-A-Gogo and bought a pair of white patent leather shoes with a square 1960s two-inch heel. I needed something blue—everything I owned was borrowed. I went to David Byrne's record label, Luaka Bop, and asked them for a good wedding soundtrack—they gave me a couple of compilation CDs. I went to the *Voice* to tell my editors I was getting married. Getting married! I had a lot to do, a long list, many, many things—and at the very bottom of that list, I added, *Tell Mike we're getting married.*

The last fragment of the tape captures that same day at dusk. The camera is pointed toward the floor, and I am dragging Mike up to the roof. You can hear the fatigue in his voice and the growing irritation. He's resisting, while I'm guiding him upstairs.

"Why are we going on the roof?" he asks.

We have to, I insist. He threatens to turn off the camcorder. I ask him to point it at me. Then, on bended knee, I ask him to marry me. "It's all set up," I say.

Then, the picture turns to snow.

He didn't say no, but his face was angry and tired. I didn't even pause to feel rejected. "Okay, can you just come and videotape Bobby and Peggy's wedding?"

"Who are Bobby and Peggy?"

"They're getting married. Bobby's my friend from the rice cake corner and Peggy is his girlfriend."

We stood by a window that overlooked Seventh Avenue in the front of the office, and Mike asked me to stay there. I looked out the window and it was getting dark and I felt more allegiance to Bobby and Peggy than I did to Mike. I felt more allegiance to love. I wanted to bear witness.

Mike was my sidekick, he was my cameraman, but if he couldn't hang with the revolution, I could not be burdened with dead weight. Mike told me his company was launching tomorrow and that he'd be at the office all night. He could see that something was not right. That I was not right, this person he barely knew was not right. He distracted me while his coworker Kelly pulled out my leopard-print address book. Mike made two calls: to my mom and Dr. Schwartz. He told my mom, "My name is Mike, you don't know me, I'm a friend of your daughter's and I think something is wrong." Mike said that when he talked to my mom, she was all business. "Like yup, yup, getting on a plane now," Mike said. "Like she had a sense that this call was coming. She asked me to try and stick close to you until you could get to Hana." My mom said when she got the call, she felt relief. She had visions of identifying me with a toe tag in some NYPD morgue.

I shrugged off Mike's inability to appreciate matrimony and took the 1/9 downtown. I had flowers for the bride and I wanted to see them down the aisle. Bobby was waiting for me in the lobby of the World Trade Center with his rainbow glasses. I met Peggy and hugged her and gave her the flowers to hold. There were Latino newlyweds, young couples excitedly strutting, on top of the world with the expansive electric city unfolding below—it was the kind of New York tradition that made me want to marry the city itself, every block, building, and broken soul.

I walked Peggy down the aisle. I gave her hand to Bobby's and signed the certificate as the only witness. They gave me the mug from the gift basket decorated with a red drawing of the Towers, hearts cascading from the top floors. It said TOP OF THE WORLD. I hugged Bobby and Peggy again. Just as they were setting off to a honeymoon dinner, Hana came running toward us thinking I had just gotten married to an old man in rainbow glasses or an elderly bookish woman. Her face was totally stricken and long, like she was too late to save me. She wasn't, it had all just begun.

The *Merck Manual* defines Bipolar I as manic patients who are "inexhaustibly, excessively, and impulsively involved in various pleasurable, high-risk activities (e.g., gambling, dangerous sports, promiscuous sexual activity) without insight into possible harm. Symptoms are so severe that they impair functioning; unwise investments, spending sprees, and other personal choices may have irreparable consequences."

Yes, on all of that. This was full-blown mania, round two.

CHAPTER 16

CHEEKING MEDS,
BARTERING FOR UTOPIA,
AND THE PASSOVER CRUISE

I'm not sure if I went home with Hana or if I insisted she come back with me to the old building on Seventh to see Mike. They knew each other from the Fire Pizza Party and now they were crucial members of Team Rescue Jaime from Herself. My mom borrowed miles from a friend and was on a redeye due to land at six a.m. the next morning. Between Hana and Mike, it was babysitting time. Hana's roommate, Jim, vacated his room and stayed with a friend without even a conversation. He could just tell something was up and that we were all in need. My mom arrived and slept in Jim's room.

I had missions to accomplish and would drag my mom to art galleries or different offices I had outstanding "business" with. We went to the Prospect Park Zoo, where I popped in and out of human-sized badger holes, thinking how profound it was to see the universe from ground level. Eventually she convinced me to go back to Dr. Schwartz. I met with him alone—while my mom waited outside—and told him I slept well at Hana's and he described me as "combative." I asked him to draw a diagram of why I should take lithium again and he did—a happy face (mine) with smaller circles surrounding and contributing to the happiness (lithium). I grabbed the drawing and drew over it—a demonic me with a curlicued kangaroo claw holding a polarized world, with chaos surrounding the globe in the form of scribble on top of scribble on top of scribble. According to The Notes, I threw the drawing at him and then said I would take the medication. My mom and I left his office and crossed the street to Central Park. It was crisp and sunny and rich and I could feel the agitation growing, that the people around me were insisting on repression, that they were monied and well fed and unaware of suffering. I felt that an invisible *they* was trying to contain me, that I wasn't special, that my inner iridescence was unacknowledged. Then out of the corner of my eye, I saw a cab hit a Corgi crossing the street. I ran to the dog, knowing I had healing powers, and held him and helped him back to the curb while others tried to stop the cab from driving away. I could feel the dog's heart racing and I held him close to comfort him. I squeezed his Corgi body and massaged his haunches. The dog had gotten out of his collar; he was hurt. We tried to find a dog ambulance or someone who could help, and a limo pulled up.

Ben Vereen (actual Ben Vereen, star of *Pippin* from the 1970s!) got out wearing a dapper yellow scarf and made one call to a dog ambulance to assuage our worries. Corgi would be all right, Ben Vereen rescued us all. And once again, like the wedding night, I felt chosen and special and connected to a larger narrative. My narrative. Ben Vereen was the narrator. I was queen. Ben Vereen just doesn't show up out of nowhere for anyone.

While my mom filled medications—lithium and Risperdal, an antipsychotic medication—I went into a bar on Seventh Avenue in Park Slope and told the bartender I had invented a drink. I dumped some mint chip ice cream (not sure where that came from) into a tumbler with two shots of vodka. I sat next to a grizzled man who hid his aging features behind tailored clothes and tinted glasses. He introduced himself as Bruce; he had been a Broadway director and insisted I leave the bar for my own well-being. It was two p.m. and he thought I was an alcoholic and gave me a stern lecture, a real monologue about the perils of drinking. The kind of monologue that comes from someone who knows, someone who was *actually* drinking in a bar at two p.m. I didn't even want to drink my mint chip ice cream vodka slosh concoction; I didn't want to drink alcohol at all but I thought, I dunno, it might taste good and I was in an inventing mood. I was making magic everywhere—I saved Corgis! Bruce instructed his driver to take me to Hana's apartment, around the corner. My mom wrote down his phone number from a card he gave me just to keep track of all my new friends: "the man who put you in a car (at a bar), Bruce" followed by his number.

We went back to see Dr. Schwartz the next day. I reluctantly told him and my mom that I would start taking the lithium and the Risperdal when I went back to Hana's apartment, that was the plan. We made a pasta dinner and Mike came over and I ate a lithium dessert. Only I didn't. Because the only reason I was cool with getting the meds was that I had learned how to cheek medication by reading books like *Girl, Interrupted* and because I learned in the ward that they checked under the tongue for a reason. It's easy to store pills in your cheeks or other crevices in your mouth, let the sink water wash by and then spit out the actual capsule. Kept that a secret for a dose or two until I told Mike that I was not being drugged, that I was still me and we could still be in love. Mike told my mom and Hana, and it became clear

ME, IN GOLD PANTS, A FRINGE BELT, TUBE TOP, AND A BAZILLION NECKLACES.

why the antipsychotic had not taken hold. I had a glint in my eye and was smiling until I realized he was a narc. This time, my mom gave me the meds and checked in my mouth, under my tongue, and in the crevices of my fleshy maw looking for any stray capsules.

Risperdal wrecked me. Like with most psychiatric meds, it's unknown how Risperdal works, but the idea is that it affects the way the brain processes things by interfering with communication among the brain's nerves. The medication stunted me, stopped me in my manic tracks. I went from frothing and plotting to drooling from the meds and crying uncontrollably. My tongue was swollen to the point where I could no longer talk. Another invisible straitjacket.

I was broken so that my mom could get me on a plane back to LA.

Hana sent me back with a pocket full of marbles, and although she was the daughter of a rabbi, one had a picture of Mother Teresa on it. She wrote me a note to be opened on the plane. It read: *Dearest Jaime, I want to remind you that as you are flying high above that: 1) I love you dearly; 2) I am holding down the NYC fort for your return; 3) you need to have patience in all this adjustment; 4) you have the most amazing fashion sense of anyone I've ever met and wear more gold than Mr. T like a rock star and finally; 5) you need to listen to your friends and family who know you MOST and love you the BEST. I love and admire you so much more than you know. Love,* h.

Even though I was seven years older than eighteen, Dr. DeAntonio, an adolescent psychiatrist, agreed to see me again since I had been his patient before. He weaned me off the Risperdal and kept me on lithium. I resisted and tried to cheek my meds again; my mom was wiser. Even with the meds, the mania did not stop. The montage version would go something like this: I was angered by restrictions; agitated by anything resembling rules; I sang to anyone who would listen; I smoked Fantasia cigarettes and left a trail of rainbow butts everywhere I went; I painted my face green with makeup; I painted over all my college canvases, making them look like garbage can oil spills; I rapped, a lot; I was convinced I was a battle rapper and changed my name to Jamya; I carried around a pocket rhyming dictionary and a pocket Webster's dictionary; my rapping was terrible and mostly centered on poop; I was obsessed with bodily functions. I thought I was Jesus and was not afraid to tell most people. On one of my thrifting expeditions I found a jean jacket from the 1970s with *Jesus*

PAINTING FROM COLLEGE ABOUT MY HIGH SCHOOL MANIC EPISODE THAT I PAINTED OVER DURING MY SECOND EPISODE.

stitched big and wide on the back—I bought it and wore it without irony. It was me, a name tag not a religion. I could touch the sky and bring back the holy. That the world didn't bow down was a mystery—but not an impediment. I had plans. I described my love for Mike and strangers would feel it acutely, like a tangible thing occupying the center of the room.

My parents all continued working, not knowing how long this would take—they couldn't afford to take off work—but Dr. DeAntonio stressed the absolute importance of doing everything they could to keep me out of an institution. He warned that now that I was an adult, I would be subjected to a much more challenging environment than NPI—that my version of bipolar was on the light end of the adult spectrum and institutionalization should be avoided. He advocated for home care and so they scrambled. About three weeks after I came home, Jeff was in charge of babysitting duties. He wrote in his journal: "She's still not close to well. She's foul-mouthed, smoking like a chimney, unable to do anything for longer than a half hour, messy, grandiose ('I'm gonna be a rock star.'), longing for New York, and often sad. Some light moments— I took her over to Abbot Kinney, to the Zephyr antique shop, and the owner there was a white-haired hippie who listened to all of Jaime's crazy questions ('Can I barter? . . . What kind of drawing would you like?') and had a normal conversation with her, and when Jaime went into the back room, I pulled him aside and told him Jaime was in the middle of a manic episode, and he said 'That's cool man. I picked up on that right away. I'm just riffin' with her.'" I remember trading him a couple bucks and a drawing for a pair of red and black and white cowboy boots that I wore throughout the rest of my episode (to match my Jesus jean jacket and gold tutu, naturally).

"POETRY/RAP"
FROM CALIFORNIA.

Abbot Kinney was different then,

March came in like a lion
Out like a lamb
What a sham
They think meds will keep me down
Bucking like a ram
In heat
Don't treat me different
Don't call me names
Cause I'm right here
I came
To steer you all left
Cause my chin is cleft
Like superman
You ran
Into someone else's arms
Because you can
Don't call yourself a fan
Try another name
Like cain or able
Cause this is my stable
And I'll crush you like a pill

full of junk shops and old Venice natives, before the street centered on a gourmand leisure class that hung out on milk crates in front of restaurants with too many consonants. Jeff would take me to the beach in hopes that it would calm me down. It had the opposite effect: "On a Sunday," he wrote in his journal, "Jaime approached a street performer on the Venice boardwalk and he let her sing a few bars of 'One Singular Sensation' [from *A Chorus Line*] and two women upon hearing Jaime's awful voice covered their ears and screamed and another man started laughing and videotaping her. The musician Cedrick told Jaime she had a lot of guts to do that and that she should follow her dreams." My memory was that the busker was pissed that I scared away his crowd but impressed that I took the stage at all. I was Jamya after all, fierce woman rapper, rhyming to the waves. My friends from junior high, Rachel and Miriam, took me out for dinner at Alejo's and then to my favorite bar, Hinano's, a dive bar where Washington Boulevard ends and the sand begins. Hinano's had live music, big bouncers, and juicy grass-fed burgers. (It's not the kind of place that you would expect to have grass-fed burgers.) I went back into the bathroom and transformed. I glittered my face like the sky was running out of stardust. I was falling from my manic high but still magnetic. I would tell people, *I write for the* New Yorker, *I'm a painter, a poet, a rapper, a muse.*

My dad's neighbor, an actor ten years older than me, who wore gardening hats while intentionally planting a feral lawn, saw me pacing the blocks in our neighborhood in all my layers and all my gilded armor. He took me to Astro Burger for fries, which I didn't eat as he described his own relationship to mental illness. The people who picked me up and helped me out knew what was happening with me. Crazy is a secret code. There were also people I encountered such as the waiter at the French restaurant Le Café du Village on Larchmont who bought into my rap and music prowess—he wanted to record together and had a garage studio waiting. Miriam picked me up at my dad's, and he told her under no circumstances should she give me money or let me convince her or others to buy anything. We walked to Larchmont and into a clothing store, Picket Fences. It was like it had been—when we were in junior high hunting for Betsey Johnson bargains. Only this time instead of searching for riotous floral patterns and checked bloomer onesies, my fashion choices were a question mark, a symptom. A Ganesh tank top hung on a sale rack. I asked Miriam for twenty dollars. She denied, so I started bartering with the sales ladies. We ran into the music producer/waiter and I asked him for the money. Miriam called my dad, who drove to Larchmont and bended to my will. Easier to buy the Ganesh tank top than convince me otherwise. I had an antique suitcase given to me by our deceased neighbor, Mr. Danjou, a former carpenter for Paramount Studios. He built sets in the 1920s. His wife was a costume designer. The suitcase was full of scrap material from ball gowns and custom majesty. Yellow chiffons and brocaded swatches were packed with folded magenta silks. I naturally unfolded them all and shredded the material. I was still working from the assumption that I would be leading a hippie cult into the apocalypse horizon and needed a fanciful cape.

Around the same time, I wrote on a legal pad: "The plants talk to us. Actively ignored or passively acknowledged, the massive destruction of both biological and cultural diversity. Quaint indigenous culture that exists on a parallel plane. Virus disease, domination, consumerism, redemptive spirit, monochromatic world of monotony, a fully conscience species of our own demise. Getting by with nothing, multicultural, pluralistic world." I took out all my paintings from college and painted big bold red slashes over finished canvases. I painted my feet and walked across my work leaving a trail of chaos.

This ain't no thrilla in manilla
I am cookie and cream and vanille
Just give me some time
To speak in rhyme
Cause I will dine
On ~~swere~~ sewar water and wine
Just pour the water bitch
There ain't no hitch
Cause I will stitch
your wound
With my teeth
Bare and bloody
I'll repeat
Give me the respect I deserve
And I will throw you a curve
So don't swerve yet
Until I disinvite your ass
from my jungle gym
That's how I win.

My mom applied for financial help from a sexual assault victims fund that the State of California had set up—she used it to pay for daycare while she read scripts (her job). She hired a Jamaican woman named Alma who watched me paint rainbow colors over any surface and braided my hair into cornrows and helped me keep my liquid green makeup in line. We spent most of our days together frequenting 99-cent stores and nail salons and grocery stores to buy more cigarettes. One thing that became very clear in this episode if not the first one was that being crazy makes people (including me, especially me) smoke a lot. People with serious mental illness treated in the public health system die roughly twenty-five years earlier than those without mental illness. Tobacco-related illnesses, including cancer, heart disease, and lung disease, are among the most common causes of death in this population (*my* population). And Americans with mental illnesses have a 70 percent greater likelihood of smoking than the general population.

My mom—and all my parents—were once again uncertain whether I would get better. Jeff's brother Tom (my uncle), a psychiatrist, told Jeff and my mom that sleep was the only thing that would bring me out of this. Sleep and time. My aunt Sally came to visit, my aunt Carrie took me to get new pants, and my grandma tried to take care of me. When I showed up (with Alma as backup) at my grandma's house, I took all her scrap material from her sewing projects and started to sew a second magic outfit-cape-slash-thing. She was such a precise seamstress and perfectionist that watching me cut every which way gave her a heart attack (not literally). She did not recognize me. She could not respond to a flurried frenzy of unmeasured energy. Alma took me home, and my mom took note, one less

MORE "POETRY/RAP" FROM CALIFORNIA.

person who could handle the babysitting. It wasn't all bad—I went to see *Saving Silverman* with my mom and grandma one afternoon and was so enraptured with the Neil Diamond tribute and the extremely underrated comic genius of Amanda Peet that I stood up and gave it a standing ovation. With God on my side and Jesus in my veins, I stood and clapped very enthusiastically. I even got my hands on the press materials later.

Dr. DeAntonio could see progress, but it was slow. The first lucid moment I remember was sitting across from Jeff at Jerry's deli in a mini mall near our house in Marina del Rey. We both had soup. I was anxious and frustrated and angry. And so was he. His voice was elevated, which had never happened before in the twenty-three years I had known him. He said, "Do you know what this is doing to your mom? Do you know what this is doing to her?" I mean, I really didn't, I hadn't thought about it. The way he said it made my recovery seem like my choice, which I know it wasn't and I know he knows it wasn't, but it shook me. It was the first time I actually heard and understood consequence. I could feel it. Another moment that stood out was when Marilyn took me to the famous deli, Canter's, where as a kid, the old ladies would give me free cookies. We waited at the counter to get cold cuts and I stood in my one hundred necklaces. A woman approached me to discuss one in particular—a blown glass medallion encased in silver, something I borrowed from my mom that she got in the 1970s. The stranger told me of the magic properties and secret meaning of the glass, the way the blue swirled meant one thing, the way the cream enamel enveloping the color meant another. And I let her talk for a while and thought, *She's crazy*. And then it dawned on both Marilyn and me that if I could recognize crazy, I was one step away from it. A week later, my mom noticed that when we left a Dr. DeAntonio appointment, I did *not* speak to every person in the elevator. I was getting better.

And then things got dark *because* I was getting better.

The lithium was working. And once again, I didn't care how. I just noticed that it brought me back. I could see clearly that I had destroyed personal relationships, professional relationships; family members saw me in a different way; the world I came in contact with knew two different Jaimes, a medicated one and a manic one, and reconciling all this was part of coming to a painful merged consciousness. It was a cold world; one second I was exuding glitter and rapping with Em, the next I was literally sifting through rubble. There was also the matter of Mike, who responded to my e-mails less and less, as they got more and more primal. Here was the first person I fell in love with, who loved me back. But was it even me? It was so complicated and it sucked. (*Love* might be a strong word for a two-week fire romance, but we both felt something. I felt something.) The realization that we would not be sitting on a gilded throne with a direct pipeline to heaven sucked. But I could not let go of the foundation, the experience that we had together, that he was part of my mania and me when many people bowed out.

Meanwhile, my mom had a get-better marker for me. Margie (Jeff's mom and the matriarch of the Maine crew) had planned a family Passover cruise in April and my mom was convinced that I would be better enough to attend and that I *had* to get better to attend. The Passover cruise meant nothing to me. She was fixated. I was entering the portion of a bipolar cycle when lithium takes hold and reality washes over like heavy mud. I would sit on the bottom bunk of Matt's old bed, still, unclear on what exactly I was supposed to do postdestruction. I was functioning again and what I saw was wreckage; what I felt was very tired; what I knew had shifted dramatically to the unknown. I had ruined the life I had built. I was burnt out. What do burnt-out people do, especially burnt-out mentally ill people? They go on Passover cruises to the Caribbean.

My mom called Margie. *Jaime will be joining us on the Passover cruise, after all.*

There were many aspects of this plan my mom did not consider, but I applaud her effort to break the cycle of the bunk bed. The first challenge was getting me there. My mom had already canceled my flights so I was on a different flight. I had a stopover in Charlotte, North Carolina, where I sat in those calming white rocking chairs near the food court, and ended up meeting them in Miami—I'm sure it dawned on my mom that if I wasn't better, I could have ended up in a different city altogether, on a different adventure, with or without pills, off the rails, riding the rails, who knows? The second ill-thought-out aspect of this adventure was that I would be trapped on a fucking cruise ship. Incidentally, four or five people die by "falling" overboard off Florida's coast each year, and the height of the particular cruise ship we were on did not fail to impress anyone in my family—cruise ships on average are about twenty-three fucking stories high. My mom had my brother Matt and cousin Meredith watching me most of the time but I remember looking down, roughly 236 feet, into those dark waters. Now, I was never suicidal. But I looked for a long time. I looked hard into that abyss. Even worse than the suicide-around-every-corner was that I spent most of the cruise in my cabin watching *Titanic* on loop, its own form of quiet suicide attempt. I brought my Discman and a mix CD that Mike made (not even for me, just him fucking around with DJing tools). I felt close to it, like the songs were an extension of Mike himself. I pretended that he made it with me in mind—the Pharcyde's "Passin' Me By" was the first track, Michael Jackson's "Rock with You" followed it, his handwriting scribbled on the surface of the CD. The cruise had bright spots. The seder was short; the octogenarian high-seas rabbi skipped everything but the four questions, paging through the ceremony with the eagerness of a holy man who respected the buffet more than God. There were frequent announcements regarding the Midnight Chocoholics Buffet (Chocolate fondue! Chocolate pound cake! Chocolate chocolate!). Meredith and I snuck out to a dance party in the ship's hip-hop club. I extended my arms and let my legs get loose and it felt good, the laser lights felt good, the cheese of it all felt good, the disappearing from me—it felt good.

When I got back to LA, it was time to plan my return to New York. I passed the Passover cruise test.

THE OFFICIAL PASSOVER CRUISE PHOTO.

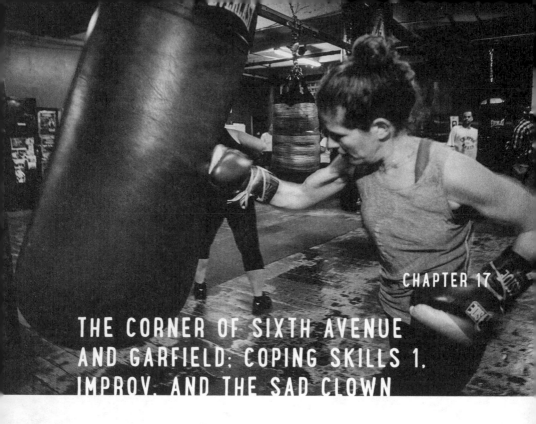

CHAPTER 17

THE CORNER OF SIXTH AVENUE AND GARFIELD; COPING SKILLS 1, IMPROV, AND THE SAD CLOWN

MIKE TOLD ME he was planning a cross-country trip in a van with his friend for June and my goal was to get back to Brooklyn before he left. But I was scared. A week or two after returning to LA from the Passover cruise, I had a phone session with Dr. Schwartz. I was supposed to have left for New York the day before, but I pulled back, feeling uncertain about finding work, securing housing, and resuming a social life that felt damaged (at best). I had already started gaining weight back and wearing more normal clothes—brown and black cords and regular blue jeans—but I was far from normal. I missed manic me, the person who was an ethereal god. The person who feared nothing. She would have gotten on a plane, sat on the pilot's lap, and sung a fully improvised set from the cockpit.

No one around me missed that person, but I was in mourning.

I wanted just one one-hundredth of that confidence. Dr. Schwartz wrote of our phone session, "She's afraid she burned her bridges with writing because her editors were exposed to her mania, but she's not sure about what she wants to write. Freelancing feels too unstable—she's looking for safety and security right now." By the end of April, I packed my new clothes and flew back to New York. I stayed with my dad's first cousins Pam and Terry and their daughter Emma, who lived next to Prospect Park. They took me in and said I could stay in their guest room as long as I needed. I got in touch with Mike. We sat in the same empty amphitheater in the park where I had performed my poop musical. We were different. Subdued. Not romantic. Not anything like what I wanted. A gut punch. In my head, we still had a chance to date. In Mike's head, he was already in the van, on the road with his college friend. We sat close to each other but I could tell he had already pulled away. Mike didn't like me for me, he didn't know me. And I didn't like me either—we were both missing this ghost. I wished for the style of Jamya, the metabolism, the flow of ideas, the genius. I was drained of my magic.

I wanted to be invisible to the world. I slept past noon most days. I tried to stay out late, walking the streets because I had nowhere to go and I knew I couldn't sleep. The nights were lonesome and oppressive and unbearably awake. My cousin Emma remembered later that all of a sudden there was this new person in her house at the same time she was approaching adolescence, a curious person slightly closer in age and experience to the traumas of teenaging. "I remember not seeing you for days on end because you would sleep all day and be awake all night. The thing I most remember is wishing you would never leave. I liked knowing you were there, even in the months when you were just occupying the second floor and I thought perhaps someone should wake you up to feed you (my parents stopped me from doing that;

I guess they realized from the fridge contents that you weren't starving yourself)." She remembered the two of us talking about life, boys, friends, family, California, college, jobs, politics—and that I was argumentative. "I remembered nights at the dinner table, early on, when your hair was in a giant Afro that matched your telling of the apartment fire or a dinner with Hana or an experience at a bar. I remember debates we had about articles in the *NYT* in which you far surpassed the fervor with which even my dad talked about them—and I think a lot of them were political, so that's saying something." She told me, "Even in what must have felt like your fog, you made a huge impact on me." It didn't feel like I made an impact on anything at the time. Sometimes I would just watch *Seinfeld* reruns quietly. Being me hurt.

In therapy, Dr. Schwartz described me as "depressed," "more depressed," "irritated," "bored," "depressed," and "slumped over in the chair." His notes had shifted from noting combativeness and ferocity to more than a hint of worry—I was lackluster. I assume he was more aware of my depression because the mania had acted as a siren, warning him about what would come next. I stopped making art; I stopped caring about art. I worried that I had moved back to New York too soon, and I thought about moving back to LA (my mom supported this; my dad thought I should try to stick it out). I started Zoloft with the lithium, but it had no effect. Mike and I spent his remaining days in New York together, sniffing this new normal from a distance. I told Dr. Schwartz that I was bored by Mike, which had to be a defense mechanism, knowing he was leaving just two weeks after I came back to Brooklyn to be with him. When he left on May 14, I was devastated. I remembered our Valentine's Day together; I walked by the bodega on the corner where I got his bouquet and fingered the flowers. This felt like a return to the days of driving Benedict Canyon.

I drove Emma to New Jersey for horse riding lessons. She would ride and I would walk through an abandoned field adjacent to the stables, and just wander through the wheat with nothing in my head or heart. We would stop at Wendy's on the way home—I would get a Greek salad wrap and Emma would get chili. One morning, after refusing many previous morning runs, I went with Pam and her sister (my cousin/aunt) Katherine on a run in Prospect Park, completing the loop. It had an impact. I finished something. I did something. One foot in front of the other.

There were glimmers of good. But it was hard. Depression is thick, endless lukewarm molasses. I couldn't get up. I couldn't see a reason to. I had nightmares about the weather. This is when depression becomes physical, clogging arteries and pores and openness alike. It's when thoughts in your head lie. Lying to you like you don't belong or deserve a smile or a chance or just a flicker of happy.

I went on job interviews, dissuading most people from hiring me. I was particularly negative with Bill Vourvoulias at *Talk* magazine, where I had freelanced before the fire. He was looking for a full-time fact-checker—the pay was decent, I knew most of the staff since I had freelanced there before, and it was a good way to pitch editors.

Yet I told him, in no uncertain terms, that I was a terrible candidate and that I was only interviewing for practice.

He said, "Everyone I talked to recommended you highly."

I said, "I'm the wrong person."

He offered me the job. I said I had to think about it; he said every other person he made an offer to accepted immediately. I still needed time, I said.

It seemed absurd to be a fact-checker when my natural, unmedicated state was based on anything but fact. I doubted my ability to do a job of any kind, let alone one that involved determining what was real. By June, I took the job. By July, I got a shared apartment with a thirty-five-year-old cancer survivor who shared my depressed state; we were both wearing depression ponchos and that environment was okay until it wasn't. I gained more weight and felt more and more uncomfortable with being me again. Apart from friends I had known forever like Hana and Sarah J. and Sarah P., I was impossibly awkward. When you are depressed you want to be a time traveler going back, going forward, being anywhere but in the here and now. I got invited to socialize with publishing friends and people I'd known before. I was nervous and with each interaction announced what I had been through. *Oh hi! It's nice to see you again, I was gone because I'm bipolar and my house burned down but now I am back and trying to . . . get back to normal!* So, I did what felt like a natural trust fall with myself—I signed up for improv classes at the Upright Citizens Brigade (UCB) theater. It was not because I wanted to be a comedian or an improv player; it was a form of therapy and forced social time. (There is a natural irony that I went to a class that taught a "Yes, and . . ." technique which is pretty much the opposite of depression, which functions more on the level of "No, but . . .") I was terrible at improv and I hated it. I was not entertaining and kept referencing Shakespeare and James Joyce and the only person I connected with was a hyperkinetic dude named Sharif who had just broken up with someone as well. Part of my recovery was connecting with other people who also had devastated hearts—trying to figure out what the Mike whatever-it-was-relationship-ish-thing meant. Sad broken-up people seem to find each other—Sharif didn't seem sad, though, just like a genie let out of a bottle. I was a better improv watcher than doer and found my devotion centered on an improv troupe named Respecto Montalban—I went to every show, practice, battle, open performance of theirs I could access.

Comedy was helping more than the Zoloft; improv people were easier to stand near than anyone who had known me through my episode, largely because the improvers didn't know me at all. They didn't care. I did not have to speak to people if they were performing. That was much more preferable. I could shout one word and it counted as participation.

On the morning of 9/11, I turned on NPR and heard about the first plane. It was early and I assumed it was a tragic mistake. I took the F to my office in the Flatiron District and saw people standing in the middle of the street looking at the plumes of gray and black and white smoke—the billowing tragedy erupting in lower Manhattan. It was the first time I felt my depression really lift. I had been unable to get out of bed for months prior, shocked by personal, self-inflicted destruction, blame, doubt, fear. I felt alone through September 10, 2001. And now an entire city—no, the world—mourned with me. It turned out suicide rates dropped after 9/11 and so did crime and murder. Soldiers with PTSD felt better. At *Talk* magazine, we watched live on CNN as the second tower fell. We thought the footage was a replay at first, until the second tower started to fall. There was an enormity, a camaraderie, and a silence that took hold. Some of the staff, including me, began clearing out, looking back toward the dust cloud of downtown. We walked uptown to James Lochart's apartment to watch more CNN and make phone calls, and I ended up sleeping on the couch of a friend who stayed up snorting heroin with his roommate. That feeling of togetherness in the wake of international tragedy was weird, it was confounding. I finally felt *okay*. I felt guilty that my first thought upon seeing unspeakable tragedy was that I felt calm and better than I had been in months. It was so selfish, so narcissistic, it was embarrassing and awful. I could not handle the day-to-day things so well—bill paying, being on time, scheduling, responsibility, living. I had a more natural affinity for chaos. So when the world spun sideways, my poles were more aligned. At the same time, Dr. Schwartz decreased my Zoloft and tried Prozac. By the end of the year I was still introducing myself to strangers with pronouncements of fire and mania, but I was leaving the house and smiling every now and then.

My writer friend Donnell from the *LA Weekly* and Amy from *House & Garden* had a going-away party at a club in DUMBO, when DUMBO was still industrial lofts and Gleason's, the world famous boxing gym. He introduced me to a writer named Brett who for some reason took pity on me and invited me to play pool at Lucy's in the East Village on a random Tuesday night. I sat on a stool and Lucy, the squeaky-voiced Polish matron, opened a bottle of Żywiec and Brett introduced me to a whole new round of friends: Mason, a Shakespearean actor who ran a monthly comedy night; Dana, an editor at *Spin*; and Ned, a mysterious entrepreneur. There was a group of dudes playing pool most nights at Lucy's and I was more than happy to be folded into their company to cultivate crushes on all of them like a rotating roulette wheel. As if being broken up has a scent, Mason found me first. We swapped heartache, talking about how much we missed our people, what we did wrong, what we did right. A month later, he invited me to bartend at Moonwork (his comedy show), where I got the kind of behind-the-scenes comedy experience no comedy fan wants. It turns out most funny people are deeply depressed or deeply disturbed or both. The trope of the sad clown felt especially relevant—humor masks an underlying darkness. Charlie Chaplin once said: "To truly laugh, you must be able to take your pain and play with it." In a 1978 article for *Time* magazine, psychologist Samuel Janus looked at the link between Jewish humor and tragedy. He found that "Jewish humor was born of depression and alienation from the general culture . . . comedy is a defense mechanism to ward off the aggression and hostility of others." Throughout his decades of research on Jewish and non-Jewish comedians, he also found that many of the performers he interviewed had experienced significant trauma during their childhoods. Most of the performers at Moonwork and UCB hid it well, but they were kindred spirits, I could tell. We stayed out late at the neighboring bars talking about the energy of the crowd, whose sets worked, who bombed; we broke down the room. And I cleaned up the Sam Adams bottle caps.

I was happy handing out beer and listening to comedy sets on repeat. We had Marc Maron, Eugene Mirman, Slovin and Allen, Louis C.K., Todd Barry, Demetri Martin trying out new material and then sticking around for the after-party. I was happy to set up chairs and stow them away at the end—I was happy to be part of something again. The Prozac was working, or time was working, or Moonwork saved me, or Lucy's or Respecto Montalban or whatever, I was getting better. I stayed on Prozac for three or four months and then Dr. Schwartz decreased the dose until I was back to just lithium. *Talk* magazine folded; I started writing music reviews for the *Voice* again; I interviewed to be a reporter for the *National Enquirer*; that didn't work out but I saw the desk where a reporter had died from anthrax; I fact-checked for *Men's Journal* and *Glamour* and signed on to help launch *Radar*. I dated some people; I mostly pined for Mike, who was back in Chicago. I stayed in touch with him; we talked for hours on the phone late at night and every time it felt like my mania had some validity to it, like if I could legitimize a relationship with him, it would somehow make me less crazy, make my episode less surreal. In March 2002, I told Dr. Schwartz that I had an idea for writing a book about my manic episode, "but rather than treat it as a personal memoir, she would treat it as a subject to investigate, as if she was reporting on someone else. (She wants to interview me.)" The same month I planned a trip to visit Chicago, ostensibly to see my cousins and Aunt Sally and Uncle Aggelos, but it was really to see Mike. Dr. Schwartz noted that I had fantasies of getting back together with Mike and I didn't "deny the likely outcome of more misery." I told Dr. Schwartz I didn't want to rule out the possibility of something good—a possibility that was super small—but that I also had "nothing else going on."

A couple years later, I wrote about seeing Mike in Chicago for the *Voice*:

> We walked back to my aunt's house, his arm hugging my shoulder. Everyone was asleep. He took off my clunking boots. We lay on the leather sofa cringing from the sound two bodies make against leather. His arm snaked around my waist, his head on my chest. His mouth parted in sleepy gasps, my heart pounding in what-the-fuck. We moved against each other for warmth and for wondering what happened. We lay still. He grew heavy. I grew tired of his weight. I rolled to the floor with my head on his lap.
>
> He brought me closer, lifted my arms to his shoulders, my body to his. Tired and looking for a fit, I moved my legs to his waist. We grazed face to face but thought better of it. We fell back asleep breathing what used to be until 4:30 became too late for napping and too late for us.
>
> I walked him to the door and didn't kiss his cheek, knowing the dinner we talked about having would turn into a phone call of sorry and a mouthful of not mine.

. . .

WHEN I MADE it back to New York, I was clear about my disappointment. When I moved to New York initially, in 1998, I had unlimited hustle. I pitched nonstop to anyone who would listen. After the fire, I was less and less confident about sending pitches and writing. I didn't feel like I was a real writer. I started fact-checking at *Sports Illustrated for Women*, which required late-night closes. There was a chaos to the last-minute edits, swapping profiles in and out of an issue, and designs upon redesigns, but watching Susan Casey, the editor in chief, mold issues from a subject I had always wished to read about (WOMEN'S SPORTS! FINALLY!) was overwhelming, almost moving. I thought I was finally in a space I could own—something I believed in, somewhere I could pitch and write. But *Sports Illustrated for Women* folded just a couple of issues after I started working there. I sat in the back of the conference room where Casey gathered to tell the staff and I stifled tears even though I BARELY worked there. I felt like the black widow of magazines (three in one short six-year career!). In retrospect, I was probably more akin to a canary in a coal mine as journalism and magazine publishing advanced into the digital age. I went back to fact-checking at *Men's Journal* and then got hired as a reporter/researcher at *Sports Illustrated on Campus*, a college edition of *Sports Illustrated*, because the managing editor, Meesha, had worked with me at *Sports Illustrated for Women*. For the first time I had a full-time job that included writing regularly— I interviewed Larry Holmes; covered college wrestlers making weight; went on a cross-country roadtrip in an RV with two other reporters during the NCAA March Madness tournament; I played water polo with Tony Azevedo and the Stanford water polo team. I was happy to report on the lesser-covered sports, but it was clear that my job there would always be dictated by the fact that I didn't breathe and sleep and die by sports, and I was not a dude (although the gender disparity was more of an issue at the main mag than at *On Campus*). I traveled for work and stayed in real hotels and expensed meals and had to get a cell phone. My paranoia had subsided but I still had my suspicions about tracking and brain damage. I was bad at using the phone and would drain the battery talking to crushes or my mom or dad while I was on the road. I had no idea that little flip phone was powered by lithium-ion batteries. (Lithium everywhere!) I got into trouble with inter-office crushes and I knew my days at *SI* were not forever days. I did not want to be trapped by genre, which is why I never got far as a music or culture critic either. I always felt that a good story was just a good story, and I wanted the freedom to write about anything. Although it's entirely possible that I just wasn't that good at criticism or sports writing. One of my last stories for *SI* was an interview with Shirley Muldowney, aka "Cha Cha" or the "First Lady of Drag Racing." She was the first woman licensed by the National Hot Rod Association (NHRA) to drive a Top Fuel dragster. She won the NHRA Top Fuel championship in 1977, 1980, and 1982. She was a chain-smoking badass and as we sat together in lawn chairs in Joliet, Illinois, talking to her fans, she told me of all the sexism and all the bullshit she faced as a female driver. But she didn't care—she was driven by the speed and the adoration and the competition. She told me to stand on the starting line of just one race and I might get a sense of what she experienced as a driver. I did and could feel the hot asphalt erupt beneath my feet. I worried that the heat might melt the soles of my Vans. The sound reverberated like a bomb; that starting line was a full body experience, sensory overload. I had never been to a Top Fuel race or a NASCAR race and I could see the appeal;

fans approach drivers. They see the engines. The sport is felt and participatory. Everything is accessible.

The morning after *SI*'s 2005 Christmas party, I boarded a plane to Los Angeles still drunk and wrecked from the party. I was groggy from two hours of sleep and ready to pass the fuck out in a back-row seat. But when I walked through first class, I noticed an extra-wide black man with a face tattoo. I assumed this was a hallucination, or maybe some kind of Christmas wish fulfilled by boxing fairies. I had been fixated on Mike Tyson since I had seen the Barbara Walters interview from 1988 with Robin Givens, the interview in which Givens says that Mike Tyson is manic depressive and on lithium. "Michael is a manic depressive, that is just a fact. When he's in a manic state, he has enormous amounts of energy. . . . He doesn't sleep," Givens says. She explains his temper, his violence, his abuse as instances when Tyson is out of control and manic. Tyson responds by saying, "This is a situation in which I'm dealing with my illness." Givens, controlling the interview, concludes that Tyson's disease went untreated for so long because he was dominant in the ring, such a brute force, being used by his trainers. (Shortly after the interview, Tyson's manager at the time set up a one-hour doctor's appointment, which cleared Tyson of any psychiatric disorders, in order to sanction a Frank Bruno fight. Boxing, a sport always known to be free of corruption.) I had always wanted to interview Mike Tyson. A year before that plane ride, I had begun training at Gleason's with the idea that if someday I got the opportunity, I would have a sense of the sport from inside the ring. I found a trainer who taught me how to tape my hands and wrists in yellow wraps, how to jab, how to punch, how to slip and counter. I learned the basics of boxing and was hooked. On that plane, that morning, though, I sat in complete disbelief. *That could not be Mike Tyson.*

By the time the plane landed, I had drooled all over the seat tray in front of me and assumed that the face-tattooed person was in fact a phantom. Besides, I was sitting in the last row, he was in the first, I would never catch up to him. But I got to baggage claim and sitting on the edge of our designated area was Mike Tyson, by himself. I have never been so starstruck. I hovered. A girl ran up to him and asked for a picture, which he obliged. But he looked devastated, in sweats, his thick musculature resting on the baggage wheel. This was before his cameo in *The Hangover*, and his book and one-man show. I have to imagine it was among his many low points.

I walked up to him and said, "Hi, I'm Jaime Lowe, I'm a reporter for *Sports Illustrated*, if you're ever interested in talking for an article, I'd love to talk to you."

I gave him my card. He shook his head and said, "Why can't anyone just want to talk to me. To go out to dinner and just talk to me."

"I'd go out to dinner with you."

He didn't seem to hear me or care. It was hard to believe this was the man responsible for such quick brute force and aggression in the ring. He just seemed sad and human. Sad like I had been sad. Our bags came, his baggage undoubtedly heavier than mine.

In anticipation of Mike Tyson calling me some day, I continued to box. I wanted to know what it felt like to get into the ring, to fight, to punch, to be punched. That's when I met Fluff (not his real name, but his chosen pseudonym), a sixty-one-year-old former boxer, former photographer, current member of the Iron Knights of Newark. He was married to a preacher named Pam and trained at Gleason's. He taught me to extend my jab, to turn my glove, to slip, to punch, to move. A few months into training, Fluff asked me if I wanted to spar. I said no, but he got the headgear anyway and we got in the ring. He chased me around, pulling no punches. After two rounds, three and half minutes on and thirty seconds of rest between, I wove through the ropes, gassed out but completely enchanted. It was not fight, it was dance. After that, I'd show up every Saturday morning to spar. Sometimes with Charlie, a cavernous-chested but thick-backed dude who would sip hard liquor between rounds. I didn't like sparring with him because he was erratic and threw haymakers that sometimes landed. He couldn't see straight. Sometimes I sparred with Carlos, little George, big George, Maureen, Yuko, Devon, Sonya—whoever was there. The first year of sparring was like dating: I was aggressive and angry and I chased and was occasionally chased back. As I learned and watched and practiced, I realized it wasn't about emotion. Mike Tyson was at his worst when he was emotional. Boxing looks like revenge, like hate. But it's something else, it's a kind of feral sport that makes everything disappear. In the ring you react and act; you inhale and exhale; you are calm in an environment that mimics war but the only way to win is to be buoyed by breath.

I felt most powerful when I was so tired that I couldn't move. After sparring some mornings I'd go home and crawl back into bed with an egg 'n' cheese and spinach and watch a movie I'd already watched a dozen times. I had a rotation. *Blue Crush*—favorite scene, when she's standing in the ocean and asking for guidance from a dopey NFL love interest and he says, "Be the girl on the beach who doesn't ask the guy what to do." *Laurel Canyon*—favorite scene, Christian Bale is talking down a naked mental patient. She says, "You don't understand the naked. Naked is intimacy. I am here with you. There is no shame. There is no separation. And . . . I am not ill." Bale responds, "Yes, you are ill, Gloria." She says, "And I have no need for a green synthetic nighty used to conceal the essence of my simple skin and my aching soul in the barren desert that is this land." And of course the sexiest Frances McDormand ever as Bale's loose-cannon music producer mom. Or *Tootsie*—every scene is my favorite scene. I'd have a headache some days, I'd sleep three hours on other days. Bright lights were too bright sometimes. I might have been concussed. Sparring consumed me. I worried about my abnormal brain and thought, I dunno, maybe boxing is like a self-lobotomy? Maybe the exertion helped me calm down without anyone saying *calm down*. Maybe the discipline subdued a frantic personality. Boxing and my morning crew—Zerline, Cindy, Kevin, Ian, Fluff—gave me a place to go, something to do with my tensed-up fists. Life went on, inside and outside of the ring.

I was still working at *Sports Illustrated* but searching for music articles that felt important. My friend Max gave me his all-access badge to CMJ, and I went to the old Knitting Factory in TriBeCa. It was *rumored* that Ol' Dirty Bastard might perform and as one a.m. approached, two a.m. followed, and by three a.m., he emerged. I wrote in the *Voice*, "He took the stage looking like he was fresh from a coma, tears trailing down his cheeks. ODB didn't even seem to notice he was crying. The crowd chanted, begging for the hallucinatory diatribes from his drunk days. Buddha Monk and his Brooklyn Zoo posse filled in words when Dirt's jaw was slack and his mouth open in exasperation. One dancer stripped. ODB didn't even notice. He was paralyzed, lost onstage in a shell of what used to be. His eyes were quiet too." He didn't notice, I thought, because he looked like he was on meds or not ready to be onstage after being in prison. The *Daily News* and the *New York Post* had printed rumors that ODB was suffering from schizophrenia and getting treatment at the Manhattan Psychiatric Center on Randall's Island. I felt that this performance did not bode well.

The concert was a starting point for an article that led to the last interview with ODB and focused on his mental health and the stigma surrounding mental health—it ended up running in the *Voice* after he died of an overdose in 2005. I quit *Sports Illustrated* to work at *Radar* 2.0; *Radar* 2.0 folded (my magic as the black widow of magazines returned) and I considered a longer project on ODB. I thought RZA or GZA would have written something; they didn't. And eventually the *Voice* article led to a book, *Digging for Dirt: The Life and Death of ODB*, published in 2008. I loved ODB the rapper, but my interest in him was his magnetism and how his career careened into this tragic end. Of all the Wu-Tang MCs, he was the one to watch, the rapper that everyone thought was crazy. People called him crazy all the time. I thought he needed a diagnosis. That was probably overstepping since I am not a psychiatrist, but I was so interested in him and his behavior. For this little westside white girl from LA who was deep in therapy and looking for people to relate to, ODB was not the obvious choice. But I related to his outbursts and his self-destruction and his grand presentation; I related to his declarative state of being. He was ODB and no one would fuck with that. He was a walking manic episode in my mind. Obviously he had experiences and a life that I could never relate to, but for three years I tried to report everything I could on ODB. I shared an office with a promoter at Gleason's and would write to the sound of the speed bag and the thumping of sixteen-ounce gloves connecting with flesh.

After my book came out in late 2008, everything broke. The year before, I was fixed up with a friend of a friend who I fell in love with. We went to dinners, we ate hamburgers and Di Fara's pizza, he met my family, we went to bars. I tried to encourage him not to go to bars. He was not the right person for me and I spent a year tethered to drama. I was proud of the relationship. My first one, at age thirty-two. We broke up in November 2008 and then again in December and then finally in January 2009. He had been cheating on me and I had been reading his phone obsessively, imagining him with others. Around the same time a ten-million-dollar lawsuit was filed against me in response to the book. The lawsuit—frivolous and dismissed—felt like someone slowly dripping acid into an open wound; the breakup was worse. The financial crash made working again seem impossible. In 2009, I made seven thousand dollars above the New York State poverty line. Adjusted to the city, I was just barely getting by. My brain was tangled. I couldn't stop lengthy speeches from looping in my head. They were angry diatribes, reenacting conversations. Lines I wished I had said to various people. Anger and frustration that felt like shards of glass plunging into my brain. One neighborhood friend said he would see me walking around, talking to myself. I had nowhere to go, no boyfriend, no project, no future. I worked nights at ESPN as a late-read copy editor and my hours were lonely and disconcerting. I had been back on lithium for seven years and for the first time I was questioning whether it worked. I felt like I needed more. I needed something else.

I was desperately looking for a magic salve or a brainwashing routine that could quiet the storm of hating on my ex. I used to walk the bridges. It wasn't aimless, I was looking for someplace to go. Something to do, to be needed somewhere. I kept boxing, sparring every Saturday at Gleason's with my surly trainer. I would finish my workouts by stretching my body out long, looking up to the uncovered rafters, comforted by the parallel and perpendicular lines of the open ducts. It wasn't enough. My brain worked overtime the minute the endorphins dropped. I looked for light in Zen Buddhism with intensely calm monks on State Street, meditating in the dark, while incense smoke wafted through crouched bodies. I learned how to breathe there and how to sit still. I learned how to say "I don't know" and how to really mean it. I learned how to clear my head. Some days it worked; many days it didn't. I remember one Sunday being terrified of meditation and going deep into what felt like a vision, a dance of some sort in the bull's-eye of a Rorschach test. I would sit for hours with my eyes at half-mast and I would emerge less frantic. My friend Jeb said that when we spoke on the phone after those sessions, I sounded tranquil. I would try anything to lift the veil of my brain loop. I went to a scarf-laden lady who tried to sell me my future self downloaded into a crystal. I loved crystals and said sure. (Quartz crystals are made of lithium and I keep one strung around my neck at all times.) I mantraed under a Magnetic Rainbow Helix with 5-D Star Tet and Casual Ring. It was a mobile. But sure. I rode Harleys with the Iron Knights of Newark and I held my twenty-five-year-old neighbor's waist for two hours as we raced the yellow-painted lane dividers. But not even a gang of men in leather could clear my cloudy heart and spiked brain. I surfed with dolphins and a longboarder named Chad. A man in a beret and a fake fishtail braid who reeked of Marlboro Reds read my aura for thirty-five dollars. He printed out my white-lavender computer-generated aura prognosis: "Others are instantly attracted to you as you sparkle and glow with a mysterious inner light. You also seem to be a magical fairy-like creature." His assistant told me my head chakra was blocked. So she waved her hands around my head and said, this might hurt a little at first but you *will be so much more open*.

I wanted my head chakra unblocked so badly. Nothing helped.

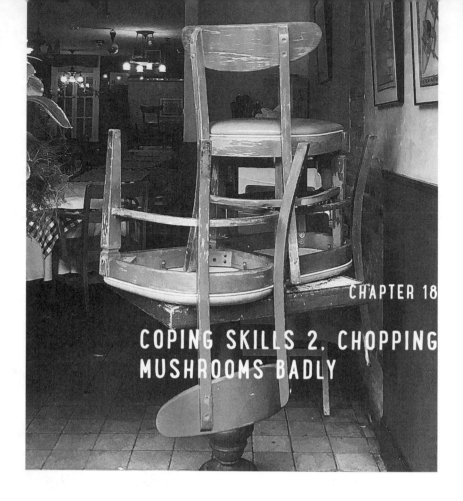

CHAPTER 18

COPING SKILLS 2. CHOPPING MUSHROOMS BADLY

SARAH J. GAVE me a battered copy of *Eat, Pray, Love*, which I had ignored for all the years it claimed to be God's gift to women. But when I started reading it, I was surprised, I couldn't stop. I could relate to the way Elizabeth Gilbert wrote about being broken and I was envious of her solution. Obviously journeying to Italy, India, and Bali was not possible. I thought, *I don't need to travel anywhere, New York has all of what she sought out*. I could do it myself, I had my days free. I had already found my Zen retreat with the State Street monks. After three months of spirit questing and meditating and granola making (I had some idea that I could parlay my granola recipe into a small business; this was not the case) and listening to Justin Timberlake (only one song, "What Goes Around Comes Back Around") and Tina Turner (only one song, "Better Be Good to Me"), I was feeling better enough to get better.

One night, I ended up with my friend Karey eating my usual rigatoni with eggplant and ricotta salata at a back table in the Brooklyn Heights neighborhood restaurant Noodle Pudding. We were both launching into our tireless updates of breaking up and breaking down when I heard a screech—like a possum being Tasered.

The pink-cheeked woman sitting next to me burst into hysterical, high-pitched noises, the kind of bellyaching, screaming cacophony that was from either indescribable joy or burning pain. Her dining companion was a man who had been bringing out dish after dish from the kitchen, describing how each one was cooked— seared tuna, pastas, soups, small roasted vegetables, scallops, and grilled artichokes, tiramisu, and hot, hardened biscotti.

"What did you say to get her to laugh like that?" I asked.

"It's the wine," he said with a heavy Italian accent and a lisp. His eyes widened like punctuation, then narrowed. "You guys need more wine." He waved over our waiter, who approached, bottle in hand. The restaurant was about to close, but you'd never know it.

At our table introductions ensued: The lisp man was one of Noodle Pudding's chefs, Fredo.

He removed the potted plant between our tables. "Come, drink with us."

He had been a photographer before he was chef. When Fredo talked of food, his arms took on a classical conductor's poise— gesticulating with each ingredient. "When I was on vacation, I was staying on an island in southern Italy and though it was an island, the people were land people, farmers. So I went swimming off the coast and there were sea urchins everywhere, up and down the rocks. I jumped out of the water and got a table knife and plastic bag and jumped back in and hacked away until I filled the bag. I went home, made spaghetti with olive oil and garlic—just a little garlic, not the way you Americans use garlic—and opened each urchin and let the roe cook on the hot pasta." Fredo then made a gesture from his elbow to his fingertips to his mouth, perfection. His lips were pursed together in a kiss as if tasting the dish all over again.

Fredo wrote out a menu of what he would cook for me if I ever agreed to have an affair with him, which I had clearly stated I wouldn't. He asked for a date, to make out, to have an affair, to spoon, but it all seemed like a show, like he was coming on way too strong for it to actually carry meaning. He was playing a character. But when Fredo spoke of food, he was being real. Pure joy, hedonism at its best. The menu he wrote for me, which was a love letter that I'm sure he'd written to many, many ladies, was beautiful: oysters on the half shell with Franciacorta, an Italian champagne; crudo, raw marinated tuna, swordfish, snapper, scallops with citrus zest with a sauvignon blanc; spaghetti with sea urchins and more Franciacorta; whole roasted wild fish, red snapper with tomatoes, garlic, olives, and parsley; lemon sorbet, fresh fruit; "rest"; and coffee and grappa. The menu was written in block letters and he hunched over the paper thinking about the right combination as he wrote out each course. I was flush just from reading the meal. Fredo countered with flirtatious self-deprecation: "Eh, sex, I'm only good for one round. BUT it's a bery, bery good one round, like at least seven minutes."

He couched every advance with the proclamation, "No, I love my wife. I would never leave her for anyone and I hope to God she never leaves me. That is the truth. I love my wife and kids." And then he quickly added, "C'mon, Yaime, please, let me give it to you once, why do you deny me 'appiness?" (Fredo never so much as tried to kiss me on the lips, now or then.) The attention, that night, felt good and unreal. I was happy and welcome among strangers and passing time at a restaurant after closing. I saw the veil lifted and, lo and behold, there was even more beauty behind the gauze. It was like being back at Moonwork—allowed into a space with new friends in an unexpected place after a period of darkness and isolation.

I don't know how that night ended. I don't remember, my brain was marinating in red wine and my intestines were indistinguishable from the mounds of pasta I had eaten. I got several texts from Fredo about playing pool on Monday, which I deflected. Every excuse I gave, he'd respond with perfect, fine, I can wait, we can do something after you make granola/box/levitate. Finally, I said, no, I really had to make granola. And he responded by saying, "You can cook in my kitchen, anytime."

"Really?"

"Sure, come whenever," he said.

So I did. Again, I had nothing else to do.

There are two Noodle Puddings—the one at night, filled with stories and Ella Fitzgerald and tea candles and hot plates of fish and pasta and cold plates of carpaccio and arugula often helmed by the restaurant's owner, Antonio Migliaccio; then there is the daytime Noodle, the quiet, fast chopping of ordering and prep work and tasting and small intimate lunches of what wasn't eaten the night before.

When I arrived, the restaurant looked closed and the windows were locked. Everything was still and stacked like furniture Jenga. But below there was activity—the metal rabbit hole that connected the sidewalk to Noodle Pudding's basement kitchen was flung open, tempting curiosity. I looked through the open passageway and saw a splintered plank and stacks of vegetables, roots poking through cardboard, leafy greens itching to bust out of their crates. I walked into the silent, wooded room, the polar opposite of the night before. There was the hum of the espresso machine and the walls still vibrating from the previous night's conversations. I saw Fredo, hunched over the paper tablecloth tallying the checks, writing on the back table the food that was eaten, the food that needed to be sold—meals reduced to chicken scratches, meals reduced to brass tacks. He looked up.

"So, Betty Blue, you want to learn to cook. You want an espresso first?"

We walked to the brass and copper antiquity that sat on the bar and he cleaned it and made a shot.

"Sugar?"

"No, I take it black," I said.

"You should take sugar, it'll make you sweeter."

He handed me a spoon, which I rested on the saucer. I don't put sugar in my coffee.

"So, you want to learn how to cook?" he said again, surprised. "Okay, let's start, here's an apron."

He took me to the kitchen and showed me the small stations for cutting, peeling, and dicing; he showed me the two overheated ovens and the stovetop. He stood me in front of a cutting board, which had already been placed on a wet napkin so that the board stayed in place on the metal counter.

"I am not a chef, I have never been trained; you want to learn how to make French food and French sauces, go to the Culinary Institute. Here, I will teach you how to love."

And with that Fredo gave me a sharpened knife and introduced me to the prep cooks Poncho and Cunyado. In between speed bouts of slicing and grilling, they'd look at me suspiciously. They'd half smile and pretend to understand but really they just wanted to get through the vegetables, the deboning of the chickens, the red sauce, the stocks, the lettuce, the chard . . . the prep. I tried to focus on my tasks and whatever was on my cutting board. I helped make a cold snap pea soup by shelling the peas, blanching them, and sieving them through a metal cone that looked like a contraption from my grandmother's kitchen. I drained the blood and fleshy juice from a rack of pork ribs by running my fingers perpendicular to the bones, and then I sliced them, three ribs a portion, and prepared them to be braised. Fredo took me downstairs to gather carrots, celery, and onion for stock and we stopped to examine the fish being delivered hours after the morning catch.

"Look for clear eyes and a dark red behind the gills. This is beautiful, perfect fish," Fredo said.

"Probably a good test for boyfriends as well," I said.

"Mmm? You want a boyfriend? Why can't you American women just have fun?"

We put the black cod, brook trout, and headless salmon on ice to be descaled and filleted by Juan when he arrived at four. We gathered the celery, carrots, onions, and parsley in the basement fridge, which was the size of my kitchen and stocked chock-full of fresh vegetables from the Queens market. Most of my first day I was reprimanded for not knowing how to cut . . . anything. First Fredo showed me on carrots: "Like this, your fingers go like these, otherwise you end up in the ER. I'm not going to the ER today." I tucked my four fingers under and chopped very deliberately.

"Ugh, you are bery, bery slow. Like this." And the pile would vanish in seconds. I would resume at a glacial pace only to have Fredo clucking behind me.

"I don't like the way you cut. Your body positioning is all off. Do it like this."

He demonstrated again, and again cut a hundred carrots and lifted his hands to display the same pile I had been laboring over for an hour, only now diced to pieces.

"Protect your fingers and you won't get cut, you work too hard with the knife, make it easy. Eh?"

I stood in front of the window and chopped. I tried to make it meditative, but I wanted to chop correctly, like Poncho and Cunyato. I could see them arriving from downstairs with whole vegetables in the tubs and leaving with those same vegetables finely chopped. They were machines. I'd already helped prepare two entrées, the soup, some stocks. Slow chopper was okay for day one; no one really cared what I did or how fast. The space was calm in every way, except for the cartoonish stovetop, which was crowded with overflowing pots and pans and cauldrons filled with lava-like sauces. There was a pot of red wine on fire, luminous with blue flames circling the alcohol, and a giant cauldron of Bolognese that took two men to carry—a vat of slow-cooked meats and fats and tomatoes.

As much as there was to do before the real line chefs showed up at four, Fredo made time for lunch. He relished this task, cooking for four—Cunyato didn't sit with us for reasons unknown, but Fredo made a plate for him and set it aside. For lunch, Fredo sautéed pasta with a roasted yellow pepper–based sauce . . . parm, bread, and mineral water. Fredo may speak often and obsessively of sex, but he's clearly in it for the food. When he talked about ingredients and flavor and freshness, there was a sense of gravitas, a balletic grace to the way Fredo combined ingredients, his arms floating in free form, dropping fresh-cut herbs and spices over iron skillets. Some chefs look tight and hurried when they cook; Fredo looked like he was doing an interpretive dance, moving with the food and the heat.

When I asked exactly how he made this hot, delicious mess on our plates, he said, "When I talk of food, I talk of love and I cannot talk of love with you so I will not tell you what I made today. I cannot." He said this like I had violated him. I had underestimated the power of someone cooking specifically for you, tailoring a menu to suit you and only you. Our lunch was intimate. At the end of the day, I gave Fredo my apron and he said, "Keep it, just in case you want to come back." I said I did, that I loved my first lesson in chopping. "Ah good, well then I can't be that awful if you want to come back. Whenever you want, stop by."

I came back the next day.

"So"—Fredo started many sentences with the word *so* and followed it with a dramatic pause—"you want to chop again?" Fredo positioned me next to six different crates of mushrooms, each one requiring a damp washcloth cleanse and individual rubbings to get rid of dirt. I cleaned and cut porcini, crimini, shiitake, chanterelle, oyster, and enoki for the garnish. I sautéed each of them in garlic-infused oil, white wine, red pepper, and chopped parsley until a metal tray was filled and one of the specials was done. I didn't slice my finger and I didn't set my hand on fire. It was a good day so far; I was progressing from stock maker to mushroom lady. Fredo introduced me to my favorite task yet, pitting olives. I looooooooooved pitting olives. I would pound each olive with a mallet until it split and remove the pit. With each thud, Fredo would jump slightly.

"Easy, easy. This isn't your ex-boyfriend."

I liked the meat grinder too; it satisfied the Sweeney Todd in me, the way the raw, marbled flesh of wild boar shoulder oozed out of the metal grinder; it just looked cool and I liked wearing the plastic medical gloves and sticking my hand in the ground raw flesh. Making the duck ravioli fillings required grinding and mashing and elaborate hand mixing with ricotta cheese. I was starting to really get into the kitchen. I didn't know what to expect and now I never wanted to leave. That afternoon, the owner, nicknamed Toto or Tony by all the neighborhood regulars, stopped by the kitchen after the market in his paint-splattered work boots.

"Eh, Tony, this is Yaime," Fredo said.

I thanked him for letting me chop in his kitchen.

"Yaime, it's my pleasure." Antonio had a kind of singsong melodic way of speaking. It was almost operatic, like every syllable was infused emotion. Toto treated me like family, like a daughter. I shelled fava beans; made a bean dish whose name translates to "jumps like a flying bird"; cooked ravioli, aka "little purses filled with cheese"; I cut more carrots and celery and onion in more ways than I thought possible . . . big chunks for stock, diced for seafood salad, thinly sliced for the rabbit, shredded, and medium cut. Fredo still thought my knife skills were lacking. "You are going to slice your finger off. I know it. Not like this. Like this." Fredo and I ate lunch together—pancetta and fava beans over penne with ricotta salata, pea soup; on very good days we'd split a chocolate hazelnut torte. Sometimes I'd stop in on my way to work and have an espresso. I'd eat at Noodle Pudding for dinner with friends and I'd be treated like a princess—Fredo bringing out special olive oil and small bites, Marcelo filling our wineglasses and Anthony (Toto's son) with the tiramisu.

I'd ask Fredo how he was each morning. "Depressed," he'd answer, then lift up his hands and look around, like it was obvious. He always answered either "depressed" or even "suicidal," in spite of his generally good mood. He complained about his family life ("Nico decided to dump a jar of cinnamon in the living room, then took off his diaper and paraded around with it, then he thought it was a good idea to stay up till midnight!"). Then would rescind everything: "No, no, no, I love my wife and my kids, they are the best thing in my life." I once mentioned being unsure of motherhood or family and he said dismissively, "Well, you are going to miss out on the best thing this world has to offer." I took Fredo's near-constant chatter about sex and cheating and attraction to be more of a front than a reality. He would flirt with a broom if a broom had an ass.

Lithium allowed me to function, but during this breakdown, breakup, or whatever was happening, Noodle Pudding saved me. The food, the people, the wine, and having a place to go cannot be underrated in the realm of treatment. In *The Hidden Life of Trees*, Peter Wohlleben writes about how forests act as a family, pooling resources and protecting each other, sending messages and nutrients through an elaborate roots system. Noodle Pudding was like that—a forest made of pasta. I lived alone, Randy (a regular who lived upstairs) lived alone, Fredo seemed alone in this world, alone in his kitchen. There were times when the isolation felt awful. But at Noodle Pudding, we were alone together. Noodle Pudding was my friend; it sometimes felt like I was dating the whole restaurant. I chopped for about a year until Marcelo and Fredo opened AlMar, a different Italian restaurant, in DUMBO. And when ESPN moved to Bristol, Connecticut, I lost my night job. I started waitressing at AlMar and was the world's worst waitress (according to Marcelo). I stressed out customers by overapologizing and by empathizing with them when their orders were late. I'd explain over and over again how sorry I was that it was taking hours for a cloud egg sandwich—something that looked cool but took a while to execute, hence the massive delays. I had anxiety attacks over any-thing that went wrong (dishes piling up, slow orders, mistaken or-ders, no orders, wrong change).

It didn't matter; I quit to cover the Women's World Cup in Germany for ESPN.com. I spent the month in Germany criss-crossing the country via train, haunted by the night rides, feeling the ghosts of relatives from generations previous who had taken very different train rides to gas chambers. Most of the tourna-ment sites were in German suburbs or industrial towns. On the trains, outside the cities, I felt like a curio. I'd been to exotic places but this was different. I talked with Germans who had heard of Jews but never met one. There was extreme care with every conversation, as if these strangers were observing a museum exhibition—a Jew. Most of the people I met in Berlin and Ham-burg were friends and friends of friends and expats. I went to the Schlagermove parade—picture a city vomiting 1970s kitsch for an entire weekend—and thought, *This is manic, how is this normal?* I went to an abandoned waterfront building occupied by anarchists who lived with pit bulls in sweaters under squatters'-rights laws. I met a fellow journalist, Jack from Melbourne, and we lived in the bubble of the World Cup. I offered him a piece of chocolate at the opening ceremonies in the press seats and we followed each other around, reporting our stories in tandem. Between matches, we'd sit close at beer gardens on the Spree in Berlin or walk among the street paintings of JR or BLO or Os Gemeos. It was the first time I dated someone I could talk to about writing and journalism, someone who was smart. On our last night, we watched the final in Frankfurt and took the last train to Berlin, huddling in the cold train car. We slept on my friend's couch, clutching each other for a few final hours. He was staying on to study German and I of-fered to stay longer. The offer was met with hesitation, and I had by now learned to keep moving. I had a flight to catch back to Los Angeles. I would be house-sitting for my aunt Carrie for a month. Jack and I FaceTimed—he in Berlin, me sun-drenched in front of magenta bougainvillea. I spent the month swimming and running stairs and trying to write. My writing was thinly masked fiction and bad. I felt far from magazines and worried that I'd never work again. But I didn't know what else to do, and I was running out of money.

Matt, in a fit of generosity, took David and me to Japan to see the town he once taught in. We rode trains south to parts of the country that looked like Japanese mountain paintings—like screen prints Opa had in his study, jagged new crags of rock reaching for the moody sky, sliced with small inconsequential lines where a train might be. We were that train, rolling on the edge of rock and over cold waters. When we got to Nakamura, we rode bikes to a bridge and we jumped off that bridge, plunging into cold river waters; we ate the hottest, fattiest ramen on the hottest, fattiest day, sweating chilies and pork into the night. We sang karaoke with judo instructors and traded sake shots. I stayed in Asia longer (nothing to do again). I visited friends in Beijing, danced at one of the best hip-hop parties I've been to with a playlist of early 1990s tracks that would make Bobbito jealous. I traipsed around without a real game plan. I got stuck in industrial China (thirty-six hours in Jinan!) with no money or credit cards or ability to say "bank" in Chinese. I ate unidentified skewered chewy objects. I stayed at an elephant sanctuary north of Chiang Mai volunteering to help the vet treat wounds, and to feed and wash the giant pachyderms. I practiced Muay Thai with a tiny Thai Rastafarian and had a near-death experience on a scooter in the middle lane of a freeway during a monsoon. I stayed in Asia, e-mailing Jack half hoping he would meet me there. He didn't.

I returned to the States with no job and no direction and no real home. I thought I might move to Los Angeles, I thought I might go back to New York, I didn't know where to go. I went to a Robyn concert at the Hollywood Bowl with a friend and felt her sing directly to me through her crop-top sheep-looking sweater and platform sneakers. "Dancing on My Own," "Call Your Girlfriend," "With Every Heartbeat" radiated heart and love and strength. She was femme and fierce and obsessed and didn't give a fuck. I had heard her before but felt her now. She came into me and somehow guided me back to my New York perch feeling independent and hopeful, still miserable in the day-to-day but compelled to return to my life. On the eve of my thirty-fifth birthday, I went to a matte-gray testing center with standing cubicles to take a standardized test for a city job. It was the last day I was eligible to apply to the New York Police Department, which an elderly black cop had convinced me might be a good idea when I was at the Occupy protests (I had gone to them in Oakland, New York, and San Francisco). He stood calmly next to one in downtown Brooklyn; his rationale was to try to do good from within. He showed me his gun and said, "I've never discharged a bullet. It's a stable paycheck and you can try and do right by the community." I took the test and got a near-perfect score—I wondered if I was a natural fit or if the bar was too low. I thought about applying to nursing schools (Oma on her deathbed said I should be a nurse, so maybe?). I applied to grad schools and I applied to every job I might qualify for. I went home for New Year's, spending the actual eve with my mom and cousins, all of us in some state of feral funk. My mom kept trying to go to bed (I explained to her you can't invite people over for New Year's and go to bed at ten p.m.), and my cousins and I kept spontaneously bursting into tears. One ran out the door entirely, opting for a sob on the curb. There was no rationale to it, just general malaise. We needed a family massive cry fest. One glimmer of sweetness was that Jack e-mailed me to wish me a Happy New Year, and I was grateful that he remembered. It had been a better year with him in it. I decided to return to New York, and within a week I read a blog post on Ol' Dirty Bastard that enraged me. It was something I had reported in my book (I had painstakingly published his FBI file after several FOIA requests on ODB and Wu-Tang Clan were sent to me) and I was pissed it was repurposed on the blog by a writer I really respected and liked. I wrote an angry letter—the only one I've ever written in spite of my "aggressive" tendencies—and got the most polite, delightful response from the writer, H. It was an unexpected reply; his posts were usually biting and aggressive and cut to the bone. We realized we both boxed at Gleason's and when he said, "Hey, let's get a drink someday." I responded with, "How's Monday?" By the time we met for our second date, I had accepted a job offer to become the executive editor at an in-flight magazine and we were swooning. Job and dating were in sync as if they had never been off-kilter. In fact, after we ate dinner, we walked back to my apartment for "tea" and when the conversation paused, I said, "I think we should kiss now." And that was it. I lunged across my small navy sofa and haven't looked back. (Aggressive worked for me in this particular instance.) The first six months of our dating was like pure ecstasy, not unlike a manic episode. I barely slept, was running on fumes and glowed. Life was good for a couple of years. I would get my blood levels taken but not as often as I was supposed to; Dr. Schwartz would scold me but I saw no reason to worry. I was working; I finally had a boyfriend who I loved and who loved me back (novel accomplishments). Life was really good; lithium levels were fine if not a little high. Dr. Schwartz reduced my dose from 900 milligrams to 750 milligrams.

Then in 2014, I saw my primary physician, Dr. Matthew Lane, for a routine checkup. He sent me to the nearest emergency room. He was alarmed at my combination of high creatinine levels (which Dr. Schwartz had already been monitoring), damaged kidneys, and heart-attack-level blood pressure (185/130). At Mount Sinai Hospital, I sat in the emergency room next to an elderly Orthodox man who yelled through curtains in pain. H sat next to me on my gurney. The room was packed with people in much more immediate and real pain than I. Within days, I was told I should phase out lithium and start another medication, or face dialysis and a kidney transplant in ten years.

Suddenly, those pink pills, the ones that had saved me, were hurting me.

I realized I didn't know what they did in the first place, that I had never thought to ask where lithium was from and how it ended up coursing through my blood and shaping my brain.

PART 3 —

THE TRANSITION

CHAPTER 19

THE BIG BANG, THE THIRD ELEMENT EMERGES, HOSTS ALIEN LIFE . . . MAYBE?

I TOOK THE train to the emergency room. It was faster than an ambulance. I felt eviscerated, thunderstruck. I knew lithium would not be forever. Dr. Schwartz and I had been aware of higher-than-normal creatinine levels. But I chose to ignore the implications of those test results, thinking they might level off or be insignificant long term. I did not think about lithium one way or the other. It was not something special. I took it for granted. It was just like Dr. DeAntonio had initially said: if I were a diabetic, I'd need insulin. Just a medication. That it was a salt always in my body, changing my chemistry, guiding my personality toward a more rational state, never really fazed me. It was a medication that had always been there for me, invisibly. But now that my kidneys were eroding, I felt differently. Dr. Schwartz consulted Dr. John Mann, an expert in bipolar disorder at Columbia, and he referred me to Dr. Maria DeVita, a nephrologist practicing at Lenox Hill Hospital on the Upper East Side. Dr. DeVita talked fast and listened intently; she didn't miss anything. She issued more tests to confirm what was already clear.

The test results indicated that my kidneys were working about half as well as they should—at 48 percent function. Dr. DeVita told me that if I were to switch medications to preserve the kidney function I had left, "the time to strike was now." I had to choose between my kidneys or risking my sanity. It didn't feel like an obvious choice; just two bad options. Switching meds might mean the return of cornrowed, Eminem-obsessed Jamya and many seasonal gourds. It had taken a lot of work to recover from the damage of the last episode. Yet dialysis felt so extreme, something out of a *Mad Max* sequel—tubing up and cleansing my blood until I got a stranger's kidney quilted into my insides. I didn't know what to do. When I had anxious days, H helped me through with his preternatural calm. Some mornings, I would ask him to lie full body weight on top of me, a thunder jacket. I spoke with nephrologists who had all seen manic relapses and been terrified by the results; I spoke with psychiatrists who watched patients stand by lithium and try to function after kidney transplants, and who felt a psychic relapse might be worth the risk—each doctor fearing the disease she didn't know. I was living in Crown Heights at the time and walked by a dialysis center on Dean Street whenever I made my way toward downtown Brooklyn. I tried to picture lying on a gurney three times a week for four hours at a stretch, feeling depleted, sick. Not manic. But sick all the time. Not boxing, not standing on my head or riding the subway to my annual visit to the Cyclone and a Nathan's hot dog. Just sick, dominated by treatment. If I could avoid it, shouldn't I at least try? I thought.

I watched the videotape that Mike made on Valentine's eve again. I saw the wild hair, swirled eyes, and heard my gnarled, gravelly voice. I thought about how I felt on that night, ruling the world, performing, recruiting, revolution in the air. I thought about the energy, that magnet at my core. If I gave up the lithium and took another med and that med didn't work, would that be me again? I could not return to her. I wasn't sure I would survive it, that my parents would survive another episode. I worried that H would never make it through. I was not ready to let go of the medication that had worked for more than twenty years.

I needed to know more about lithium before I let it go. So I set off on a spirit quest and scientific quest, an expedition to understand the third element.

The beginning of lithium is the beginning of everything. Imagine when the universe wasn't even one second old, nearly fourteen billion years ago. There was no space, just a very dense, single point in the universe. There wasn't really even a universe in the traditional sense of the word. It was about ten trillion degrees and made up of neutrons and protons. It was so scalding hot that those neutrons and protons couldn't stick to each other—they just careened around like restless teenagers, slamming into each other. Within the first three seconds of the formation of the universe, the elements present—overwhelmingly helium and hydrogen— exploded into a raging storm of superheated energy. It was violent, tumultuous, restless, hot, and raw. Lithium was there in such small quantities that only one part lithium matched one billion hydrogen atoms—its presence almost seemed mythical, nearly invisible, but not quite. After two minutes, the universe *existed* and it was made up of hydrogen, helium, lithium, deuterium, and tritium and *that was all* for billions of years. For the first 380,000 years after the Big Bang, the intense heat from the universe's creation made it essentially too hot for light to shine. There was a period of darkness before stars and other bright objects were formed. What is a world without light, without shadows and stars and a scale of grays? What was this darkness? What was this universe? What existed before time and space? What was this manic burst of energy followed by deep, sedentary darkness? These were questions that a manic person is not really allowed to ask because the origin story of earth, of the universe, of the world, seems kind of far out.

Galaxies and stars were formed. The other naturally occurring elements came later. Many scientists think the sun and the rest of our solar system came from a giant, rotating cloud of gas and dust known as the solar nebula. As gravity caused the nebula to collapse, it spun faster and flattened into a disk. As the universe expanded, it cooled. At one stage, the temperature of the growing universe was similar to temperatures in the cores of stars like our sun. According to a 2009 article in the *New Scientist*, "The existing amounts of hydrogen and helium match theory perfectly—so well, in fact, that cosmologists claim this is the best evidence we have for the big bang. Things aren't so good for the third element, lithium, however. When we count up the lithium atoms held in stars, there is only one-third as much of the lithium-7 isotope as there should be." There have been recent theories that lithium is made during some supernova explosions; it's also one of the few elements produced in interstellar space by high-energy cosmic rays. But unlike most other elements, lithium is destroyed by its stars. This depletion is known as "The Lithium Problem," one of the few aspects of the Big Bang theory that doesn't make sense. The amount of lithium, or lack thereof, just doesn't add up.

In 2005, Neil deGrasse Tyson, ambassador to all things astrophysics, wrote: "Lithium remained a rather rare element, distinguished among astrophysicists by the cosmic fact that stars hardly ever make more lithium, but only destroy it. Lithium rides down a one-way street because every star has more effective nuclear fusion reactions to destroy lithium than create it. As a result, the cosmic supply of lithium has steadily decreased and continues to do so. If you want some, now would be a good time to acquire it." One of the theories surrounding the Big Bang is that there should be three times as much lithium as can be observed. I asked Tyson whether this lithium destruction was still in effect and he wrote me, "The circumstances surrounding lithium, as detailed in that quote, remain unchanged. What the quote does not address is that Big Bang nucleosynthesis, a cottage industry among cosmologists, predicts three to four times as much lithium as is observed in stars that should have nicely preserved that lithium abundance from the beginning. This is called the Lithium Problem and, last I checked, it's still not resolved." The Lithium Problem, an unsolved galactic mystery of universal origins! Astrophysicists debate where lithium is most present—some have said stars rich in lithium can host alien life; our own sun lacks lithium as do most stars that host planets; others have said they found brown dwarfs to be lithium-rich; lithium lives in asteroids and dying planets. It is everywhere in space, on earth, in me, on me.

I have these galactic leggings from the Fulton Street Mall, tight spandex holding in my body. My lithium body. The leggings make me think of the microcosmic universe of the cells that make up our bodies and of the celestial macrocosm mirrored in the night sky. I had too little lithium, too much lithium. I had a lithium problem too. I imagined wearing my leggings and being weightless in space, tethered to nothing, floating free among Hubble images—near enough to the explosions of dreamlike rainbow clouds to feel them, to taste them, to absorb them in my haze. I'm not afraid among the stars because I can feel a permeation, a subtle intake of lithium's fairy dust floating with me like an invisible shield, what it has always been. My medication *is* stardust.

The beginning of lithium is the beginning of time, the darkest lightest moments of our universe. With that astrophysics primer, I wanted to travel to one of the grandest, most delusional places of all, the world's largest reserve of lithium. I wanted to make a pilgrimage to the wellspring of my sanity, in Bolivia.

HER BODY HIT the mat like a stunning shock of weight, her purple petticoats blooming like a bouquet; her opponent, wearing red, grabbing her by the waist dragging her across the ring with the kind of showmanship that was definitive—she would make mincemeat of the woman she loathed, this purple petticoat monster lady. She pulled her foot, pranced about, making faces, and threw the purple lady's tiny top hat into the audience; she mocked the lesser of the two as if she was dragging out the punishment; she enjoyed it, the choke holds, the slamming, the shaming, the predictability of it all. And as if rising from the dead, the meeker of the two—the Cholita in purple—gathered her petticoats and her strength and fought back, clawing away for comic justice. Popcorn flew into the audience, water splashed, limbs split and splayed. The Flying Cholitas, a group of female wrestlers who perform in the same vein as Lucha Libre wrestling, crashed into each other and audience members in the tented gym. The gym was one death-defying winding bus ride from a hostel in the La Paz city center. The Cholitas performed in El Alto, meaning "the high" or "the heights," the mostly Aymaran town that was hastily built into cliffs as high as thirteen thousand feet above sea level. The city looked down on La Paz; they were connected by a red line funicular. The Cholitas wore traditional Bolivian dress— intricate long braids, bowler hats, and multilayered skirts, colorful and stacked wide with ruffled rainbow skirts. The tiny top hats came into being after hat manufacturers in Manchester designed bowler hats for the British railway workers in Bolivia and made them accidentally too small. The hat designers convinced Bolivian women that little bowler hats were all the rage in Europe and the trend took off (just another example of how the white man took advantage of native culture). I looked at the Aymaran women wrestling and I thought Jamya could step into that ring.

How did I end up here, thinking deeply about mania and witnessing it in the form of awesomely psycho lady wrestlers? I had been in La Paz for a couple days, adjusting to the altitude before I could make my way to the Salar de Uyuni, the largest salt flat in the world. These women, who had famously fought to gain financial control of their wrestling franchise, were a curious greeting. They clearly knew their audience—mostly tourists—but at the same time I couldn't help wonder if life's outward absurdity was a reminder that my inward absurdity wasn't so weird. Here I was on a mission to see the largest quantity of my favorite medication, which now had the potential to kill me, sitting ringside next to visions that could have spilled from a hallucinatory mind. I was staying near the Witches' Market and collected talismans and amulets that promised fertility, luck, and longevity. I stopped short of buying a dried llama fetus, used as a burial sacrifice to the fertility god Pachamama. I clambered up steep, cobbled alleys, out of breath, wondering: Was it the altitude or my kidneys or both? Pampered street dogs looked at me, judgmental of my inability to adjust to the heights and the air. I panted, they panted. Would I always think my internal organs were at half function? It's not helpful to imagine a persistent sickness, to be diagnosed with something that can always be blamed. It certainly doesn't help an already obsessive, borderline hypochondriac mind. The thing was, when I watched the Cholitas, I did not feel weak. I did not feel powerless. I felt like a warrior, like them. I wanted to wear the tiny hat. I climbed through the city and found a street vendor on a corner that served chicharrón fresh from the fry. I took in the valley, the churches, the graffiti, the other foods that tasted less good, like a fast-food dish that looked like a meat Frisbee with a fried egg on top. After I adjusted to Bolivia's altitude, I flew from La Paz to Uyuni, a nowhere zone of dust and Aussie bars and the promise of "real American breakfast." The people who gather in Uyuni are there for one reason, to see the salt flats. Toyota Land Cruiser four-by-fours parked in front of the guide shops with jagged stickers that read *Salt Life*.

If there is an earthly environment that looks like the beginning of time, it is the salt flats of Bolivia. The vastness of Salar de Uyuni is intensified by its mind-bending, flesh-burning, breathtaking altitude. The salt flats spread out twelve thousand feet above sea level (a little lower than the height of the Cholita fights). The flats look like ice interrupted by ruptured crevices that form "crack polygons" from thermal contraction. This part of southern Bolivia consists of four thousand square miles of what were once prehistoric lakes, now dried up into crust and brine. Parts of the desert landscape have been used to test Mars rovers before missions. Gazing out at the horizon in Salar de Uyuni is like looking back into those earliest moments of the universe or maybe what a brown dwarf might look like six thousand light-years away. Aliens could hide at the optical illusion horizon, or behind the rusted-out abandoned railcars. In one direction, there is nothing to see but vast, glaring white; in another direction, psychedelically colored landscapes. The place feels like a hallucination. And this trek was equal parts soul tourism and complete manic realization. I was alone. H stayed behind out of respect for my spirit quest. I went with a group and was paired with a family of four who were trekking through South America for six months and homeschooling; the other four-by-fours were populated by a British couple, Australians, and a Finnish librarian who made enough money to work one year and travel one year, alternating at will. The drivers were Bolivian and well versed in lithium lore. The trek was about the flats, the dizzying, undeniably trippy flats. There was an island populated by century-old cactuses, a bloodred lagoon, flocks of hot-pink wild flamingos, a Bolivian guide who wore a surplus *Shock and Awe* army shirt, and piles of the blindingly white crystalline substance. Lithium salt piled everywhere, surrounding me, enveloping me. I stood on top of a small mountain and felt the lithium in my veins. I could hear the tiny vibrations sing back to me. I walked the crusted, jigsaw surface. I wanted to feel and taste its granularity and saltiness. The far-off Andean peaks floated dreamily, with no visible foundation. As I ran between the salt mounds, cracks accompanied each step. My hiking-boot footprints flooded with milky saltwater. I was so breathless, so thirsty, so thrilled. If ever there has been a perfect backdrop for a grandiose delusion, it is the Salar de Uyuni.

After a few days of off-roading, our group stopped at a camp and slept in a building made of salt bricks—a lithium igloo. We each had our own room and I huddled next to the wall, hoping to absorb some lithium. I wanted to lick it, to taste what I had swallowed without noticing. I sat in the nearby hot springs, in water naturally laden with high concentrations of lithium, and watched the steam rise on the moonshine horizon. If I soaked in this warm bath long enough, I thought, maybe it wouldn't feel so bad to let go of my medicine—or maybe I wouldn't have to. Maybe in a world like this, I wouldn't need it. This was obviously a fleeting thought, but there I was soaking in the Altiplana trying to make sense of my body and this world. This world around me, which included a green blob plant named llareta that lived in this landscape too. It clung to desert mounds, kelly-green, and looked like alien moss except that its surface was hard and it had black sticky goo inside. The plant, our guide told us, was one of the oldest living things—some as old as three thousand years. Older than the sequoias and the Greek civilization that wrote of a lithium cure in the first place.

On my last day in Uyuni, the tourist town suffocated by sand and glaring sun and pockmarked with graffitied railcars and tall rusted-out artistically whimsical metal creatures, I thought about how the town was once a stopover for narcotraffickers hoping to move coca to Chile or Peru. Now trekkers wearing hiking boots and sunglasses and well-placed scarves walked through Uyuni largely unaware that the spectacular visions they came to see (a check off their South American bucket list) are also the future of Bolivia's economic stability and possibly the world's. I could see off in the distance the state-owned Bolivian lithium plant. None of the drivers knew much about it; they barely knew anyone who worked there. An estimated 50 percent of the world's lithium supply lies beneath the Salar de Uyuni in southern Bolivia. The increasing global demand for lithium has prompted many proclamations, including claims by Bolivians that the landlocked socialist country will become the "Saudi Arabia of lithium." The danger of relying on any natural resource for national income is known as the "resource curse." It seems like an almost too easy and obvious parallel to my dependence on lithium. Internationally, economists have been forecasting a lithium economy for decades, and it may well be that every car, computer, and wearable electronic device—not to mention our energy storehouses—will depend on lithium batteries the way I've relied on medicinal lithium for the last twenty years. If I were especially good at being bipolar (and entirely off my meds), I might invest all my money—and that of those I could convince to give me money—in lithium.

Whether Bolivians would benefit from their own resource is

still an unknown. Their processing plant is starting to catch up with international competitors, but it's not running at the same pace as mines in Chile, Western Australia, or even Nevada, which might be a good thing. Many indigenous people in the region that encompasses Chile, Argentina, and Bolivia have been exploited by firms flocking to the neighboring Atacama lands to mine "white gold"—but they rarely distribute the wealth of the operations equally or even fairly. "One lithium company, a joint Canadian-Chilean venture named Minera Exar, struck deals with six aboriginal communities for a new mine here. The operation is expected to generate about $250 million a year in sales, while each community will receive an annual payment—ranging from $9,000 to about $60,000—for extensive surface and water rights," the *Washington Post* reported in 2016. Some companies see indigenous communities as small hurdles standing in the way of big profits. Bolivia's lithium is more protected—after years of exploitation in silver mining, President Evo Morales is more cautious with their resources. Morales said in an interview that Bolivia's lithium is "like a beautiful lady, very much sought and pursued." Morales is determined to use the natural resource as an economic boost. National firms will get first crack at extracting the element, but if local companies can't do it, then the state will allow private companies to invest—with the understanding that most of the profits would go to the Bolivian people.

A few years ago, a friend of mine published a book about lithium and batteries, and when it came out, I had a small panic attack— what if there wasn't enough lithium for me *and* the batteries that power all of our electronic devices? *Should I stockpile lithium, in case of emergency?* I thought. It was a short-lived panic attack; I quickly learned that batteries don't need much lithium and that it's wildly abundant on earth already. But I also learned that the trick is in the extraction process. In fact, lithium and its various methods of extraction are considered the Wild West of speculation and mining right now. Trade magazines prophesize who will land the big contracts and who will really be able to provide the amount of lithium necessary to sustain the electric car market, solar energy, and electronics.

Lithium plays a critical role in Elon Musk's mass-produced Tesla fleet and his planned expansion of his solar power company, SolarCity. He's banking on lithium to power both, and he's not alone. Nearly 70 percent of the demand for the raw materials that make up new lithium-ion batteries will be coming from China. Prices for lithium carbonate were up 47 percent in the first quarter of 2016 from the average price in 2015. A Goldman Sachs report suggested that demand for lithium could triple within ten years to 570,000 tons a year. As Musk builds his billion-dollar gigafactory in northern Nevada, an industrial park next to the world's biggest data center, the company would manufacture its own lithium-ion batteries. And where will the lithium be coming from? As part of the development deal, Tesla is constructing a new highway connecting the gigafactory to Silver Peak, Nevada, where the Silver Peak mine, now owned by conglomerate Albemarle, has been the only operational lithium mine in the United States.

If I thought the Salar de Uyuni was remote and desolate, I was wrong. Silver Peak, Nevada, has a population of about 350 people. It's haunted and burnt by a sun-drenched landscape littered with a dusty collection of rusted-out car frames, employee trailers, and white barren hills. The one moving piece: a processing plant with endless pools in various stages of evaporation. The mine resides in Clayton Valley, a hot spot to at least a dozen different lithium prospectors hoping to tap into the "white gold" rush. The brine deposits that Silver Peak Mine has been extracting are part of a catchment area of approximately 540 square miles that includes at least five adjacent basins, according to the United States Geological Survey (USGS). They're all hydrologically linked, which makes the area one of "the best-known deposits in the world" for lithium because of its expansiveness. This is because (like the climate in Bolivia) Silver Peak is arid; the basin is closed, tectonically active; and there's an elevated heat flow from hot springs or young volcanoes. Hundreds of lithium junior mining companies are searching for lithium deposits in South America, Australia, and Nevada, too, and there are at least a dozen companies—with names like Lithium X, Nevada Sunrise Gold, and even "Elon Project," named after Elon Musk—looking at Clayton Valley.

A few hours south is the Nevada National Security Site, previously the Nevada Test Site, an area established on January 11, 1951, for testing nuclear devices. Among all its other miraculous applications, lithium is also crucial in nuclear fusion reactions. Nuclear testing at the Nevada Test Site began with a 1-kiloton-of-TNT (4.2 TJ) bomb dropped on Frenchman Flat on January 27, 1951. The images of the nuclear era became so iconic that tourists would flock to Vegas hotels to watch the mushroom clouds from the atmospheric tests that could be seen from almost a hundred miles away. Local lore, I was told, is that the winds would blow residue of uranium north to the Valley and as silver mining dried up, outfits looking for alternate ways to make money "found" uranium. After more testing, they thought the soil was naturally rich in uranium. But they found lithium instead. Though *mine* is the word used for extracting lithium, it's not quite right. The process is a mostly sun-driven evaporation process, with pools of brine captured in various stages of evaporation until the liquid transforms into salt. It's also misleading to call Silver Peak a town—there used to be a gold mine and a silver mine here, like most of the abandoned places in the middle of Nevada. But all that ore had mostly run dry. What remained was a frontier mentality and a load of cash to be made by sifting something else from the earth.

In August 1966, Foote Mineral dedicated its plant in Silver Peak to prospecting for the lithium-laden brine that lay beneath the surface of the high desert hills. No one had thought to exploit the brine before because the technology simply hadn't been developed. The company first established a method to extract lithium from the underground pools, then established its plant in the mineral-rich land. "The sun does the majority of the work," USGS geologist Brian Jaskula told me. "They have this dry desert area but underneath it is a running brine solution. The process begins by pumping the brine into a big series of evaporation ponds. . . . The brine is pumped into trucks and brought over to the processing facility and certain chemicals are added like soda ash to make lithium carbonate. It's made and bagged and shipped off to customers. It's pretty amazing because it's so low tech." David Klawitter, a mechanic for Rockwood, showed me his swollen, red hands painted with a permanent layer of grit. "The lithium burns sometimes, but it's fine; it eats sockets, though, rusts them up solid. You can see what it does to the trucks." Tankers rolled by transferring the brine to various different pools. "We make medical-grade lithium here; we're processing a pure form of lithium, the purest." Rockwood Lithium, purchased by Albemarle in 2015, is the only operating lithium plant in America and sits on the fifth-largest deposit of lithium in the world. It's more accessible than the findings in Afghanistan because there isn't war breaking out above the brines. Its processing facilities are more advanced than anything in Bolivia, and the final product is easier to transport. But China, Australia, and Chile are capitalizing on an open market.

When the operation began, there was already a community of miners from the days of the gold and silver mines, a volunteer fire and police force, a bar called the Shifting Sands Saloon, and its rival the Dead Coon Saloon, which hosted local weddings that ended in bruises and brawls, new mothers-in-law included. It's the kind of place where bodies were found mysteriously at the bottom of the town well. Silver Peak, when asked what it wanted from the spoils of mines, requested a swimming pool for the kids to offset the 100-plus-degree summer days. Along another dusty road between Silver Peak and Goldfield are the remnants of concrete pools near Alkali Hot Springs. There are two plunging tubs with a hose funneling in lithium water at around 100 degrees Fahrenheit. The springs were once the bathing grounds for tent city miners and cowboys like the Earp brothers, prospecting for gold at the turn of the century. The baths are still soothing, though the pool is full of catfish now.

Only 1 percent of lithium produced goes toward medication, but I imagine this is the spot where my pink pills come from. I like to think I was just ahead of the trend, that my taking lithium was prophetic to a future in which we all depend on lithium. I made my way to an old gold mining town, appropriately named Goldfield. I'd heard of a natural spring nearby and thought I might soak in lithium waters again. No one had a clear sense of where the hot springs were, except for a nudist website with vague instructions. There were no roads or roads with names or roads that made sense to me, so I pulled over to talk with an old miner who told me about the springs location but only after I bought a gold chip mined from his nearly inactive mine. He said to turn around, turn left, and then make another left and look for an oasis—an actual patch of paradise in the middle of the sand. I didn't see one person or car or tree on the ride through the dirt roads. I was driving a tiny rental car that left a hurricane of dust announcing my presence. In some patches the road was only one-way and I drove cautiously, mostly nervous about being alone. When I pulled up to the springs wearing my bathing suit under layers, a truck was already parked there. That made me more nervous. The man I saw was an elderly gentleman with a Wilford Brimley mustache and a hunting-plaid shirt. He told me the waters were healing and pointed to a young man soaking in the hot springs, his "nephew." I noticed his nephew had a fresh gash on his temple and seemed mentally impaired, like he couldn't talk, or wouldn't talk or had been locked in a basement too long to know if he should talk. He wouldn't make eye contact with me. "It helps him calm down," Brimley Mustache said. Wilford Brimley kept talking up the waters, and I kept imagining myself chopped up in the Clown Motel (a real place) back in Tonopah where I was staying. I thanked him for chatting and said I had to go. "It's a shame you can't stay for a soak," he said through his mustache. But I had my Bolivia waters still fresh in my veins.

CHAPTER 20

LITHIUM'S LORE AND
THE TRANSITION TO DEPAKOTE
(TAKE 1)

LITHIUM WORKS IN mysterious ways and as I bid it good-bye, I wanted to get a sense of how it went from ancient Greek soaks to a pink pill. Despite the fact that people have benefited from its use for millennia, how lithium works on brains is largely unknown. "It has so-called trophic or fertilizing activity on the brain—that is, it stabilizes membranes," James Kocsis, a professor of psychiatry at Weill Cornell Medical College in New York and an expert on lithium, told me. Lithium acts on many levels throughout the nervous system and within the functional integrity of the cell, including transmitting signals to the brain through cells. But the actual mechanics are a mystery. One way to think about its effect, though, is suggested by a 2007 UCLA study that found that bipolar patients taking lithium had significantly more gray matter than their counterparts in the study—both bipolar patients not taking lithium and people without bipolar disorder—especially in the region associated with a person's capacity to maintain attention and emotional control.

In the second century AD, Soranus treated manic patients with the alkaline waters in his town, which contained very high levels of lithium. Since the fourth century BC, Therma, Ikaria, has been a known center for hydrotherapy—it's even referenced in historical texts and archaeological remains for its ancient baths and facilities, which delivered "the cure" via its potent hot radion and lithium springs. Herodotus recommended bathing twenty-one days in a row at the Apollon Spa in the center of Ikaria. One of the first references to lithium in a neurological context appears in 1870 by a neurologist in Philadelphia named Silas Weir Mitchell—the same doctor who controversially employed bed rest for women suffering from nervous disorders. (Remember, "The Yellow Wallpaper"? That guy.) He recommended the compound lithium bromide as an anticonvulsant and a hypnotic for epileptic patients. Psychotropics were just starting to show results by newly implemented medical establishments. The following year, William Hammond, professor of diseases of the mind and nervous system at Bellevue, became the first doctor to prescribe lithium for mania: "Latterly I have used the bromide of lithium in cases of acute mania, and have more reason to be satisfied with it than with any other medicine calculated to diminish the amount of blood in the cerebral vessels, and to calm any nervous excitement that may be present." Two decades later, Danish psychiatrist Frederik Lange explicitly referred to lithium in the treatment of "melancholic depression" and treated thirty-five patients with lithium carbonate. At the turn of the century, French physician Roger Reyss-Brion said the popularity of a fizzy soda tablet called "Dr. Gustin's Lithium" may have undermined some medical testing because lithium was effectively being administered as a medicine already in the form of over-the-counter soda: "It's quite simply for that reason that you don't have a lot of manic-depressives in Marseilles," he wrote. It's also thought that mineral springs in France have unnaturally high amounts of lithium. More lithium in the waters, less need to medicate people because they're getting small doses every day. Lithium may be the true reason why the French can sit in cafés for hours, eat cheese, and sip coffee slowly. They may, in fact, have a natural lithium chill embedded in their geography.

But by the early 1900s, medical lithium had largely been supplanted by other treatments. Ironically, in the 1930s and 1940s, the makers of 7-Up included mood-boosting lithium citrate in their soda formula, back when the health-minded sect of society was lithium-happy. There were "Lithia-Beers" and even a lithium version of Coca-Cola. Researchers now have come close to identifying why lithium functions as a mood stabilizer—it affects the levels of serotonin that act as a messenger regulating aspects of the nervous system such as sleep, memory, appetite, mood, sex, endocrine function. And studies have found that when lithium is prescribed chronically (for more than three weeks), the increase in serotonin is focused in the hippocampus rather than scattered all over the brain. However, the National Alliance on Mental Illness remains opaque: "Lithium is a medication that works in the brain to treat bipolar disorder." It never explains how.

In 1947, John Cade, a psychiatrist working in a hospital outside Melbourne, Australia, rediscovered lithium's medicinal potential. Cade was among the first to conclude that mental illness included bodily manifestations and thus should be treated with medication, not just talk therapy. "It required a change in how people understand mental illness," I was told by Robert Beech, an assistant professor of psychiatry at Yale University who conducts studies on medical lithium. He described this insight as a shift from "more psychological, Freudian explanations to a biological explanation." There seemed to be a cycle of psychohistory: Freud saw physical symptoms as evidence of troubles in the mind; later psychiatrists found physical symptoms were in fact biological; some doctors later combined both theories. What remains is a constant debate in psychiatric circles: What is the best combination (if any combination) of analysis and psychotropics?

Cade, whose father was also a psychiatrist, was at first simply trying to isolate the cause of mania. Having noticed that the urine of manic patients was unlike that of his stable subjects, he figured the distinguishing component, uric acid, was responsible for the mania. Seeking to produce that mania in his animal subjects, guinea pigs, he needed a solution in which to supply the uric acid to them, and used lithium urate (and later, lithium carbonate, the exact compound that I was taking). But his guinea pigs became lethargic; instead of inducing mania, he had accidentally discovered a treatment. Cade became convinced that lithium could cure many of his patients' symptoms that we now associate with schizophrenia, bipolar disorder, PTSD, and dementia. To test its safety, he ingested lithium himself; later, he began a trial with nineteen patients. The ten manic subjects experienced a significant shift in mood and function, but one of Cade's subjects died, probably from a high dose, which halted any significant steps toward employing the element as a medication. The therapeutic range of lithium is relatively small and has to be monitored closely, but that wasn't known when Cade conducted his research. It didn't help that toward the end of the 1940s, lithium's use as a table-salt substitute for congestive heart patients in the United States proved lethal in at least two instances. Cade proved lithium's efficacy nonetheless, and he did it by using the scientific method, a significant hurdle to the psychiatric community that had been previously regarded by some as a pseudo-science. Not only that, but Cade's research marked the beginning of the psychopharmacological era.

Lithium trials continued in a number of countries regardless. Mogens Schou, a physician who specialized in clinical chemistry and happened to have his lab located in a large psychiatric hospital, tested Cade's theories in double blinds; Poul Christian Baastrup set up his first lithium study in 1957; G. P. Hartigan, a psychiatrist in Canterbury, England, had noticed that lithium treatment seemed to inhibit mood swings in both manic and depressive directions after a small clinical trial. He spoke about his findings in 1959. Schou encouraged Hartigan and Baastrup to publish their findings, but both were reluctant. Schou wrote to Hartigan about lithium's efficacy: "I am asking about this not only out of interest in the use of lithium in psychiatry; but also because one of my brothers has been suffering." Hartigan responded, "In your brother's case, it should be well-worth trying." Schou administered lithium to his brother and his brother had no more bouts of mental illness. The three psychiatrists, now aware of each other's continued trials and patients, started collaborating on research, convinced it could be a miracle drug. However, the British psychiatric community protested the findings, writing them off as a "therapeutic myth." American psychiatrists were starting to champion the drug but its use was debated. The Food and Drug Administration (FDA) was still reeling from thalidomide the "wonder drug" and its consequent birth defects. Doctors and boards approving new medications were especially cautious. Barry Blackwell, an anti-lithium psychiatrist, wrote in response to an editorial written by American psychiatrist Nathan Kline, that lithium would "join

Cinderella's godmother in the pages of mythology. To transform 'just plain old lithium' into the elixir of life on the evidence available is an achievement second only to converting a pumpkin into a stagecoach." In response, Kline wrote, "Dr. Blackwell's delightful letter reads as though it was written by one of Cinderella's spiteful step-sisters. . . ." But research in the States began nonetheless: Samuel Gershon's arrival from Melbourne in 1960 at the Schizophrenia and Psychopharmacology Joint Research Project of the University of Michigan at the mental hospital in Ypsilanti, Michigan, introduced lithium to the U.S. Several other lithium studies began, as well: Nathan Kline at Rockland State Hospital in New York, Stanley Platman in Buffalo, Paul Blachly in Portland, and Eugene Ziskind in Los Angeles.

After dosages approached uniformity and careful monitoring became routine, lithium in various compounds was recognized as an acceptable treatment. Lithium gluconate was approved in France in 1961, lithium carbonate in Britain in 1966, lithium acetate in Germany in 1967, and lithium glutamate in Italy in 1970. Among the drug's champions was American medical resident Ronald Fieve, who began experimenting with lithium in 1958, after his adviser at Columbia University returned from Australia with tales of Cade's experiment. "It was so effective," Fieve told me, that he was "treating the most severe bipolar 1 patients, and this lithium brought them back to normalcy in 10 to 15 days." Fieve described running a lithium clinic in 1966—the first ever lithium clinic in the States, part of the New York State Psychiatric Institute and Columbia Presbyterian in New York City. The clinic was well regarded by Governor Rockefeller—it was a place where patients who were thought to be hopeless were rebounding and functioning. Fieve hosted Cade for a dinner in the 1970s and they swapped lithium stories. The breakthrough was that a medicine could cure a mental disorder, something that was and still is controversial and not fully resolved. "We needed a certain approach because thera- pists were still trying to talk to manic depressives, as if they could fix them," Fieve told me. "I was becoming an expert in psycho- pharmacology. We used the clinics to house and treat these people. They were oriented toward drug therapy instead of only talk ther- apy. It was a medical approach to psychology. We still have that same paradigm, you come in, you get an examination, and after a thorough history of the family and your medical history and tests, we start patients on the lithium if they need it."

When I talked with Fieve, in his eighties and still practicing on the Upper East Side of New York, he had not let go of lithium, including the medication's uses beyond psychiatric implications. He's been conducting a study on how lithium salts could possess cytoprotective actions, a process in which chemical compounds protect cells against harmful agents. It might prevent a variety of disease states such as cardiovascular diseases and neurode- generative disorders. He's not alone in the belief that lithium could treat other illnesses. De-Maw Chuang of the Mood and Anxiety Disorder Program at the National Institutes of Health in Bethesda, Maryland, found that lithium might help treat other brain conditions such as stroke and Alzheimer's disease. In 2003, Chuang conducted several experiments. He gave lithium to rats after they experienced a stroke and studied the rats and their cells. After five days there were 30 percent more stem cells than nor- mal. Meaning, lithium was potentially prompting the brain to replace damaged brain cells with healthy ones. The medication could act in a regenerative way, not just as a psychotropic. The most promising study was published by Chuang and several other colleagues from the National Institute of Mental Health and the National Institute of Health in 2014. In it, they argue that so much of lithium's research has been related to "the protective and regenerative properties of lithium focused on neurons; in contrast, limited research has been conducted into lithium's effects on white matter, which also plays an important part in Traumatic Brain Injury–related pathophysiology." In other words, lithium has the potential to act "as a neuroprotective agent in a variety of neurological and neurodegenerative disorders, including cerebral injury." But in spite of more than ten years of trials, the study, titled "A New Avenue for Lithium: Intervention in Traumatic Brain Injury," was more of a plea to continue research. Unfortunately, continued research into lithium's application in this realm seems unlikely. One of lithium's characteristics—that it is an element on the periodic table—makes it unpatentable. There's no incentive to continue studying lithium's effect on brains because there's no money in it.

After Bolivia and Nevada, my spirit quest had more than piqued my curiosity. I saw lithium's vastness (salt flats and galaxies far away), I saw its future (batteries and tech and electric cars), I felt its past in the waters (soak, soak, and more soak!), and I spoke with doctors and friends and family again (what should I do?). The plan was for Dr. Schwartz to prescribe Depakote, a medicine used to treat bipolar disorder as well as seizures and migraines and epilepsy. It's also used for delirium tremens caused by withdrawal. The thing was—and this coursed through my brain—the only way to know whether it would work was if I *didn't* have a manic episode. And the idea of waiting for that terrified me. I had been with H for three and a half years, we were living together, and he didn't know what it was like when I was manic. I described it on our first date and would pepper conversations with jokes about that time I scaled a building to shower a city in glitter and granola, but there was nothing I could say that would prepare him. I worked really hard to be in a relationship and all of a sudden it was at risk. I worried that if I became manic again, I might run off and ride the rails or that I'd be accidentally unfaithful or that I'd insist on wearing metallic unitards and Mexican wrestling masks (both actions that straddled the line of manic and normal for me). Or that, worst of all, I just wouldn't be me, and he wouldn't be able to remember who I was or that I was in there somewhere, at all. I worried that without lithium I could lose my job, my partner, my home, my mind, again . . . because I'd already been through all this.

I don't believe in God, but I believe in lithium.

I have seen this mysterious substance completely change my life—allow my life to unfold. But I had to let go.

If I were to give up on lithium, the miracle drug that was no longer a miracle for me, what drug would replace it? Lithium had been my longest relationship yet. Lithium wasn't easy at first either; there were imperceptible shifts and doubts about who I was and how the drug affected me. I have never really resolved those doubts, except to carry on with the assumption that I am a better me with medication than without. So I looked at other options. I was pretty sure that I would try Depakote. But there was fear. (I wished then as I do now that there were a real structure in place, like Alcoholics Anonymous, for people with mental illness to drop in and get some casual group therapy driven by peer counseling. I even have a good acronym for it—MIA— Mentally Ill Anonymous.) I was told that the transition would not be an instant switch. I'd start Depakote, see how my body reacted to the new medication while on a full dose of lithium. We would slowly increase the dose of Depakote over months until I was on two full doses of mood stabilizers. Then we'd gradually decrease the lithium. That was the plan. In September 2015, I took my first Depakote. It was large and difficult to swallow and I resented it.

Depakote, the brand name for valproate, valproic acid, or divalproex sodium, did not have the same appeal as lithium. For one, it was a real drug that the pharmaceutical industry had made billions from. It did not come from primordial stardust; it was not an essential element in calming waters; it did not make fireworks red. It was a tested and proven drug with an unglamorous origin story. Beverly Burton, a chemist in Würzburg, Germany, synthesized a mood stabilizer compound during early fatty acid research in 1882. For the compound to be impactful, Burton had to figure out how to transform it from liquid to salt form, which he couldn't. Consequently the compound was shelved. By the 1940s the compound was investigated in Europe as a potential oil replacement during wartime, then shelved again until two decades later when Pierre Eymard under the supervision of George Carraz used valproic acid to dissolve khellin, a plant with potential antispasmodic properties. In the same way that Cade had mistakenly used lithium to dissolve uric acid, Eymard intended to use valproic acid to dissolve khellin. Instead, he found that it prevented epileptic seizures. In 1962, Carraz transformed the liquid into a salt by adding a nitrogen group to sodium valproate that would enhance its psychotropic properties and eventually become valpromide (used for epilepsy) and valproate (geared toward manic symptoms). The medications were tested on patients in a Catholic ward in France, and the nuns proclaimed success in "personality strengthening"—that the patients suddenly looked younger, had less gray hair, and were less irritable. But valproate and valpromide were selling well for epilepsy, or as anticonvulsants, so drug manufacturers did not continue to test their effect as a mood stabilizer. Yet, papers were published in France and in Germany chronicling the effectiveness of Depakote on mania, and by the early 1980s psychiatrists in the United States were starting to use the medication off-label. In 1987 and 1991, Abbott Laboratories filed for a patent on a new stable semisodium valproate. Its formula differed from the original formula in Europe by one sodium ion, making it distinct enough to be considered unique. Charles Bowden, a psychiatrist trained in Fieve's lithium clinic, developed a far-reaching clinical trial for Abbott and got a license application to study its effect on mania. The drug was patented in 1995—a year and a half after I was first hospitalized—and Abbott made billions. The company, Abbott Industries, and its spin-off AbbVie, reported a Depakote sales peak of $1.5 billion in 2007, but when the drug went off patent in 2008, sales dropped. Lithium—because of its status on the periodic table of elements and because it's been used in medical practices for more than a century—has never been a big moneymaker. I can take home lithium from the pharmacy without health insurance for about seventeen dollars a month, whereas a full dose of Divalproex (the form of Depakote I was taking) costs closer to seven hundred dollars a month, a completely prohibitive cost if you don't have health coverage. In 2012, Abbott paid a $1.6 billion fine for remarketing the drug as a way to treat agitation in elderly patients with early dementia and schizophrenia when it wasn't FDA-approved for those applications. This barely dented its overall profit. In 2012 a class-action lawsuit was filed against Abbott by mothers who gave birth to children with birth defects and cognitive dysfunction as a result of allegedly taking Depakote during pregnancy. In the lawsuit, the plaintiffs claimed the natal risks weren't clear on the warning labels and that Abbott should be held responsible. By mid-2017 alone, 695 lawsuits have been filed nationwide. (The outcomes of these cases are pending.) Suddenly, my medication went from an anarchistic punk-rocker to a villain of a John Grisham novel.

What's most significant about Depakote's rise to prescription power is that it was one of the first drugs that was actively marketed when a simpler, cheaper alternative was available. There was no incentive for doctors to prescribe lithium when Abbott would send boxes full of samples and swag. Patients would begin treatment on Depakote and were reluctant to switch if it worked.

When I looked at the pill, I was hesitant. I hated it. And then I felt it in my body and hated it more. I almost instantly gained seven pounds and I was bloated all the time. I couldn't stomach any food that I was used to. Lemons, hot sauce, kombucha, grease, cheese—any food that was acidic or complicated to digest—became my enemy. Even raw vegetables. I was limited to crackers and soup for the first weeks, and I still felt rough with every bite. I was more dehydrated than I'd ever been on lithium and couldn't speak for long periods of time without getting extreme dry mouth. For someone who talks a lot, this is a major problem. I chewed gum, I carried water with me, but I felt like I was so dry that I had turned into one of those old, kind creatures in *The Dark Crystal* who moved so slowly and whose skin was so cracked that it was hard to tell them apart from the desert they walked on. My skin was dry and I cried a lot. More than I ever have. Dr. Schwartz said some of the intensity could have been from taking both medications at the same time—they could have been interacting in some way that amplified the side effects. He wasn't sure, he said, because it's different for every person.

Another gross side effect (and you should stop reading for the next few paragraphs if you're squeamish) was a complete change in bowel movement schedule—I pooped all the time and sometimes with very little warning that I was going to need to. That kind of indigestion is not something a person can live with easily. At least not this person. Mania is much more appealing. I felt lethargic; I could barely wake up and when I did I would want to stay in bed, comatose. But Dr. Schwartz and friends who had been on Depakote said I should try to power through, that my body would adjust, that it was possible that the Depakote could still work. What was more troubling than the physical side effects were the mental and emotional ones. I didn't feel like myself. I was drowning and far away, irrationally angry, disturbed by things I would normally find okay. I snapped at H, I snapped at my mom on the phone when she would suggest I keep a diary. Nothing seemed to soothe me—not boxing or painting or my favorite pastime, watching bad police procedurals. L.L. Cool J, Scott Bakula, and Lucy Liu had helped me through many rough times but not these.

I felt off. I didn't have the words at the time, and I still don't fully, but it resembled what had always happened a few days before my period when I wasn't yet taking the kind of birth control that regulated my hormonal cycle. During my period week, I would turn into a lunatic. For those days, every part of my life was falling down. I would pick fights with H, assume we needed to break up, want to quit my job, be angry at the weather, glare at the moon. My gynecologist suggested a different birth control and all of sudden my monthly outbursts were tamed. I know it was the birth control that was responsible because when my pharmacy would send me home with the generic form of Generess Fe (which happened more often than not because of my insurance company), I slipped right back into the k-hole of psycho anger and flailing about. That was how Depakote felt on week one. That was bad.

The worst, worst part of trying to assess a new medication was the not knowing. Not knowing whether your feelings are valid, whether the symptoms are real, whether what you're feeling is coming from the medication or from one thousand other life variables. How would I—and Dr. Schwartz and those around me—determine which side effects were bad enough to stop taking it? Week two, I felt the same. Week three, same. Week four, I wanted to murder Depakote. Week five, I was barely able to keep it together at work without fistfights and naps in the nap room. Week six, I called it. I felt too bad and I didn't like it. I couldn't see transitioning to life like this. I thought I would happily sacrifice a kidney to stop feeling this way. This wasn't me. Dr. Schwartz agreed, and I went home and flushed those horse pills down the toilet. (Not literally, they were too big to be flushed! And I would never subject the fish to that torture!) I was eager to try the other possibilities—Dr. Schwartz and Dr. DeAntonio and the current literature had all listed Tegretol as the next drug to try. Then Lamictal was next up, and a handful of others were in the wings. It felt like I'd be fine, with plenty of options, 90 percent sure. There were so many options that it would be okay if my body rejected the first one. The world of psychopharmacology was ripe with fruit. That was what it always seemed like on pharmaceutical ads—that life was one pill away from being a blissed-out golden retriever chasing a red balloon on a lazy Sunday. That we all could be happy, would be happy, should be happy. (No one ever pays close enough attention to the litany of side effects speed-read while the golden retriever is chasing sunbeams.)

Next batter! Tegretol. Aka carbamazepine. It was also developed as an epilepsy medication in the 1960s by Swiss chemist Walter Schindler, but it was hard for me to care if it had a cool or uncool backstory. I just wanted it to work. The pills were normal-sized capsules, half yellow and half black like a wasp, Wu-Tang pills. They were already an improvement from Depakote's horse-ness. The first couple weeks went smoothly. I didn't feel markedly different. Tegretol seemed to be working. Great, this was going to be easier than I thought. The most frequent side effects, particu-larly during the initial phases of Tegretol-taking, were dizziness, drowsiness, unsteadiness, nausea, and vomiting. I didn't feel any of that. I took regular blood tests to confirm that the Tegretol was not adversely affecting my kidneys or thyroid. All the levels seemed great, more perfect than one might imagine. Then I went for my routine physical, got all my annual labs done, and my primary doctor, Dr. Lane—alarmed once again and saving the day once again—inadvertently found that the Tegretol was causing a toxic reaction in my liver. When he told me, my eyes got hot and wet. He said it was a rare side effect. Lucky me. I felt like my options were dwindling and that maybe finding another miracle medication might not be in the cards. That I might not have an option at all. And I was not into the idea of another damaged internal organ.

It was a blow to my liver, my kidneys, my body. I put on my headphones, played one song because I could not think of another anthem I needed to hear: embarrassing but whatever, Chum-bawumba's "Tubthumping (I Get Knocked Down)." I tried really hard to internalize the exuberant horns and the relentless up-tempo. I got teary in spite of the persistently perky chorus that defied the reputation of the anarchist band. I wrote in my medica-tion diary that I was "sad that one path of survival, one scenario was erased. I'm not dead or dying, just sad. Sad that one thing didn't work when I felt certain that it would." But then, I knew I still had lithium. At least I had that. A lot of people don't have that. About 3.5 million people with mental illness receive no treatment. I wrote, "Fucking internal organs. I'm ready to carve out my spleen and hand it to the Pharma Gods. I will give you this, just give me that. Give me something to make me feel ok." But wah wah, so many people have to juggle combos of meds and have all the side effects I was experiencing and can't get a break from mania or depression or anxiety or obsessive thinking. I had twenty years of a good run and I knew I was still lucky to have an option in lithium.

CHAPTER 21

THE CALM WATERS OF BAD KISSINGEN

AROUND THE SAME TIME the Tegretol got flushed down the toilet (again, not literally, I love fish), my cousin Gavin e-mailed. He had been researching my paternal grandfather's family and it turned out that this magical place Opa had described visiting every summer before the war—Bad Kissingen—was known for its waters. Bad Kissingen was among the most popular spa towns in Europe during the turn of the century, largely due to the confluence of seven natural springs loaded with minerals, including lithium. During its heyday, Goethe, Schiller, Otto von Bismarck, and Chopin spent summers taking in the waters—bathing in them and drinking the licensed medicinal waters for cures from ailments or just to alleviate stress. It was called the water cure. I decided to go to Bad Kissingen and then to a lithium conference in Rome to gather intel. I wanted to see where my paternal grandfather, probably the calmest human I've ever met, soaked and swam and ran through the virgin woods as a child. I wanted to talk to international psychiatrists and see what they thought about my lithium situation. I'd been trying to get in touch with the godfather of bipolar disorder, Dr. Jules Angst, for months, but a language barrier prevented any real communication. He was set to lead the meeting and I thought, if I sat in front of the very person who chaired bipolar disorder's definition for the *DSM 5*—the standard classification of mental disorders used by mental health professionals in the United States—that maybe he could help guide me toward a solution or an understanding. I talked with Dr. Schwartz, who thought that when I returned, we should consider trying Depakote again. I said I would think about Depakote and that I would think about the lithium/kidney option as well. Maybe the Depakote side effects had been psychosomatic. Maybe I was ride-or-die with lithium. I was back to the beginning with no questions answered, no medication issue resolved.

On the flight to Frankfurt, a man as thick as he was wide as he was tall, with an army cut and an army-issue backpack, sat down next to me. He was clearly military. He immediately unloaded several small bottles of booze and arranged them in the seat pocket in front. He introduced himself and we started talking. He had completed four tours in Iraq and had just finished cyberintelligence training in Norfolk. We had six or seven hours to kill and it was easy. We talked about General David Petraeus's strategy. We talked about the time he missed a chopper because he went back to get some gear for the flight and took the next one. The first chopper crashed. His dad saw that he was on the manifest; his wife was completely distraught until they realized he was alive. It was fate, he lived. What surprised me the most was how openly he talked about the emotional residue of war. The way it haunted him and changed him. We talked about PTSD, and he kept saying, "It's a real thing. It really is. No one wakes me up in my house because they're not sure *how* I'll wake up." He explained that he had been trained to behave a certain way, and being in civilian life was not the same. "I will sit down, like right now and assess a situation and figure out who I might have to take out and who I might be able to save if it came to a survival situation. I feel like I am constantly aware of everything in front and behind me and reevaluating what might be a problem. I can't stop that. That's just who I am now, it's who I've been for too long."

He explained that he got anxious in situations that he couldn't control and with certain things that he couldn't handle. "When my wife was giving birth there was something about the smell of the insides of her body that brought me back to when I was in Iraq and to those dead bodies and I could not handle it. I buried my face in her hair and just inhaled the smell of her shampoo until it was over."

It turned out his mom was from Bad Kissingen and that his dad met her during World War II. He gave me some advice on what to do (soak in the waters). His eyes glowed as if I were about to visit heaven on earth. "It's one of the most beautiful places I've ever been." We landed and parted ways. I took three trains to town— Bad Kissingen is located in Bavaria on the southeast edge of the Bavarian Rhön nature reserve. I walked a block toward my hotel and all my senses were struck. Bad Kissingen was like a Disney movie, hillsides covered in electric-green trees, birds tweeting the happiest tunes, and rainbow flower beds erupting every few feet. It was immaculately planned and laid out. I could feel the trees reaching over and talking to each other, sheltering the smaller woods.

There was a perfect, lovely river flowing through town and paths that led to horse pastures and museums. Everything was lush and dewy and new and spring—tall trees with neon-green leaves were dying to unfurl further, reaching for insurmountable heights. I could see why this was a place of rehabilitation. Since its most glamorous days, the city has been recast as a holistic treatment center where health tourists travel to treat anything from diet issues to stress to athletic rehabilitation to internal organ cleansing. (This included a water specifically designed to help kidneys that I found particularly interesting—here, I could drink kidney cleanse water and lithium water.) It was also a place of rest and relaxation.

A local historian and retired government employee, Sigismund von Dobschütz (called Dobie by friends), had been in touch with my cousin and was involved in documenting and establishing markers or "stumbling stones" in front of homes and businesses owned by Jews who were killed or forced out of the region during World War II. Jews were officially banned from Bad Kissingen in 1934, but somehow and for some reason they stayed on much longer. I've heard refugees and residents of war-torn countries explain this all the time: *Why would I leave my home? I have nowhere to go. The war will stop soon.*

Dobie offered to meet me at my hotel and take me on a tour of Opa's childhood, and of the town. I had the same feeling that I had when I was in Germany covering the Women's World Cup—like it was a familiar place, one that I liked instantly, but that the country itself would constantly be apologizing to me. That I was a curiosity. Nonetheless, I loved this town immediately and Dobie greeted me warmly. He was somewhere between his late fifties and late sixties, it was hard to tell with an ever-present waft of cigarette smoke being carefully released. He figured living in Bad Kissingen was so calm and so health-centered that smoking a cigarette couldn't be all that bad. He was practical like that. He had a timeline of where my family lived, what they did, how they left, and pictures of the property they were associated with, and he planned to take me to each place.

"Vell, are you ready?"

I don't think I actually was ready. I had prepared for the beauty, the embrace of medicinal waters, thinking that my time in Bad Kissingen would be a calm way to approach my decision. A link to the historical use of healing waters. I joked with H that it was a way to do research while sitting in a spa and getting a massage. But thinking about Opa loving this place—the place he spent summers with his grandmother and great-aunt—and that he was forced to leave made me reconsider my visit. It wasn't only about the waters; it wasn't only about me. I read once about the migration routes of the monarch butterfly across the North American continent. A couple of years ago they were mapped in detail and researchers found that for monarchs to complete their full migration they had to make it north out of Mexico to southern Canada, then return and fly back to Mexico for the winter, and it took as many as five generations to complete one full migration. The butterflies instinctively knew the route and stopped at the same trees as previous generations, dying along the way, their offspring continuing the journey where previous generations left off, as if an internal compass led them in the right direction. I thought about Opa, about PTSD, and about the possibility of something the psychological community calls intergenerational trauma. I wondered if I am carrying the emotion my Oma and Opa could never express. I thought about how the Holocaust was such a prominent feature in my first episode and how dying by gas chamber was pretty much every Jewish kid's worst nightmare since it was one that was real and drilled into our heads early. It was discussed in every grade of Hebrew school and regular school.

But Oma and Opa simply would not talk about it. Both were

relatively lucky. Oma, age twenty-three, left Germany in 1937 with her younger brother Fred, sixteen. Opa, twenty-two, emigrated from Berlin around the same time. They all ended up in Chicago with a small assortment of uncles and cousins but little close family to speak of. They were fixed up through mutual friends who all belonged to a young Jewish association in Chicago. But once they moved to LA, to their mid-century middle-class dream house perched off Mulholland, the Holocaust was never mentioned again. I could talk about it at length with my great-great-aunt Paula, Opa's aunt. She escaped from Berlin in late 1942. Disguised as a French woman, she lived in the brothel district of Brussels. The Gestapo raids made her feel unsafe enough that she would practice hiding on the roof as they rounded up neighbors. She ended up moving hours outside town to hide in the woods, collecting mushrooms. "Dressed like a peasant woman to avoid attention I went every day, in the morning and afternoon, to the woods to gather mushrooms . . . what I could not sell I dried. I eat mushrooms every day for lunch and for supper. For many hours every day I walk through the woods. I know every mushroom spot in the neighborhood. The peasants think I am a half-wit and the children laugh at me and call me names," she wrote in her diary.

Eventually, she was forced to return to Brussels, where she stayed, again, in the brothel district—she learned that the original family that took her in had been carried off, "deported to Poland. How lucky I am that I left in time, forewarned by some kind of apprehension." She wrote of Jews turning in other Jews, and the Gestapo extorting anyone uninvolved or unwilling to be part of the persecution. She survived and she hid until September 3, 1944, when the Allies crossed into Tournay. She wrote, "the Palais de Justice suddenly began to burn . . . when it began to burn the beautiful dome began to cave in, another picture rose in front of my eyes—the burning synagogues on the 10th of November 1938

Berlin. I began to cry as I had not cried for many years." One week later the synagogues of Brussels were open after five years of war. Paula wrote, "Most of the people were crying, as there is probably hardly a Jew who has not lost some of his beloved ones." As a kid, I remember visiting her with my dad in a Sherman Oaks Jewish retirement home. She would pinch my cheeks. She lived to be 100 and died the day after my Bat Mitzvah. She did not have a problem talking about the Holocaust or keeping it in the collective memory. As she got older her memories slipped in and out of German until she reverted back to her native tongue. But for Oma and Opa, the topic was off-limits. Now, seeing a piece of what Opa left behind, this botanical wonderland, I could understand how complicated it was. They were survivors, too. They moved on, they assimilated, and they looked forward rather than inward. Trauma is hard to face every day (especially if you don't have to) but they may have been onto something—recent studies have shown that the mind is driven more toward the future than the past. It is what differentiates humans from animals, the ability to collectively plan for a future, that ability to fantasize. The brain is constantly rewriting and reshaping the past, using memories as an archive. Here, I could see both past and future. The butterflies flitted by and I felt what M. Gerard Fromm described as generational trauma, or "what human beings cannot contain of their experience—what has been traumatically overwhelming, unbearable, unthinkable—falls out of social discourse, but very often onto and into the next generation as an affective sensitivity or a chaotic urgency." I did not feel it acutely and not in the exact way Fromm describes the condition, but there was something about a visual articulation of my Opa's environment that communicated his trauma silently and deeply.

Bryan Stevenson, founder of the Equal Justice Initiative, spoke about generational trauma and slavery and the contemporary black experience in the fall of 2015. I saw him in a Q&A at MoMA talking about his project, a museum and memorial for lynching victims. He described it as an effort to mark every place a black or brown person had been strung up to die. He spoke of the importance of remembering trauma, visualizing it, and categorizing it for current and future generations to understand. He spoke of Germany as a role model, which was hard for me to hear until I saw the Stolperstein, or stepping-stones, a physical reminder of Nazi atrocities. It was just a square brass plaque with a deportation date but it was a grave reminder of what had happened. An acknowledgment at least.

"Vell, let's get going," Dobie said, with the same German efficiency and enthusiasm that I remembered emanating from Oma and Opa. I pictured them in their hiking boots and their walking sticks, ready to conquer the Matterhorn or Yosemite paths or the fire trail down the road from their house. Our first stop was a hotel that Rosamunde Löwinsky (Opa's grandmother) ran during summers from 1915 until 1920, when Opa was a toddler. She did not own this building. The building was nondescript and peacock blue and now called Bayerischer Hof, located on Maxstrasse 4. I tried to feel my lineage, but I did not. It just seemed quaint

and occupied by others. It was as if someone had painted over my family's history and occupied it entirely. In later years, between 1921 and 1932, Rosamunde bought and ran with the help of her daughter Else (Opa's aunt) Hotel Löwinsky. (Rosamunde's son, Erich, my Opa's dad, tragically and ironically died fighting *for* the Germans in World War I, as did many Jews who put national identity ahead of religious identity.) The main building was gone, but a parking lot remained with lime-green leaves sprouting between rusted iron gates and cement brick pathways leading to rugged woods. The trees were tall and swaying; this space felt more like a Lowe spot. I could sense that a young Walter Lowe might have been here, hiking through this. This place was further off the beaten path, a few blocks from the small town center. It was shrouded in growth and green, trees and birds, and wild flowers in bloom. I could picture Opa's boots, worn from climbing trees and rushing past these woods. Maybe that play and exploration could only happen after he helped Rosamunde with the guests and Else with making the beds. My Opa's tranquility, I could feel it here. The overgrown parking lot functions now as a second parking lot for what was the Fürstenhof sanatorium and is currently being renovated to

become a medical spa hotel. After Rosamunde and Else sold Hotel Löwinsky in 1932, half the buildings were demolished; the other half were demolished in 1960, surviving longer than most of the area Jews.

Dobie explained in great detail Else's path. After selling the hotel,

DINING ROOM IN
BAYERISCHER HOF.

Else and Rosamunde lived in an apartment in town until Rosamunde's death in late 1940. A year later Else, single and fifty-eight years old, moved into the house of the Jewish merchant Samuel Hofmann in September 1941. Dobie handed me archived photos of the buildings, showed me the apartments, drove me around to understand where my family had been and where they had been forced to go. After only eight months in the Untere Marktstrasse, Else Löwinsky was instructed by the Nazis to sell her property. She had to do it within a week and was sent to Würzburg on May 20, 1942, for "short-term evacuation." She lived in a retirement home and stayed there for four months, until September 23, 1942, when she was sent on the Nuremberg Transport and "was deported to the Theresienstadt ghetto as number 283." She was forced to conduct a "home purchase contract" for accommodation and care in the ghetto. The Nazis took her remaining possessions. Else had 375 Reichsmarks left.

Dobie tracked down Else's death certificate from the Theresienstadt ghetto. She died on October 12, 1942, at 5:10 p.m. As the only relative in the ghetto, Else's aunt, Martha Gerson from Berlin, was called. The cause of death was listed as a heart defect. But Dobie found a letter from June 27, 1946, from one of the survivors from Theresienstadt, Emilie Schloss, who also came from Bad Kissingen. She said simply: "Fraulein Löwinsky took possession of herself." Else, like many others, committed suicide. It was hard not to look at the buildings, the properties, the places she had been and be struck with sadness. I wanted to cry. But Dobie was so gracious and on track and helpful; no need to deal with a sobbing American coming to terms with genocide. I wondered if Else suffered from mental illness before the war or because of it. War, it seemed, was a collective mental illness. We are never not at war—with each other or with ourselves.

In 2014, Dr. Anna Fels wrote an op-ed titled "Should We All Take a Bit of Lithium?" for the *New York Times*. And sometimes I think, yes, we should. There would be less aggression, suicide, and a calmer state of mind. Some experts have heralded lithium as the next fluoride, especially after scientists found that suicide rates were lower in areas where the drinking water had higher concentrations of the element. In the October 4, 1971, issue of the *New York Times Magazine*, a feature was published called "The Texas Tranquilizer," in which University of Texas biochemist Earl B. Dawson claimed that El Paso had lower rates of suicide and crime and fewer admissions to mental hospitals than Dallas because their water supply was heavily laced with lithium. For centuries travelers have soaked in the Chianti Hot Springs outside of Marfa, Texas. Within the past few years, the lithium-in-the-water question was raised again. And again, the response was severe—augmenting the water supply amounts to mind control, *Brave New World* tendencies, and human modification. More recently, a researcher from the Medical University of Vienna, Dr. Gerhard Schrauzer, also conducted a survey that looked at twenty-seven counties in Texas over a decade and found a consistent inverse relationship between lithium levels in water and suicide, violent crime, and rape. A century ago society was more open-minded about soaking in the waters and taking them in; it was even considered in fashion.

In the center of Bad Kissingen is a fully gorgeous, multiwinged, ornate palace with an old wing completed in the early 1800s and a new wing finished in 1913 in the neo-baroque style of architecture. The early buildings of Bad Kissingen were commissioned in the 1820s and 1830s and became known worldwide after the Bavarian king's first visit in 1833. The aristocracy and the bourgeoisie followed, along with artists, writers, and musicians. H. J. Heinz of the ketchup dynasty (a known hypochondriac) and George Bernard

Shaw took to the waters. Czars and emperors under assumed names came to truly relax. In 1877, Otto von Bismarck said: "I owe my health to a loving God and the healing waters of Bad Kissingen." Bad Kissingen was just one of many spa towns in Europe and the United States at the turn of the century. In an October issue of the *Lancet* from 1894, a doctor examined the effects of lithium-rich waters in the Welsh region of Llangammarch, concluding that the water was certainly therapeutic, if not curative for a variety of illnesses. At the turn of the century therapeutic waters were all the rage.

The town now is still considered a central place for the elderly and the infirm. You cannot walk down a street without seeing a walker or an arm brace or someone in recovery from one surgery or another. Bad Kissingen has seventeen hospitals, sanatoriums, and rehabs and about 250,000 guests per year. When I was there, the gardens surrounding the main buildings were carefully planted in rainbow eruptions of petals in different patterns, each area more manicured and colorful than the next—murals and figures from Greek and Roman mythology lined the gardens. There were long halls for walking, an instrumental action in drinking the waters. To provide a soundtrack for the scene, Bad Kissingen features twice daily orchestra recitals—at ten a.m. and four p.m. They play on stage for an audience that I could imagine Oma and Opa sitting in; the orchestra holds the Guinness world record for most performances per year. The stage rotates so that in summer they play outdoors to audiences in the garden.

Dobie took me to the drinking waters (there are both drinking and soaking waters in Bad Kissingen). There were bartender-esque figures behind long sinks, mixing formulas of the different waters in small clear glasses. I took the waters from the Rakoczy spring and the Pandur, the two springs with the highest lithium content. The mineral water mixologist sloshed the liquids back and forth between two cups and handed me one cup, which I drank. It tasted metallic, soapy, salty, and a little tinny. I walked off my medicinal waters to aid in their flow within my body and felt nothing in particular beyond what my lithium was already doing to me. The amount in the water was minuscule compared with my medical dose. Still, I wanted to taste the more subtle version. And the next day I was planning to soak. Lithium, inside and out.

I planned to go to the new state-of-the-art theme park–esque therme KissSalis. I had heard about German spas and was bracing myself for an all-nude experience with proud misshapen pasty bodies. The nudity didn't really bother me—it was more the double helplessness of being naked and not knowing the language. (I had been to a nude beach once in Jersey with a bunch of swingers, and the funniest part was the casual nature of it all. One dude walked around with a plate of crudités offering vegetables. "Baby carrot?" he kept asking earnestly. "No, thank you.") I knew there were strict rules regarding German spas and what if I did something wrong? I did online research and there seemed to be a consensus that most facilities are coed naked. There was a mineral water pool in the basement of my hotel. A perfect place to practice, plus it was where the hotel stashed free apples. I changed into nothing and dipped into the empty pool, feeling vibed out by the whole thing. I chickened out and grabbed a towel. As I left, two elderly couples in bathing suits descended on the pool. Close call. Not nude in the hotel. Noted.

I walked to KissSalis the next day with a bathing suit, a change of clothes, and a book. It looked like a glorious mall—modern and made of glass, boasting eight indoor and two outdoor pools and more than ten thousand square feet of relaxation. There was less protocol to follow than I thought. All the common areas were clothes on, the saunas were super naked and coed. Easy to navigate that.

I jumped in and went to the outdoor current pool first. I moved with the water and an elderly woman moved at her own pace in front of me, jogging in a circle with the happiest old face on earth. She wore dark round steampunk glasses and a big black bathing cap whose shape resembled the Coneheads. She had the biggest no-tooth smile as she babbled and waltzed with the water. Indoors, in the main pool, a column lit from within with other-worldly presence dominated the center of the open building. Underwater aluminum stretchers lined the edges so that bathers could watch the almost imperceptible rainbow transition. The column changed colors slowly—one minute pale blue, the next pale green. I felt like the pillar had power; it could stretch to the moon and lord over its earthly tenants. Maybe the column could reach to the galaxies far away, drawing lithium down? There was a fire hose–strength waterfall that I sat under for minutes, hours, days? Who knew. Time was not relevant to this place. I went to the saltiest indoor pool, a nearly pitch-black room with holes poked into a ceiling blanket to mimic a night sky. I hitched my heels to the edge and floated effortlessly. Classical music played underwater. And I basically took a nap on the surface of the water. I felt liquid.

CHAPTER 22

WHEN IN ROME
AND THE LITHIUM RECKONING

RUINS OF CARACALLA IN ROME.

The conference in Rome was a lark, mostly an effort to track down the mysterious Dr. Jules Angst (real name). In July 2015, I'd received a manila envelope in the mail from a scientist who had read the article I wrote about my kidneys in the *New York Times Magazine*. Dr. Ed Ilgren sent me a bio of himself and his work researching how lithium exposure through natural water sources in Chile affected indigenous populations. Over dinner, he made it clear that he was worried for my safety, and insisted that I find Dr. Jules Angst. Dr. Ilgren introduced us over e-mail, but because of a language gap, Angst and I could never quite connect. So I found myself searching for his next lecture, and if I had to go to Rome, I would suffer that fate. It was sort of a kill-two-birds-with-one-stone kind of trip: I could find the mythical Angst and I could pick the brains of leading international psychiatrists about my kidney/lithium predicament. At this point, I was asking cabdrivers, inanimate objects, anyone who would listen what they thought. Most people didn't have an answer—no one could.

When I got to Rome, I had business. I had to find the ruins of Caracalla, one of the largest bathhouses of Rome commissioned by Septimus Severus and completed by AD 235. These baths, the second-oldest in Italy, had been in use until AD 537—1,600 people at one time could use the cold baths, tepid baths, hot baths, steam baths, and the open-air bath, which was the size of a modern Olympic-sized swimming pool. Part of the bathing experience that I liked best was its simplicity and ability to transcend millennia.

I had already been a spa convert—I'd spent evenings pouring ice-cold water on my head while schvitzing in the East Village and gone to Korean spas for soaks and scrubs in LA and New Jersey and Queens, feeling more at ease with the world upon exit than I ever had with a Xanax. One winter night at the Russian and Turkish bathhouse in the East Village, Hana and I had taken to the soaks and the heat, sweating out the city. We steamed, we saunaed, we went to the back room where Russian men slap other Russian men with platka leaves for vitality. The sensation of going hot and cold, the extremity of the temperature shift in body and air, felt so alive, like an external heartbeat. In the back room, when we were at the brink of heat, skin crisping, we would dump buckets of ice water over our heads and bodies. Hot and cold and hot and hotter, then coldest. Finally when our bodies had an internal temperature of warmer than normal, we made our way to the roof deck. We lay steaming on the sun chairs, looking at the rooftops, the fire escapes, the back alleys of the East Village we had once traipsed through—and we watched the first of winter's snowflakes fall delicately, kissing the roof and our skin. Our breath escaped; each flake that touched our bodies melted.

After Bad Kissingen, I was a total convert to healing waters. The lineage of treatment only added to the allure. So it was a formal, almost ceremonial homage to the ruins of Caracalla, to the Romans, the O.G. bathers! It seemed like they did everything in the baths—Romans would conduct business, read, buy perfumes, get massages, watch athletic performances, socialize, and soak in these facilities modeled after Greek baths. The main buildings were constructed in such a way that the visitors could easily walk from one facility to another, with a main corridor between the two entrance halls. The ruins now stand nearly one hundred feet tall and are an extension of a southern area of Rome surrounded by parks populated by tall, top-heavy stone pines. The Roman use of baths was more social than medicinal, but the complex was impressive. I'm not sure what I thought I could absorb from sitting there on yellowed grass and in minimal shade—a return to a Roman time when melancholia and mania was first thought of and considered? Or just a sense of the reliance and importance that this society once placed on relaxation? It used to be a sign of empirical strength to be able to build such an enormous and architecturally complicated complex devoted to leisure, to calming the mind. Now, I sat under the trees mostly, to take it in and to think. This was my spirit quest, my way into a decision and a plan.

That night I ate pasta at trattoria Lilli, a no-frills family place that felt like a Noodle Pudding; there were more Romans than tourists, all laughing through goblets of red wine. Again, I was reminded that Italians know how to relax and take in life, without much effort. For a nervous Jew with a damaged kidney on a lithium quest, this space was a welcome respite. The unassuming white tablecloths and simple pasta dishes reminded me of my favorite form of therapy—slurping noodles until olive oil dripped down my chin. Eating bread soaked in olive oil, olives soaked in olive oil. I ordered a big bowl of caci e pepe, cracked a Moretti, and settled into some easy reading about lithium. I thought of the epitaph of an ex-slave, Tiberius Claudius Secundus, at the baths. It read "*Balnea, vina, Venus corrumpunt corpora nostra; sed vitam faciunt balnea, vina, Venus,*" which translates to, "Baths, wine, and sex spoil our bodies; but baths, wine, and sex make up life." It's as good an epitaph as any, and in Italy it seemed like lithium and kidneys and health mattered less. I did not want my epitaph to read, "Lithium and obsessive thinking spoils your body; but lithium and obsessive thinking make up life." That is a shitty epitaph. There was fresh produce and tomatoes that tasted like hummingbird nectar, gelato that dripped from thumb to elbow, and people who yelled affectionately. A woman in a stall near the conference made me pasta and took offense at my not eating enough. Everyone seemed to stroll through life at pace with the sun and the moon and the cycle of storms. I thought maybe it was New York or my life, or that stress was just too stressful for me, that I need to remember that cosmic space of soaking in KissSalis. *Or* if I could combine both and soak in waters while slurping pasta, well, that would be a good life, too.

I woke up the next day and walked to the conference, completely uncertain if Angst would be there and what a room full of psychiatrists would be like. The eighteenth International Review of Psychosis and Bipolarity was a three-day affair organized by the group's director, Russ Pendleton. There were papers that seemed relevant, like "Nothing New Under the Sun? An Update on Current Treatments for Bipolar Disorder and Beyond," chaired by Dr. Dina Popovic, or "The Issue of Tolerability in the Long-Term

Treatment of Bipolar Disorders," chaired by Dr. Andrea Murru, and the last day's presentation was especially interesting to me: "Past and Future of Lithium Therapy," chaired by Dr. Paolo Giraldi and Dr. Leonardo Tondo. The conference was the all-stars of international psychiatry—with doctors traveling from Israel, Serbia, Tunisia, Austria, Canada, and the United Kingdom to try to penetrate the impenetrable: mental illness, its treatment, and its study. The chair and president of the group was the elusive Dr. Angst. To get to the Hotel Nazionale where the conference was located, I walked through alleys and cobbled streets, making wrong turns only twice. I had practiced the day before so that I could spot landmarks, a clear sign of the anxiety I felt that I might never find the conference or Angst or satisfy the reason I came all this way in the first place. The upside was that, either way, I'd experience Angst. The conference room was yellowed and taupe and windowless and could have been anywhere—Cleveland, Vegas, the Frankfurt airport. The main presentation room had the feeling like it was a vessel for PowerPoints. But there was Dr. Angst, eighty-nine years old, sitting on a bench with his wife, who it turned out had actually been the one responding to my e-mails. I introduced my-self.

"Ah, I thought you were a Portuguese man based on your name."

DIRECTIONS TO THE IRPB
CONFERENCE IN ROME.

He shook my hand and we sat to talk about the history of psychiatry, medication, and why anyone would study brains and emotion in the first place. His father was a technical draftsman and his mother managed a bake shop and he was an only child. When he was young, Angst picked up his father's entomology hobby, and noticed that butterflies that came from different altitudes had different wing patterns. He experimented by taking low-altitude butterfly larvae and birthing them in freezing temperatures in the refrigerators of the city slaughterhouse. The result: a high-altitude wing pattern. That was the beginning of his belief that health—including mental health—was a holistic issue, affected by environmental factors that shifted the expression of genes. He explained that he started his studies, alone, in a library in Zürich, poring through the pages of Jung and Freud. He became disenchanted by his own practice of analysis. It was then that he decided to become a psychiatrist. He thought taking time with patients was essential and more important than the theories and methods of different schools of analysis.

Angst said he had schizophrenic patients who didn't change long term with analysis, so he shifted his focus in the early 1960s to study psychopharmacology. "In order to diagnose and treat patients, one has to examine their physical condition as well as their psychopathology. I didn't feel a connection to analysis. Devoting enough time to patients is essential. More than fifty percent of the time now is documenting what you are doing at the computer. It hasn't become very ameliorating in terms of human relationships," Angst said. We talked about how we have ways of measuring the heart, blood pressure, ways to map the body with numbers and guidelines—I explained that from my experience it seemed like tracking mood was impossible. Dr. Angst countered that he and others had developed a series of questions—the Hypomania

Checklist, a thirty-two-question self-assessment survey. I thought back to my adolescent self-assessment and was wary. If you are manic, you are likely to answer delusionally. And what could a survey really show? And that seemed to be the crux of why treatment is so hard—there's no way for a doctor, especially a doctor just meeting a patient for the first time, to be able to identify what is manic for one person versus manic for another. For all Dr. Angst knew, I was not a writer, not working on a book at all, and that I was in the throes of an episode, interviewing experts as part of a manic episode. And maybe I was? I was eating barrels full of pasta, talking to random strangers, and I was here for a slightly bizarre and complicated purpose, almost *grandiose*.

I could see how my questions, repeated to all the psychiatrists there, might come off as crazy—I didn't have papers to prove that my kidneys were busted, or that I was taking my lithium. Even though Dr. Angst had developed this survey, he knew that the reality was that "even if you could measure mental illness, you couldn't define *normal* based on statistics. An individual is much more complex." Angst and I talked about times when he was depressed—once when he was depressed over a love affair, and once when he was briefly suicidal after unsuccessful back surgery for disc hernia with paralysis. He had felt a range of emotions in his lifetime but he was not predisposed to manic depressive disorder, though it seemed like he had a window into it through his patients and through his own experience. He wouldn't go into more detail because he said it felt too personal, but he was open to sharing how his professional life was shaped by lithium, if not by taking it, by believing in it as much as I did. He was among the first advocates for lithium in Europe by showing with Paul Grof that bipolar disorder could be improved by lithium. At the time, the UK psychiatric community believed that manic depression was unaffected by lithium treatment. He had even traveled to Australia to meet Dr. Cade in the 1970s.

Angst brought up two things that I hadn't really thought about. He mentioned the concept of trust and that with "compliance and trust, a lot of what you have is the placebo effect. The effect the patient has that he believes in you, whether you are giving a placebo or an active drug." More than half of the positive treatment responses in mood disorders are due to placebo effects. In one study, when patients were treated with clonazepam or an SSRI (a type of medication commonly used to treat depression), 60 to 70 percent of those with panic disorder become panic-free during a ten-week treatment period. During the same period, half or more of patients with panic disorder who were treated with placebo become panic-free. Angst believes that there's the potential of a placebo effect in all psychopharmacology—that the patient's trust in medicine is built through her trust in care. "It is essential to look at human beings in their whole development; we should study humans from intrauterine development to the end of life. Such a long-term perspective is also important brain research. You have to follow changes over time, without which you lose this continuity," Angst said. It's not a new approach. Hippocrates urged physicians to make frequent visits with their patients and directly inquire about their situations without intermediaries, laypersons, or nurses interfering. This effort was to inspire confidence among patients so that they would feel comfortable trusting their doctors. Because once again, how do you know if medication is working in mental illness? You don't, you only know when it's not working.

Angst spoke with a slight Austrian accent and had a hard time hearing my questions over the din of the conference and the tittering psychiatrists who filtered in and out of the lobby to get coffee. Nevertheless, we talked about the artists he's treated, and he mentioned that van Gogh had a manic spurt of production before his death in July 1890. I thought back to my days of unstretching my canvases in the backyard of my dad's house—hovering over old paintings, painting layer upon layer over a finished piece, each slap of paint more genius than the next. In college I painted an homage to my NPI stay in high school; it was a huge canvas, maybe eight feet tall. There was a section devoted to me in a hospital nightie, my butt exposed and the back of my red hair flowing, running from nurses and needles. Another section was an elaborate ink drawing of the pipes I thought would poison me. This was a painting I made when I was sane, thinking of crazy times. When I was manic the second time in 2001, I unrolled this mammoth canvas and painted over every inch.

My dad and Marilyn were just glad I was occupied with something even if it was guttural manic painting. The most striking new image was a serpentine black figure with hot-pink hair streaked out this way and that, a demon really—I wrote *ERASE HER!* across the breast of the figure. You can see my footprints winding around in paint

DETAIL OF MY PAINTING OVER MY COLLEGE PAINTING, WITH THE WORDS *ERASE HER* SCRAWLED ON THE CHEST OF THE FIGURE.

showing the path of concentration, where I was focused. I flung red paint. I bathed in it. I was dripping in paint and walked across the painting leaving a trail; I put stickers on it that said *SPECIAL HANDLING, STAT*; I wrote *smoking peace pipes* next to nuclear-looking storage tanks. I tagged most of my college paintings with silver spray paint and splattered fire-engine red across surfaces. I took carvings I made in printmaking workshops and made other new quick-fire paintings, all demon faces, some with glitter, some without.

The comedian Chris Gethard and so many other comedians/artists say and I would agree: the myth that medication stunts creativity is bullshit. (He spoke more eloquently and emphatically about it in his one-man show *Career Suicide*, in which he explains that you can't be creative, you can't write a joke, if you can't get out of bed.) Medication allows for function, which is the first step toward doing anything—creative or otherwise. My creative spurt wasn't really a creative spurt at all, it was the opposite: destruction. After my medication kicked in and I was coming to, I looked at that canvas and thought of it as ruined. I rolled it up and pushed it out of sight—a piece I had worked on for months in college was all of a sudden slashed, taken hostage. But now I see it as this relic, a canvas in which I was exorcising a part of me. The paint articulating what I couldn't.

In his final weeks, van Gogh painted a number of landscapes of the wheat fields. During van Gogh's time in Auvers, where he died, he made even more paintings and drawings—he completed seventy works including sketches during his stay from May 1890 until his death on July 29, 1890. On July 10, 1890, van Gogh wrote to his brother, Theo, about two of the canvases, saying, "They are vast stretches of wheat under troubled skies, and I did not have to go out of my way very much in order to try to express sadness and extreme loneliness. . . . I'm fairly sure that these canvases will tell you what I cannot say in words, that is, how healthy and invigorating I find the countryside." In a letter two days later, he wrote to his parents, "I myself am quite absorbed in that immense plain with wheat fields up as far as the hills, boundless as the ocean, delicate yellow, delicate soft green, the delicate purple of a tilled and weeded piece of ground, with the regular speckle of the green of flowering potato plants, everything under a sky of delicate tones of blue, white, pink and violet. I am in a mood of almost too much calm, just the mood needed for painting this." He speaks of mood just weeks before his suicide—an alternate mood, one of calm and near elation, but certainly not depression. Depressed people don't paint; depressed people don't see glory in wheat. There are other theories about van Gogh's death—that he did not commit suicide—but his letters certainly speak to the self-awareness of his disease and the fluctuations of his mood. Some of his greatest works were completed before his death. "The positive aspects are important," Dr. Angst then said. "What I have seen on lithium was that it didn't change creativity, lithium made it more consistent. There are so many creative people who are mentally ill. I have treated so many artists who were bipolar and addicted and they are very inventive during manic episodes, but taking lithium doesn't stop that."

I asked Angst what he thought drove that special kind of creativity, and he said something I had heard before: "You are deviant in your thinking, you leave that normal pathway to jump somewhere else in your thoughts, and that is creative. Being unconventional in your emotional jumps, you go away from the usual in a positive sense." In *Setting the River on Fire*, Kay Redfield Jamison wrote about how Robert Lowell's madness was inspiration for his poetry and then later braided his experiences into his work when he was lucid enough to actually write. He was one of the earliest patients on lithium and wrote to Elizabeth Bishop in 1967, "I have a new doctor now, and there seems to be real hope that my manic seizures can be handled by a new drug, lithium, and that all my giddy reelings come from a kind of periodic salt deficiency in some lower part of my brain." Lithium allowed him another decade of productivity, but in 1975 he suffered a toxic overdose and had to be hospitalized. He died of heart failure two years later. According to a study from Oxford University the life expectancy of people with mental illness is much shorter than their counterparts: "The average reduction in life expectancy in people with bipolar disorder is between nine and 20 years, while it is 10 to 20 years for schizophrenia, between nine and 24 years for drug and alcohol abuse, and around seven to 11 years for recurrent depression." I worry about my life span sometimes. As I was writing this book, both Patty Duke and Carrie Fisher passed away and I cried because I felt like I knew them and I felt like they were shouting about things that I needed to hear. And shouting with confidence and aggression. The kind of aggression underappreciated by male therapists.

Years after the fire, I was chatting with Mike and asked him why he stuck around and why he helped me through that time when it was clear I was not normal. He explained that he didn't know what my normal was, so it was difficult to gauge at first, but that also "I was always a little jealous of what you went through . . . you've had an experience that so few people have had. You've lost your mind entirely. It's almost like you've been someone else." There is something to be said for crossing over into a world lacking inhibition and reserve. But there is also danger in that.

Dr. Angst asked me, "What happens when you don't take lithium? Have you tried?"

I explained my history, my compact answer of no. I can't risk another episode. But sometimes I pine for a medication-free life and wonder if I might not be sick at all. The further away you get from it all, the less intense the memory. But then I think about everyone around me—my mom, dad, Marilyn, Jeff, Hana, H— and no, it's not an option. Being on the mild end of the spectrum of bipolar allows for this kind of wishful thinking. "The diagnosis is a label, directions for treatment," Angst said. "But the whole human being, the patient himself is a whole complexity of other phenomena which has to be taken into account. He has to be considered as a whole."

I asked Dr. Angst what he would do in my situation. "All drugs have side effects. The kidneys are extremely important, I wouldn't know what to do. You have started very early with the lithium? What happens when you lower the dose? Have you tried? The anti-epileptics also have side effects. I wouldn't know what is the best." He sounded sad for me, which wasn't my intention. But I think he might have also been sad that there wasn't a clear answer. "At some time in their lives, everyone has physical pain and problems, so everyone must have pain and problems of the soul." Then he paused dramatically and whispered, "Everyone has a brain, which plays a major role in mental illness. I think everyone is— temporarily or not—a little mentally ill."

I went back into the conference room, where a graduate student was speed-reading through her findings, ending her paper on cannabis by saying, "Thank you for your attention." The actual presentations were for the most part interesting but deeply specific and beyond my level of understanding. It was hard for me to understand why researchers would study cigarette consumption in schizophrenics rather than the broader, more mysterious elements of why people are mentally ill in the first place. Some of the presenters had ideas that translated beyond academia. A Canadian researcher presented the idea of GPS tracking for the bipolar to identify when their patterns might deviate from the norm: faster moving, more shopping, going to new, farther afield places. It was an interesting concept, but there's no way in hell you'd get a bipolar or schizophrenic patient to consent to being tracked. We all think we're being tracked anyway. One clinical study looked at "feeling sensation seekers" and used a cartoon zebra whose stripes were unraveling just underneath a thought bubble that read, "I think it's stress." I asked every psychiatrist after their presentations and at coffee breaks, what should I do? One Italian psychiatrist—Dr. Guilio Perugi—got excited when I described my situation:

"Are you cyclothymic?"

"No, I don't think so—I don't know what that is. Is that different than bipolar?"

"It's a more chronic state, happening more often but milder," he said, while holding a cup of black coffee that sloshed back and forth. I watched the liquid drip on the cobblestones below as we talked about healing waters and kidneys and my various questions. Russ Pendleton, director of the conference but not a psychiatrist, sat with me at the end of three days and explained that most psychiatrists go into the field because they have had a certain amount of personal experience or exposure to mental illness. I asked him about one conference attendee who, like clockwork, would ask a deeply complicated question after each presentation, complicated to the point of absurdity, baffling most presenters who tried to respect him but would, more often than not, move on delicately.

"Oh, ya. He's almost always in a psychotic state but very clever. He was diagnosed ten years ago and basically learned psychiatry. He comes every year; his papers are very chaotic." I felt overwhelmed by information and psychiatrists but comforted by this

community. I talked with the psychotic presenter and asker-of-
questions—what would he do? He didn't know, either; he had
taken an eighteen-hour train to get to the conference and was set
to head home, as was I.

I thought about the psychiatric advice I had picked up. Most
said Depakote. Try the Depakote again. Do not give up on your
kidneys. I couldn't do anything *right then and there in Rome*, so I
decided for the last night to try pasta instead. I felt that if I could
face-plant in pasta, that was enough of a healing experience.

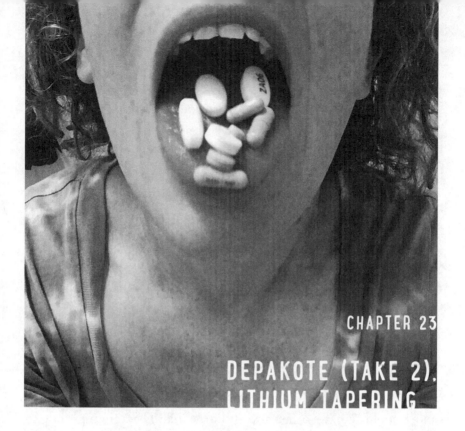

I GOT HOME. I got to work. Same drill. We would slowly increase the dose of Depakote over months until I was on two full doses of mood stabilizers—the lithium and the Depakote. Then we'd gradually decrease the lithium, until I was only on the Depakote.

There were relatively few options left for me. I am a classic case of bipolar 1 with symptoms that are primarily expressed as mania as opposed to depression. Most of the other medications used to treat bipolar disorder are geared toward bipolar 2, which leans more toward depression than mania. Lamictal, Seroquel, Abilify won't stop the manic.

I did what I should not have done and pored through Depakote chat rooms. The members wrote of agony—the hundreds of pounds gained, the lethargy, the dry mouth. I thought of Dr. Angst's theories on placebos and how the Internet sleuthing counteracts all trust. I instantly worried that these side effects would affect me too. The things I worried about most were vanity-based—I didn't want to gain weight or lose my hair. I considered my hair to be like Samson's—I wasn't me without it. Every morning I watched my drain clog with what was once my defining feature. It made me feel impotent and ugly and sad and even sadder that I was so vain. It made me angry too. I didn't want to have to sacrifice more of me. So I kept training at Gleason's, barely keeping up with Fluff, now seventy-two, who would grump about, telling me how much he hated Gleason's and everyone there and yet he would show up four days a week to brag about his daily two-and-a-half-hour workouts and to fist-bump other trainers like Chicken and Blimp and Don and Darius and Devon and Heather. I didn't spar even though I craved the ring every Saturday morning. I couldn't give up my days and I couldn't have other bodily harm, like head trauma, not to mention the real possibility of kidney punches. I used the gym as a meditation. I shadow boxed, Fluff yelling, "Extend your arms" and "Stop hunching your shoulders," disappointed that after ten years I had learned nothing, repeating the same bad habits. Some days I could imagine an opponent and slip and counter and throw combinations with the same ferocity as if I were fighting. But I was just circling the ring, losing myself in the effort of it all. The speed bag was a mantra; I'd count to the thump of the teardrop-shaped bladder hitting the wood, my feet moving in time. Sometimes I would go the full round without fucking up, counting to twenty and starting over again, practicing the same Zen ritual I learned from monks on State Street. I would breathe with the ball, knowing where it would shift based on the angle I hit it. Some days my arms were tired but I took my Iyengar yoga standing-tall lessons and elongated my rib cage to reach farther up to use the advantage for a better angle. The stink of Gleason's was comforting, the red paint on the walls, a blanket. While I was there, I was generally not aware of kidneys, lithium, and so on. I was there to punch and get tired and be so tired that I could fall down at home. Boxing made me feel strong, even if I wasn't.

This time the Depakote felt different. This time I was determined to will the medication to work. The side effects weren't as bad. I wasn't crying every day. I didn't tear up at the mention of cheese. My hair fell out and I still had a hard time with digestion, but it wasn't *so* bad. I wasn't *so* outside myself. I thought this Depakote could work. I was optimistic. H was optimistic. My mom, who called every day to hear the tenor of my voice, was optimistic. My dad, who out of respect for my time, would call once a week, was also optimistic. Maybe that gang of psychiatrists in Rome was right. Maybe I was experiencing psychosomatic symptoms the first time—almost a year before—that my body and mind didn't want the Depakote. Maybe I wasn't ready to accept it then, thinking that there were other options. Now here I was swallowing those horse pills with aplomb. And feeling fine enough. Sure, I was tired but I was on a lot of heavy-duty mood stabilizers.

The first month of Depakote went well, increasing in 250-milligram increments every two weeks. I carried water around with me to anticipate dehydration. My mouth was always chalky. But that first month was okay. It seemed milder, easier, less invasive. Then I refilled my prescription and noticed that the pills were slightly different. They were gray and oval; the other ones were larger and white and had the stamp *AN* 757 on them. The corners were rounded slightly. I checked the orange pill bottles—one was called Depakote DR (for delayed release) and the other was called Depakote ER (for extended release). I asked Dr. Schwartz if there was a difference, and he said that I should check with my pharmacist. My pharmacist said, no, it should be fine. I checked online and couldn't find conclusive information—except that delayed release had a shorter life span and needed to be taken twice a day, whereas extended release could be taken once a day. Why any pharma company would distinguish medication with the words *delayed* and *extended*, which are nearly interchangeable in application, was beyond me. Within a day of taking the Depakote DR, I was sobbing again. Bloated again. Angry, irritated, fat-feeling, hair-losing, sobbing, sobbing, sobbing. I wanted to join a death cult—I wasn't suicidal but I could see virtue in dark corners, and staying in bed. I was scheduled to work during those weeks and seeing people regularly was a saving grace. The problem was, we were also increasing the dose at the same time, so I assumed that my symptoms were just a reaction to the amount or interaction of both medications. I kept taking the DR, sure that the slight increase in amount was what was affecting my body. I kept sobbing.

After a month, my general state got so extreme, I considered ditching Depakote again and staying on lithium. When I went to Gleason's I felt a little barfy but worked through it. I was mad at Depakote. I was mad at not knowing whether it would stabilize. It made me feel possessed, like I had no agency over my moods. The opposite of what it was supposed to be doing. My medication was making me depressed, overwhelming me. I shadow-boxed and pictured a Depakote man, and just started throwing jabs and punches at a giant pill head. In my mind I had him trapped in the corner. Then later when I was hitting the heavy bag I had this war chant going through my head: "de-pa-kill, de-pa-kote." I think if I did yoga I might have been embracing the medicine, welcoming it. But it was hurting me and it was hard to take and my instinct was to fight back. I had just started to decrease the lithium and, of course, I had the thought that maybe less lithium was making me loopy. Dr. Schwartz urged me to keep taking the Depakote, and I did.

In mid-October, I refilled my prescription again. And within twenty-four hours I felt . . . better. Clearer. Something was different. The pill was back to the original shape and size from two months previous and the bottle read *ER*. Two days later, I still had side effects but they were mild by comparison. I wasn't murderous, I could eat reasonable amounts of cheese, and I didn't feel like there was an alien baby violently growing in my stomach. I called my friend's mom, Norma Juzwiak, a pharmacist in New Jersey, just to figure out if there was, in fact, a difference. She said, yes, of course, people have different reactions to different formulations of every medication, and Depakote was no exception. Why wouldn't the pharmacist know or warn me, I asked? She said, they should have. Most don't know the difference because its original application is for epilepsy. I kept a diary at the start of my lithium decrease and after I started the ER version for a second time, I wrote:

> 10/24/16: Last Thursday I decreased the Li from 750mg to 500mg. I have felt jittery and nervous since. Not manic, not euphoric, just edgy, like I have to stop every ten minutes to remind myself to breathe and slow down. I feel like everything I hold, I will drop. I feel the opposite of a bath, like tiny bolts of energy are shaking my skin. The Depakote ER is better, but I'm worried it's too much better. There doesn't seem to be an easy day when I'm not thinking about it. I'm trying to get to the other side. Upside, I'm not sobbing.

> 10/25/16: Still vomit-y. Just ate an apple slice and coffee and threw up some apple chunks while brushing my teeth. Not the worst ever, but gross and on my sleeve and less fun than flossing.

10/26/16: I'm running late and stacking tasks in my head. Need to remember to breathe; added one more necklace and had to remind myself that it's just one more . . . necklace, not a manic episode. It kind of looks like rosary beads and I'm thinking of it as protection (but not in a religious way, not manic).

10/29/16: The low-grade real anxiety is hidden beneath outer work anxiety—what if the Depakote doesn't work? What if these two years of transition were futile and I end up back on lithium, broken from another episode, nursing a broken kidney that just breaks down further with each miracle pill? I guess that fear won't go away, at least not in the first year or two of Depakote. Drank water and coffee and then barfed it up. Maybe skip acid stuff?

10/30/16: Decided to give up coffee.

11/6/16: Realized my frequent pooping is prolly from Depakote; also there's weird mucus in it. A friend on Depakote calls them "Depa Deuces." Eating papaya to try to help the digestion issues and switched to tea.

11/7/16: Started zinc for hair loss. Saw Hana yesterday and started crying. Feeling a little stuck in this place and angry that my body doesn't feel like mine. Not sure H understands but pretty sure he's tired of hearing about it, which I get. I am tired of hearing about it. It feels all consuming.

11/14/16: Lowest blood pressure yet, post Trump. Confirms my belief that huge catastrophe is easier for me to handle than small things. Just after it was clear he won, I had a wave of calm. I had a dream election morning that he won and because of the tightness of the race and the constant watching and waiting, I think I was relieved. All this eclipsed my meds, my side effects, my focus on myself. The chaos and catastrophe got me out of my head.

12/5/16: Depakote feels a lot smoother, less intense side effects. I got my period for the first time in a while since I've been on birth control and I think Depakote is affecting my hormones. Still losing hair, still have some left. Feeling a little less dramatic about it all.

THE ENTRIES BECAME more sporadic but covered my side effects and how I felt in general. Everything got calmer with time; I barfed periodically but for the most part Depakote ER seemed like it was taking. This was all luck—if I had been prescribed the DR initially in the second go-round, I never would have stuck with it. I might have been on the road to dialysis and a kidney transplant. This miscommunication or accident or psychopharmacologic lapse, even more than my mental condition, seemed insane.

So I called a psychopharmacologist, Dr. Richard Brown, an associate professor of clinical psychiatry at Columbia University to try to figure out a more specific answer. Brown was one of Depakote's earliest advocates. The drug had been approved in France in the 1960s and in Germany in the early 1970s, and by 1982 Dr. Brown was using it to treat bipolar disorder off-label in the United States. "From 1980 to '92, I lectured and helped psychiatrists use Depakote," Dr. Brown told me. "People were screaming at me and called me public health enemy number one. They said, 'You're going to kill people with this drug.'" I asked him why I would be prescribed two different kinds of Depakote interchangeably, and he said, "What's happened is that most psychiatrists have no clue that ER is better than DR, and many prescribe generic DR. And because it's been off-patent for several years there's no economic incentive to educate doctors on how to use Depakote effectively." He explained that Abbott launched Depakote DR first and Depakote ER second. He said most psychiatrists were just unaware of Depakote ER's improvements over the first formulation. It lessened the side effects and made the pill easier to tolerate. But Schwartz had prescribed ER and yet the pharmacy doled out DR? Sometimes, that happens for insurance reasons, sometimes it's just a lack of information, sometimes it's a mistake, he said.

Dr. Brown also said that there is a clear hierarchy in the psychiatric community and the medical field in general—that being a psychopharmacologist is looked down upon. "The typical training program doesn't give psychiatrists what they need to know about how to prescribe medications. Two thirds of psychotropics aren't prescribed by psychiatrists anyway—it's an internist or a general practitioner. Psychopharmacologists are thought of as people who are not that smart." But obviously there is a difference in what kind of medication you are prescribed, down to the make and model. "There should be a separate specialty board in certification in psychopharmacology, and that has been stymied by the old white guys, and they're afraid that they wouldn't be able to practice anymore because they would never pass that certification. It comes down to money and turf and prestige." Depakote isn't the only drug that is prescribed early and often for depression and bipolar disorder without enough information. "Tegretol could work really well but it has a lot of side effects. It can wipe out your white blood cell count. You only use it if everything else has failed. Lamictal is okay but it only works for one out of nine people and that's only for depression. So eight people aren't actually seeing results. A lot of doctors think Lamictal is for mania and aren't told otherwise." (Dr. Schwartz had worried about Lamictal as an option for me, and therefore it was low on the list of possible medications.) Brown went on to say what many mental health advocates and those with mental illnesses have expressed for years—mental health is simply not treated the same as physical health. Not by insurance companies, politicians, or the field of medicine. "For thousands of years people haven't treated psychiatric patients with compassion and respect, and they have been discriminated against. There just isn't true mental health parity; health insurance companies do not treat it the same way."

Dr. Brown and I continued talking about how politics and lobbyists have no business dictating access to medication, and yet in the United States, they do. He made the point that in countries with government-provided health care systems there is a way to track patients and the side effects and efficacy of drugs after the drugs have been released to market because the patients are a ready-made study. The government and health care system has a control group and access to all their subsequent reactions. We also talked about holistic approaches to mental health and how Eastern medicine considers mental illness.

He ended our talk by telling me that when I was off the lithium entirely, he wanted to give me some mushrooms. His great-uncles had been mushroom farmers in the hills of Kentucky, and he knew of some that were curative, specifically for kidney dysfunction. "I don't think we really know exactly how they work, but we know these mushrooms help kidney function and improve the function. It's probably a tubular issue. It's a brand of cordyceps, it's also called cordimmune. Call me when you're off the lithium and we'll talk about it."

I then asked him if being open to other psychiatric methods like breathing or mushrooms made the mainstream medical community skeptical of him. He paused and said yes. But he was the first person I talked to who incorporated medicinal, analytical, and alternative approaches to mental illness.

One night when H was away, the sky shook and lit up like war. It was four a.m. or five, still dark and scary. I was startled when I heard half a dozen loud baritone booms, each followed by an immediate shock of light. I checked my phone for bomb alerts, I thought the city was in peril, that Trump had incited war, that attack was imminent if not *actually right now*. I grabbed a couple of the extra pillows and moved away from our windows and huddled under the duvet. I hoped and rationalized that the sound was thunder and lightning. It obviously had to be. Either way, there was nothing I could do but breathe and wait. It was just thunder, the skies opening up, but I thought about that terror of war—real bombs, sounds that indicate death and destruction, not just low-grade anxiety. I thought about what it meant to live under Trump, whose finger was this close to the nuclear codes and whose mouth was liable to make his fingers do the talking. Dr. Brown had been to South Sudan and Rwanda and had done breathing clinics with survivors of genocide, people suffering from extreme PTSD. I imagined war, living amongst the ruins of villages and family homes. I couldn't *really* imagine it, not from the comfort of my sheltered bed. Dr. Brown told me that people born with mental illness in some villages in South Sudan are chained to trees and left to suffer through schizophrenic episodes tethered on the outskirts of their communities and separate from their families. They get parasites, their disease gets worse, and it's all for a lack of mental health care and lack of basic understanding. Some facilities in Ghana sequester their mentally ill off to one "hospital," where patients ranging from bipolar to epileptic are locked in cages and medicated without monitoring or expertise.

The United States is further along in dealing with mental illness, but not by much. In 2008 when George W. Bush signed the Mental Health Parity Act into law, it required all insurers to cover behavioral health the same way plans covered any other type of medical treatment; but insurance companies found loopholes and ways to circumvent coverage. Years later, when Obamacare was implemented, in a significant move toward parity, it forbade health plans from rejecting people with preexisting conditions—including mental illness and addiction. "We have made progress expanding mental health coverage and elevating the conversation about mental health," President Barack Obama said in a statement. "But too many people still do not get the help they need." Many therapists—psychiatrists, psychologists, and those in behavioral health—won't take private insurance, exchange plans, or Medicaid plans because they don't pay providers well, which means outpatient care is still an issue. Covered treatment becomes an emergency room issue and is reactionary rather than preventive. And, according to the National Alliance on Mental Illness, in our contemporary mental health crisis, people are more likely to encounter police than get medical help. "As a result, 2 million people with mental illness are booked into jails each year. Nearly 15 percent of men and 30 percent of women booked into jails have a serious mental health condition. . . . Once in jail, many individuals don't receive the treatment they need and end up getting worse, not better. They stay longer than their counterparts without mental illness." Former congressman and mental health advocate Patrick Kennedy has said the result is that those who can afford to go out of network do; those who can't afford it often forgo care altogether. In the eighteen years I've lived in New York, it's cost me more than one hundred thousand dollars in outpatient care to see Dr. Schwartz (and that is subtracting his absence during August). I can do that because I am functional enough to work. It's my highest expense, second only to housing. But for the almost 43 million Americans with mental illness, that simply isn't an option. In October 2016, the Obama administration released a report of findings from a presidential task force commissioned to improve parity. But with the Trump administration and the Republican Congress promising to gut the Affordable Care Act, parity seems like a delusion at best. *Parity* seems like the wrong word for what is necessary—parity implies two separate entities. For mental health coverage and the study of it to advance at all, physical health needs to be regarded as something that encompasses both body and mind. Angst and his holistic approach to psychiatric health remain the gold standard. But health insurance companies and the pharmaceutical industrial complex don't seem remotely interested in pursuing a health care system that would actually contribute to overall health. In fact, the labyrinthine process for reimbursement, coverage, rules, and regulations for both doctors and patients amplifies mental illness and anxiety. Every time I'm put on hold or puzzle through a pharmaceutical query, my back tightens, my jaw locks, and I have to calm myself down and coach myself through it. Most of the time I give up.

Over the years, twenty or thirty or more friends, relatives, friends of relatives, and relatives of friends have talked with me about being diagnosed, going through moments of insanity, taking medication, being depressed, being manic, or being manic-depressed. We've swapped survival tales. But in the past decade or so, I've also known at least half a dozen people who committed suicide. People who seemed like they could get through a day but clearly—at some point—just couldn't. I was talking with Mason about how some people can push through and others can't and that it seems so arbitrary. Why meds work for some and not others? How family and community can work? And why some-times everything just fails. The bottom falls out.

"I think, we are all looking for that thing that can get us to even," Mason said. "That thing that makes it easier to just be who we are even in bad states, to get to even." I took "even" to mean functional. Beyond diagnosis, beyond medication, beyond therapy, and beyond understanding my disorder—I'm human, we are all human. Everyone is trying to get to even. Lithium got me to even.

As I decreased the dosage of lithium, I thought I would send it off in some spectacular way to thank this miracle salt for its service. After coursing through my veins for twenty-four years, lith-ium would always be a part of me. Maybe I would drive to Saratoga Springs or fly to Canada and soak in the Halcyon Hot Springs. I thought of all the ways I could honor my pills. A vigil, a ceremonial toilet flushing, a last swig with a Michelada and nachos. I thought I could sprinkle a capsule from the highest of heights, dusting my city with a light coating—the crystalline salt that has kept me sane. I thought about the Sweetwater Park Hotel, built in 1887 in Lithia Springs, Georgia, with the central focus of taking in lith-ium luxuriously. There were 250 rooms in the hotel, each with hot and cold baths pumping in water from the springs next to open fireplaces and balconies offering views of the Blue Ridge Moun-tains. I craved a place like that for a grand send-off, but Sweetwa-ter burned down in 1912 and now there's a gas station in its place. In the end I did nothing. I was tired. I was tired of thinking about it. I felt okay, I felt happy, but I knew for at least a year, maybe two, maybe for life that I'd always wonder if happy was manic or manic was happy and if lithium was the only thing that prevented my happy from becoming mania. Those last 250 milligrams coursed through my body and within twenty-four hours—lithium's half-life—the element passed unnoticed.

A couple of months after I had been on Depakote alone, Dr. Schwartz asked me, as he had every week, "How are you doing? How are the side effects?"

"I have mild indigestion still."

"But not as extreme?"

"No," I said. "My hair is still falling out. I look like a troll doll."

"But you still have hair."

"Yes, it just looks different, like alopecia has set in," I said.

"But you're not manic?"

"No."

"And you're not depressed?"

"No."

One night, about three weeks after the lithium had passed through, I was describing some mild insomnia to my mom. I told her that I was awoken around four a.m. by the nearly full moon, shining like the sun through our windows. All week the moon would wake me up, and I would stay awake staring at it. She paused on the other end of the phone. I could tell she was thinking: *Is this a manic thing?* And then I was thinking that, too. Was I communing with the moon because I thought it was cool, or was I doing it because the Depakote wasn't working? My mom listened more and I explained that I must have been stressed about something else, and I know just by questioning if I am manic, I am probably not manic. (That is the first rule of Manic Club.) But the bigger question remains: Who am I in relationship to the medication, to the disease, to my experience? How did lithium shape me? It gave me twenty-four years of sanity—to live, to grow, to love, to flourish, and to fail. It gave me the chance to fuck up my life and repair it, to function, as if I were just another "normal" person.

But here's the thing: I am among the 1 percent of the mentally ill. I am the luckiest mentally ill person. I am the mentally illest. *I was lucky.* I have a family that supports me and understands me; most don't. *I was lucky.* I was born into a family with enough money that I knew I would be financially supported if absolutely necessary and I would have health coverage no matter what; most people can't afford a Band-Aid and a neck brace. *I was lucky.* I was diagnosed young and had the chance to get treatment; most mental illnesses can fester undiagnosed for decades. *I was lucky.* I grew up in the age of mental illness role models; previous generations didn't talk about emotion or medication. *I was lucky.* Lithium worked for me almost immediately; some patients have to take half a dozen drugs and still don't feel okay. *I was lucky.* When my life burned down, my industry, family, and friends forgave me and helped me rebuild. *I was lucky.* I had several psychiatrists walk me through this shit; most people don't even get a social worker. *I was lucky.* My kidney is degenerating, but Dr. Lane and Dr. Schwartz caught it in time, and Dr. DeVita is nursing it along; some people lose their kidney function altogether. *I was lucky.* Switching meds was hard but I got the right kind of Depakote; some might have stopped at DR or one of the sixteen different versions of Depakote that affect people in entirely different ways. *I was lucky.* I get to experience all of life, one I would never trade for normal, whatever that is.

I am lucky. Not everyone is.

EPILOGUE:
HOPE SPRINGS ETERNAL

No episodes yet!

NOTES

CHAPTER 3: If Nazis Don't Get You, the Moccasins Will

28 A child's brain was once thought: According to research conducted by Dr. Jay Giedd of the National Institute of Mental Health, cited in Valerie F. Reyna, Sandra B. Chapman, Michael R. Dougherty, and Jere Confrey, eds., *The Adolescent Brain: Learning, Reasoning, and Decision Making* (Washington, DC: American Psychological Association, 2011).

CHAPTER 4: Fat and Blood and Circular Insanity

32 Bipolar disorder is now defined: National Institute of Mental Health, https://www.nimh.nih.gov.

32 The generic definition: Mayo Clinic, http://www.mayoclinic.org.

32 The use of lithium as a therapy: According to Jules Baillarger and Jean-Pierre Falret, cited in Ayşegül Yildiz, Pedro Ruiz, Charles Nemeroff, *The Bipolar Book: History, Neurobiology, and Treatment* (New York: Oxford University Press, 2015).

33 "The people ought to know": Jules Angst and Andreas Marneros, "Bipolarity from Ancient to Modern Times: Conception, Birth and Rebirth," *Journal of Affective Disorders*, vol. 67, no. 1-3 (December 2001).

33 The physician Aretaeus of Cappadocia: Carlos A. Zarate Jr. and Husseini K. Manji, *Bipolar Depression: Molecular Neurobiology, Clinical Diagnosis and Pharmacotherapy* (Basel: Birkhäuser, 2009).

34 "an animal within an animal": Robert Lee, M.D., *A Treatise on Hysteria* (London: J. and A. Churchill, 1871).

36 The real progress was made: Angst and Marneros, "Bipolarity from Ancient to Modern Times."

CHAPTER 6: Rabid Mutant Squirrels, Frontal Lobe, Beast in the Attic

51 Outside the doors of Bedlam: Jerry White, *A Great and Monstrous Thing: London in the Eighteenth Century* (Cambridge, MA: Harvard University Press, 2013).

53 But, miraculously, he survived: Malcolm Macmillan, *An Odd Kind of Fame: Stories of Phineas Gage* (Cambridge, MA: MIT Press, 2000).

CHAPTER 12: SEX 'N' EGG 'N' CHEESE

111 In 2016, however, a study by Dartmouth: Heidi C. Meyer and David J. Bucci, "Imbalanced Activity in the Orbitofrontal Cortex and Nucleus Accumbens Impairs Behavioral Inhibition," *Current Biology*, vol. 26, no. 20 (October 24, 2016).

CHAPTER 13: HYSTERICAL METAMORPHOSIS

116 In 2011, the CDC: Roni Caryn Rabin, "Nearly 1 in 5 Women in U.S. Survey Say They Have Been Sexually Assaulted," *New York Times*, December 14, 2011.

118 Erika Kinetz wrote: Erika Kinetz, "Is Hysteria Real?" *New York Times*, September 26, 2006.

118 In 2012, four researchers wrote: Cecilia Tasca, Mariangela Rapetti, Mauro Giovanni Carta, and Bianca Fadda, "Women and Hysteria in the History of Mental Health," *Clinical Practice & Epidemiology in Mental Health*, vol. 8 (2012).

120 "When these symptoms indicate": Rachel Maines, *The Technology of Orgasm* (Baltimore, MD: Johns Hopkins University Press, revised edition 2001).

CHAPTER 15: AND NOW FOR A PSYCHOTIC BREAK . . .

146 At the turn of the century when Carl Jung entered: Carl Jung, *Memories, Dreams, Reflections*, edited by Aniela Jaffe (New York: Vintage, reissue 1989).

CHAPTER 16: CHEEKING MEDS, BARTERING FOR UTOPIA, AND THE PASSOVER CRUISE

167 And Americans with mental illnesses: Kristen Weir, "Smoking and Mental Illness," *Monitor on Psychology*, vol. 44, no. 6 (June 2013), American Psychological Association.

CHAPTER 19: THE BIG BANG, THE THIRD ELEMENT EMERGES, HOSTS ALIEN LIFE . . .

212 But unlike most other elements: Malcolm S. Longair, *Galaxy Formation* (Springer, 2008).

212 "Lithium remained a rather rare element": Neil deGrasse Tyson and Donald Goldsmith, *Origins: Fourteen Billion Years of Cosmic Evolution* (New York: W. W. Norton & Company, 2014).

216 The flats look like ice interrupted: Joseph S. Levy, James W. Head, and David R. Marchant, "The Role of Thermal Contraction Crack Polygons in Cold-Desert Fluvial Systems," *Antarctic Science*, vol. 20, no. 6 (December 2008).

218 The increasing global demand: Simon Romero, "In Bolivia, Untapped Bounty Meets Nationalism," *New York Times*, February 2, 2009.

220 Nearly 70 percent of the demand: "Graphite Demand from Lithium Ion Batteries to More Than Treble in Four Years," Benchmark Mineral Intelligence blog, http://benchmarkminerals.com, May 4, 2016.

220 Prices for lithium carbonate: Stephanie Yang and Biman Mukherji, "Tesla Shakes Up Market for Lithium, Other Metals," *Wall Street Journal*, May 5, 2016.

221 They're all hydrologically linked: Teresa Matich, "The Clayton Valley: Nevada's Lithium Hotspot," Investing News Network, http://investingnews.com/daily/resource-investing/energy-investing/lithium-investing/clayton-valley-nevada-lithium-hotspot/, April 21, 2016.

CHAPTER 20: LITHIUM'S LORE AND THE TRANSITION TO DEPAKOTE (TAKE I)

225 One way to think about its effect: Mark Wheeler, "Lithium Builds Gray Matter in Bipolar Brains, UCLA Study Shows," http://newsroom.ucla.com, April 6, 2007.

226 "Latterly I have used the bromide": William A. Hammond, M.D., *A Treatise on Diseases of the Nervous System* (New York: D. Appleton and Company, 1871).

226-27 At the turn of the century: Edward Shorter, "The History of Lithium Therapy," *Bipolar Disorders*, vol. 11 (June 2009).

228 Cade became convinced that lithium: John Cade, "Lithium Salts in the Treatment of Psychotic Excitement," *Medical Journal of Australia*, vol. 2, no. 10 (September 3, 1949).

229 Mogens Schou, a physician: Per Bech, "The Full Story of Lithium," *Psychotherapy and Psychosomatics*, vol. 75, no. 5 (August 2006).

229 "I am asking about this": Frederick Neil Johnson, *The History of Lithium Therapy* (London: Macmillan, 1984).

229 "In your brother's case": Johnson, *The History of Lithium Therapy*.

229-30 "join Cinderella's godmother": David Healy, *The Antidepressant Era* (Cambridge, MA: Harvard University Press, 1997).

231 After five days there were 30 percent: Helen R. Pilcher, "Lithium Livens Up Stem Cells," Nature.com, March 14, 2003.

234 The medications were tested on patients: David Healy, *Mania: A Short History of Bipolar Disorder* (Baltimore, MD: Johns Hopkins University Press, 2011).

235 The company, Abbott Industries: Andrew L. Wang, "New Depakote Payouts Would Fall on AbbVie, Not Abbott," *Crain's*, August 20, 2013.

235 In the lawsuit: *Rheinfrank et al. v. Abbott Laboratories Inc. et al.*, case number 1:13-cv-00144, U.S. District Court for the Southern District of Ohio.

239 About 3.5 million people: Mental Illness Policy Organization, http://mentalillnesspolicy.org.

CHAPTER 21: THE CALM WATERS OF BAD KISSINGEN

247 Here, I could see both post and future: Molly S. Castelloe, "How Trauma Is Carried Across Generations," PsychologyToday.com, May 28, 2012.

247 "what human beings cannot contain": M. Gerard Fromm, ed., *Lost in Transmission: Studies of Trauma Across Generations* (London: Karnac Books, 2012).

252 In an October issue: "Sanitation at Constantinople," *The Lancet*, November 24, 1894.

CHAPTER 22: WHEN IN ROME AND THE LITHIUM RECKONING

265 On July 10, 1890, van Gogh wrote: Letter from Vincent van Gogh to Theo van Gogh, Auvers-sur-Oise, c. 10 July 1890.

266 "I myself am quite absorbed": Letter from Vincent van Gogh to his parents, Auvers-sur-Oise, c. July 10–14, 1890.

267 "The average reduction in life expectancy": Edward Chesney, Guy M. Goodwin, and Seena Fazel. "Risks of All-Cause and Suicide Mortality in Mental Disorders," *World Psychiatry*, vol. 13, no. 2 (June 2014).

CHAPTER 23: DEPAKOTE (TAKE 2). LITHIUM TAPERING

281 In 2008 when George W. Bush: Peter J. Cunningham, "Beyond Parity: Primary Care Physicians' Perspectives on Access to Mental Health Care," *Health Affairs*, vol. 28, no. 3 (May-June 2009).

281 "As a result, 2 million people": National Alliance on Mental Illness, "Jailing People with Mental Illness," https:/www.nami.org/Learn-More/Public -Policy/Jailing-People-with-Mental-Illness.

283 I thought about the Sweetwater Park Hotel: Lisa Land Cooper, *Every Now & Then: The Amazing Stories of Douglas County* (CreateSpace Independent Publishing Platform, 2016).

ACKNOWLEDGMENTS

Thanks to everyone who has helped me get to this point, one day after another. Nothing short of miraculous.

Thanks to my immediate family for unconditional love: my mom, LeeAn Lantos, for her rocking chair, a deep appreciation of words, punctuation, expletives, bargains, righteousness, Venice beach walks, softball, and for an early introduction to analysis; my dad, Stephen Lowe, for teaching me to love trees, garden-grown tomatoes, the farmer's market, soccer and sports, for more righteousness, teaching me to absorb the way music sounds and feels, how to read a book at five a.m. when the streets are silent, and for bailing me out on more than one occasion (ahem, Jinan); Jeff, for patience, piano playing, lyrical genius, strawberry rhubarb pie, making life one big goulash, and teaching me by demonstration that writing requires curiosity, diligence, persistence, and passion; Marilyn, for her fierce dedication to anything she focuses her laser eyes on, letting me play with her court suits and Attorney General's badge, Lake Hollywood walks, saving the state's water, and talking me through many rough nights much later in life than any adult should be experiencing drama; my older brother, Matthew Lowe, the order Muppet to my chaos, you've been such a crucial part of my life that I don't know how to define the love except in extreme gratitude that you haven't murdered me in my sleep for being the crazy one—you've taught me a deep appreciation of music, food, travel, diplomacy, and how to gently urge snails to remain in line; my younger brother, David Lowe, for raw enthusiasm and support in everything, sharing a love of sneakers and track suits and cool shit in general, for wanting me to hang out with his friends even though I'm an old lady, and for thinking I might have good life advice in spite of obvious functional flaws.

Thanks to my immediate friends family from LACES: Hana Elwell, there aren't words, I feel so lucky I get to know you; Rachel Benoff, same; Sarah Jacoby, same; Miriam Kramer, same—all of you basically slay me with love and intelligence and power and beauty. The fact that we've known each other since we were thirteen—well, that's just fucking amazing.

Thanks to my teacher and role model Monsy for being a loud, fierce, uncompromising woman. Arnie for rehabilitating darkroom enlargers and teaching me to process film and develop prints. Thank you to Mack for being open then, and now. Thanks to the movies and moviemakers who got me through high school.

Thanks to Autumn Bernstein, Karey Green, Erin Stack, Stuart Seaborn, Stephanie Haren, Jeremy Engel (serious shout-out to the funniest dude who is still friends with me even after I told him he's a bad kisser and the fire and I melted his records for fuck's sake . . . sorry), Greg Seibert, Andrew Nolan, Charles Heath, the Aggie, the UC Davis art department, and the *LA Weekly*, in particular Pam Klein, Harold Meyerson, and Tom Christie.

Thanks to the smashing Sarah Poulter, who on Day 1 in New York embraced me like family; thank you, Amy Osburn, who twinkles through life in an infectious manner and for calling me sparklebutt; Effie Phillips, who straddled the streets of Davis and New York with me, Aaron Samson, and Mark Bard.

Thank you to anyone who has ever given me a job or worked with me. Waking up and having a place to go is an extraordinary privilege, especially considering the people I have gotten to work with. In particular Bill Vourvoulias, James Lochart, Ethan Lipton, Chris Stone, Dana Nelson, Meesha Diaz Haddad, Caryn Prime, Robert Firpo-Capiello, Maer Roshan, Adam Duerson, Danny Habib, Chuck Eddy, Jebediah Reed, Kerry Lauerman, Orion Ray-Jones, Sophie Hoeller, Sam Polcer, Sarah Emerson, Melissa Cronin, Ben Guarino, Jenny Kutner. Deep shout-out to all the fact-checkers and copy editors and production managers, underappreciated backbones of publishing.

Thank you to the entire staff of *The New York Times Magazine*. First and foremost to Dean Robinson for enduring endless gchats and half-baked pitches and general harassment, but mostly many thanks to him for making me pay close attention to words and sentences. Thank you to Jake Silverstein, Bill Wasik, Jessica Lustig, and Ilena Silverman for guidance, faith, and for publishing the story this book was based on. Thank you to Nandi Rodrigo, Lia Miller, Steven Stern, Dan Kaufman, Renee Michael, Nana Asfour, Mark van de Walle, Rob Liguori, David Ferguson. Thank you to Kathy Ryan for taking the best photo of me ever and preserving evidence of my pre-Depakote hair. Thanks to David Carr.

Thank you to my whole big entire amazing family that I love deeply and dearly: Sally, Aggelos, Ereni, Zoe, Sofia, Carrie, Simon T., Pete, Jan, Debbie, Gavin, Kyle, Andrew, Will, Michael, Michelle, Mark, Madeline, Rachel, Charlotte, Richard, Lorna, Jill, Julie, Jason, John, Martha, Nancy, Hannah, Tess, Emma, Tom, Jessica, Lucy, Marlena, Lauren, Alex, Adrienne, Julian, Stuart, Hal, Gavin, Mia, Pam, Terry, Emma, Michael, Carol, Aaron, Nora, Leah, Katherine, Mitchell, Margot, David, Sarah, David, Jan, Meredith, Sasha, Aaron, Denise, Jake, Jackson. Thank you to all my grandparents—Irving, Helen, Walter, Henny—and to Lynn, Barbara, and Joy.

Thank you to the St. Augustine crew—the best outlaws a girl could hope for. Please know that I could not love you more and I feel so lucky that I have extended family that I consider my own. I'm deeply grateful for midnights at the Chikee, fish fries at Genung's, and an attitude toward life and people and justice that is incomparable.

Thank you to those that don't fit into any one category: Mike for being there, my awesome brother-in-law, Romeo Ymalay III, Hardy, Maya, and Eva Fischer, Niko Higgins, Levi Elwell Higgins, Zoe Ani, Craig, Maceo, and Zinnia Melzer, Ethan, Lev, and Liam Minton, Jenny Engel, Evander Bluejay, Joshuah Bearman, Zerline Goodman, Cindy Zaplachinski, Kev, Stuart and Pam, Emily Bazelon, Nikole Hannah-Jones, Dr. G, Jenna Wortham, Claire Gutierrez, Luke Mitchell, Sheila Glazer, Willy Staley, Charles Homans, Leslie Jamison, Greg Howard, Taylor Berman, Caity Weaver, Choire Sicha, Rich Juzwiak, Max Reed, Busdriver, Elizabeth Wurtzel, Adrian Chen, Naomi Zeichner, Tommy Craggs, Ally Millar, Alex Pareene, Jay Kang, Madeleine von Froomer, Gemma Gambee, Jeremy Kleiner, Oliver, Owen, and Marisol Staley, Sharif/Boobaloo and Rosie, Mason Pettit, Lindsay Fram, Jon Mooallem, Dana Shapiro, Brett Forrest, Donnell Alexander, Chris Isenberg, Jeff and Sue, Lynn and Nate, Preston and Phyllis, Shelley and Bob, Susan and Richard, Bob and Kim, Hughbie, Steve Brown, Stefanie and Tony, Jeff and Nancy, Bruce and Betsy, Linda and Michael, David and Joanna, Idene, and John and Sue. Lia Miller deserves another thanks here for cheese, chats, and smiling through tough days. The Schwadrons and Elwells. Lizzie Simon and Reyhan Harmanci for letting me into their ad-hoc residencies in the woods. Thank you to Henry Weinstein and Laurie Becklund for being my journalism role models. Griff, Cody, Nature, Maggie, everyone from Moonwork, Gleason's, soccer, Noodle Pudding, the Iyengar Institute. Anyone who's let me interview them, ever.

Massive thank-you to every psychiatrist, researcher, therapist, and historian who let me interview them and pick their brain about brains in general. Thanks to anyone who has shared their story of mental illness publicly or just in conversation with me.

Thank you to Kay Redfield Jamison, Patty Duke, and Carrie Fisher for your humor, strength, voices, and for blazing the trail.

Thank you to Blue Rider for everything. Many thanks to editor extraordinaire Brant Rumble for being patient and encouraging while I barfed this thing up, and then making it sing. Terezia Cicelova, you are a star with impeccable editorial judgment, sharp questions, and excellent instincts. David Rosenthal, thanks for including me in a roster that I have no business being on and for finally allowing me to legitimately call Mike Tyson a colleague. Ghada Scruggs for fact-checking and researching that went above and beyond. Claire Winecoff and Amy Schneider for deft copyediting. Claire Vaccaro, Marysarah Quinn, Jason Booher, and Ben Denzer for absolutely stunning design inside and out.

Firemen and women, everywhere.

Jud Laghi. Super-Agent. Period.

H, you are my love.

Dr. DeAntonio and Dr. Schwartz, I might be dead without you guys. I'm glad I'm not.

Finally, if you or anyone you know needs immediate help, call the National Suicide Prevention Lifeline: 800-273-TALK (8255) or for general information on mental health, call the U.S. Department of Health and Human Services' Treatment Referral Helpline: 877-726-4727.

INDEX

Page numbers in *italics* indicate photographs or illustrations.